International Credit and Collections:

A Guide to Extending Credit Worldwide

Edited by

Mary S. Schaeffer

Editor of IOMA's *Report on Managing
Credit Receivables and Collections*

John Wiley & Sons, Inc.
New York • Chichester • Weinheim • Brisbane • Singapore • Toronto

Copyright © 2001 by Mary S. Schaeffer and Institute of Management and Administration. All rights reserved.

Published by John Wiley & Sons, Inc.
Published simultaneously in Canada.

This publication is designed to provide accurate and authoritative information in regard to the subject matter covered. It is sold with the understanding that the publisher is not engaged in rendering legal, accounting, or other professional services. If legal advice or other expert assistance is required, the services of a competent professional person should be sought.

Library of Congress Cataloging-in-Publication Data

International credit and collections: a guide to extending credit worldwide / edited by Mary S. Schaeffer.
    p. cm.
    Includes index.
    ISBN 0-471-40675-9 (alk. paper)
       1. Export credit. 2. Country risk. 3. Collecting of accounts.
I. Schaeffer, Mary S.
    HG3753.I64 2001
    658.8′8—dc21   00-053177

Printed in the United States of America.

10 9 8 7 6 5 4 3 2 1

For my husband, Hal Schaeffer

About the Contributors

Mike Barry   Mr. Barry has worked for many years in the legal profession in the United Kingdom before setting up as an independent credit management consultant (*m.barry@creditaid.fsnet.co.uk*). He lectures throughout the United Kingdom and Europe on a wide range of credit and legal issues. He is a member of the Technical Advisory Committee of the Institute of Credit Management (ICM) in the United Kingdom and a consultant to Experian. He has written and contributed to many books and publications, edited the Croner Loose Leaf Guide to Credit Management, and has recently produced a "desk book" for credit managers explaining the changes to the legal system in England and Wales. He works with the ICM and the Department of Trade & Industry as a consultant to the Better Payment Practice Group.

Paul Beretz   Mr. Beretz is managing director of Pacific Business Solutions (*www.pacbizsolutions.com*), a company he founded that identifies and implements global strategic planning opportunities and cash-flow improvement solutions for clients in high- and low-tech industries. His teaching experience includes faculty positions at the University of California at Berkeley, St. Mary's College (California), and the University of Phoenix. He has written programs and instructed for National Association of Credit Management (NACM) and its international component, FCIB (an association of executives in Finance, Credit and International Business). He is a frequent author of trade articles, has edited books on financial management, and has authored a book for the American Management Association. He received his B.B.A. from the University of Notre Dame and an M.B.A. from Golden Gate University.

Aloysius J. Carl   Mr. Carl is a leading international credit and collections expert with over 17 years of experience in the industry. From 1995 to 2000, he served as president of The Kreller Business Information Group, Inc., an internationally recognized provider of business services including credit reports, collection services, due diligence investigations, marketing studies, and country risk reports. Mr. Carl now works as an independent business consultant working with U.S. and foreign exporters in dealing with credit and collections, e-commerce, sales, and compliance issues relating to international business transactions. He can be reached at 859-466-7025 or e-mail him at *alcarl@ix.netcom.com*

Lewis Flax   Mr. Flax, director of Marketing and Sales for Graydon America, has spent the last 10 years specializing in export credit and international finance. He has served as both an export credit manager and a bank vice president specializing in trade finance. He was previously employed by Riggs National Bank, AmTrade International Bank, and International Financial Resources. He has worked with a number of companies on projects including the development and improvement of export credit policies and procedures. He has written articles on export credit topics, frequently speaks on international credit, and serves on a number of advisory and trade boards. He received a B.A. from the University of Rochester and a master's in International Management from the University of Maryland. Graydon international credit reports are available in the United States from *creditriskmonitor.com*.

Bon Frewen   Mr. Frewen is president and chief executive officer of Coface Holding Company NA (*www.cofacerating.com*), the holding company for the U.S. interests of Coface S.A., France. He also is a director of several Coface Group companies, including cofacerating.us, Veritas Business Information Inc., and Worldwide Credit Managers LLC, a 50/50 joint venture between CNA Credit and Coface.

Jennifer Hudgens   Ms. Hudgens is an area vice president of the Kreller Business Information Group (*www.kreller.com*) in Cincinnati, Ohio, where she has worked for the last nine years. She has received seven awards for top salesperson for collections and credit report business from 1993 to 2000. She currently travels to see her clients, helps run the company's exhibit at trade shows across the country, and attends international seminars representing Kreller. She has been published in the trade publication, *IOMA's Report on Managing International Credit and Collections.*

David I. Marsh   Mr. Marsh has been a credit manager for Novus International, Inc. since the company was formed in June 1991. He was a division credit manager at Anheuser-Busch from 1988 to 1991 and was corporate credit manager at Chromalloy American Corporation from 1971 to 1986. After graduating from Washington University (St. Louis) in 1963, he worked in agricultural and international credit at Monsanto Company and then as a division credit manager for Textron in St. Louis. He travels frequently throughout Latin America and the Asia Pacific region. He is an active member on NACM-FCIB's board of directors and received the NACM's CBF (Credit Business Fellows) designation of excellence award in 1998. He is currently chairman of the Global Business and Finance group of the NACM-St. Louis.

Thomas M. Rispanti   Mr. Rispanti formed the risk management group at Creditek (*www.creditek.com*) in January 1997. He is responsible for the development of innovative credit risk mitigation products and managing all aspects of Creditek's brokerage operation. Prior to entering the fields of insurance and reinsurance, he spent 10 years in commercial banking. He has a B.S. from Fordham University and an M.B.A. from Emory University.

H. A. (Hal) Schaeffer Jr.   Mr. Schaeffer is president of D&H Credit Services Inc. (*www.dandhcredit.com*), a credit consulting firm located in Port Washington, New York. He is a popular speaker at both local and national credit events. With over 29 years of experience, he has received the CCE and CEW certifications from the National Association of Credit Management. He is the author of two books, *Financial Customer Service* and *Credit Risk Management,* both published by John Wiley & Sons.

John R. Shuman   Mr. Shuman has been manager of the Small and Medium-Sized Enterprises Trade Finance Program & Senior International Trade Specialist, U.S. Department of Commerce, International Trade Administration from 1990 to the present. He graduated from Georgetown University Law Center (Washington, D.C.), Stetson University College of Law (St. Petersburg, Florida), and New York University School of Commerce, Finance and Accounts. He is an active member of the D.C. and Florida Bar.

Riccardo M. Striano   Mr. Striano is a senior vice president of ITF, The Internet Trade Finance Exchange (*www.itfex.com*), an Internet-based exchange, providing online solutions for forfaiting and trade finance. He was formerly senior vice president of London Forfaiting Americas and has specialized in forfaiting and trade finance since 1987 in Europe and the United States. An acknowledged expert in forfaiting, Mr. Striano is on the advisory board of the FCIB-NACM. In addition to regular speaking engagements across the United States, Mr. Striano has published numerous articles related to trade and finance.

Eva Taylor   Ms. Taylor is the marketing coordinator at NCM Americas' headquarters in Baltimore. NCM Americas, Inc., is a wholly owned subsidiary of the NCM Group (*www.ncmamericas.com*) headquartered in Amsterdam.

Cynthia M. Wieme   Ms. Wieme has been in the international aviation credit industry for six years, currently serving as credit manager, Jeppesen's World-Wide Operations. Her professional background includes 20+ years in Finance and Accounting, focusing on Credit and Collections for the last 10 years. She has passed the National Association of Credit Management exam for Certified Credit Executive. She has an M.B.A. in Technology Management and undergraduate degrees in Business Administration and Management. She serves in various officer and volunteer positions for the Mackintosh Academy (for Gifted Children); The Arthritis Foundation, Rocky Mountain Chapter; NACM North Central, International Aviation Industry Group, and is a past officer for the NACM Rocky Mountain affiliate and the Colorado Federation of Business & Professional Women.

Dorman Wood   Mr. Wood earned his B.A. in Management from St. Mary's College of California. An alumnus of the Graduate School of Credit and Financial Management of Stanford University's Graduate School of Business, he is a certified credit executive (CCE) and fellow of the National Institute of Credit. He currently serves as president of the San Francisco-NCC chapter of CFDD and is a member of NACM's National Technology Committee. Since 1982, Mr. Wood has been principal and managing director of Dorman Wood Associates, a business-to-business credit solutions consultancy specializing in start-up through initial public offering high-tech firms (*www.b2bcreditsolutions.com*). He frequently speaks on various aspects of e-commerce, credit, collections, cash management, business communications, bankruptcy, and business ethics at credit group meetings, in-house training sessions, and trade association conferences, and conducts workshops and seminars.

Acknowledgments

This book would not have been possible without the wealth of material I have collected over the last six years while working as an editor at the Institute of Management and Administration (IOMA) writing two credit publications. This position allowed me to talk to the best credit minds in the industry and attend many conferences and lectures by great speakers on a wide variety of topics. For this I am indebted to Perry Patterson, vice president and publisher at IOMA; David Foster, IOMA's president; and in memoriam to John Marqesee, the company's inspiring founding chairman.

I was also extremely lucky to have chapters contributed by the following experts: Mike Barry, Paul Beretz, Al Carl, Lewis Flax, Bob Frewen, Jennifer Hudgens, Dave Marsh, Tom Rispante, Hal Schaeffer, John Shuman, Riccardo Straino, Eva Taylor, Cynthia Wieme, and Dorman Woods.

Finally, I would like to thank the many credit professionals who have willingly talked to me over the years, sharing their incredible experiences with me and the readers of my publications. There are simply too many to name. I am always impressed by the willingness of those in the credit profession to help their peers. This book is the result of that selflessness. Thank you.

Preface

As the economy becomes more competitive and companies look for ways to expand, the international arena is the obvious choice for a growing number of organizations. Thus, it is imperative that those credit professionals who wish to be successful expand their horizons to include international—and there is a lot to learn. While international used to be the province of credit professionals who focused strictly globally, this is no longer the case. In a growing number of companies, the company's credit manager is expected to handle international activity as well. This is not to say that some larger companies do not have professionals focusing exclusively on international, just that in many cases the individual with the title "credit manager" is expected to handle credit worldwide.

The approaches that work fine domestically often need to be modified drastically to work in the international marketplace. Each country is different from the next. The strategies that work in one Latin American country may not work in its neighbor. Just as southerners in this country are different from northerners and New Yorkers are different from Texans, so to are the people and attitudes in other countries. Additionally, there are concepts such as country risk, differing payment systems, different legal systems, cultural differences, and forfaiting that just are not relevant domestically.

Given the diversity of topics, it is hard for one person to be an expert on every aspect of international credit. Thus, this book contains contributions from experts in the field. Credit insurance, forfaiting, international credit reporting, and government programs are handled by experts in those areas. Additionally, several credit professionals developed chapters on their own particular area of expertise. Many consider most interesting the cultural difference chapters written by international credit professionals who have traveled extensively to other areas. Wherever possible, we have included real-life examples, although occasionally the names have been changed to protect those involved. We have also included a number of case studies.

This book starts at the beginning with a review of international credit. Some companies, when they first dip their toes into the international arena, skimp when it comes to doing credit investigations and analysis. As a result, these companies often end up selling to customers that they would never extend credit to domestically as the customer does not meet its credit standards. Yet no credit analysis is done because of the difficulty in finding credit information, because many foreign companies do not (or will not) produce financial statements, and because the statements, if produced, do not conform to generally accepted accounting practices. And guess what happens? The company takes a bath.

So, this book starts by looking at establishing an international credit policy in Chapter 1. It includes a review of the credit reporting information available and the quality of that data, which varies from country to country. An investigation of credit applications for international customers and a look at how country risk affects credit and collections are also included in Chapters 3 and 4.

Once a company has a strong international credit policy in place, it can then turn its eyes toward its collection policies, confident that lax credit policies are not affecting collections. The chapters on collections (Chapters 5 through 8) not only review the basics of collections and provide tips on speeding up collections, but include a look at invoice discounting and a report from an international collection expert that contains many real-life examples of how she was able to help her customers, often despite the intervention of senior management and the sales force.

Those expecting to do business in another country without understanding the people and how business is done in that country will run into a brick wall. Each country has its own particular nuances. Several years ago, I visited London for vacation with my then 20-year-old son. Each morning while he got some additional beauty sleep, I had coffee in the lobby and planned our day. Typically, a number of businesspeople were there, some having meetings. The conversations were merely a pleasant hum with no voices distinguishable. One morning as I was sitting I became aware of a louder insistent, and unfortunately, fairly familiar (American) accent. I started to listen. The loud speaker was obviously a salesperson intent on making a sale. The more the British customer demurred, the harder this man tried. And the more he pushed, the more the customer resisted. It was apparent to me that this sale was not going to happen. Finally, I turned to see who this fellow was. He was addressing a group of businesspeople in business suits. He was standing over them with his suitcase thrown against the wall and wearing a jogging suit. I cringed. He had broken so many unwritten rules for selling in Europe, I doubted there was anyway he would ever sell to this customer.

This book discusses the cultural differences and awareness issues in depth in Chapter 9. Chapters 10 through 12 address the issues in different parts of the world.

Establishing a relationship with the customer is of paramount importance. One of the best ways to do this is through customer visits, as detailed in Chapter 13. Obviously, when the customer is located far away from home, visiting is time consuming and expensive. Yet the most successful international credit professionals insist that this is crucial to creating and maintaining a good relationship.

Credit professionals need to develop a good relationship with the sales department when selling overseas. Sales can be the eyes and ears of the credit department, especially when trips to see the customer are few and far between. Chapter 14 discusses how the credit department can make the relationship with sales work smoothly so both groups benefit.

Credit insurance and forfaiting are two approaches widely used in Europe but rarely used in the United States, a situation that is starting to change as Europeans aggressively attempt to sell these products to U.S. exporters. Some argue, and probably correctly, that in order for U.S. exporters to compete on a level playing field in Europe, credit insurance is a must. Why? Europeans will try to get open-account terms for an extended period of time, something many U.S. credit professionals are not comfortable offering. Credit insurance makes it possible. Thus, some companies selling internationally purchase credit insurance. Although the number doing so is currently small, some in the profession expect its use to grow. Chapters 15 through 19 cover the area of credit insurance.

Government programs are extremely important to small and midsize companies looking to expand into the international arena. They can mean the difference between success and failure for these companies. Chapter 20 offers an in-depth look at what is currently available.

Recent legislation in the United Kingdom changes the manner in which companies can obtain credit information on some of their customers. Chapter 21 describes the current situation in detail. It is written by an Englishman with extensive legal and credit experience.

Bartering and countertrade are alive and well and in use by some of the largest companies. Chapter 22 explains the basics, and Chapter 23 demonstrates how a *Fortune* 500 company was able to use countertrade to make a sale where the payment options were limited.

It is not possible to talk about international trade without mentioning letters of credit. While many people despise them, many companies still use them. Chapter 24 covers the basics of letters of credit. Chapter 25 addresses some of the more common letter-of-credit problems and what credit professionals can do to avoid them.

Technology is making inroads into all our lives, and international credit is no exception. Something as simple as e-mail is radically changing the way credit professionals interact with their international customers, their international sales staff, and other parties, such as freight forwarders who are involved in the transaction. Technology is making international credit and collections somewhat easier and is drastically changing the way the job is done and the level of sophistication involved in international credit. We expect this to continue. Chapters 26 through 29 cover new technology areas.

No longer does some guy in the back office wearing green eyeshades handle credit. It is a serious job, and the executive who does it well is handsomely compensated and well educated. While M.B.A.s are not the norm in the credit profession, many who work in the field have them. Those who succeed are those who keep up-to-date and continue to study and learn. In this vein, the FCIB, the international arm of the NACM recently announced a new certification for those with serious international experience. This certification is a signal of the growing importance of international activity in the credit profession. Chapter 30 looks at professionalism in the field of international credit.

The book is filled with web addresses that the authors feel would be useful to the readers. These addresses are accurate at the time we go to print. Some will change or cease to exist even by the time the book first hits the bookstores. We have no control over this. Also, readers may know of new sites that are not included. We have attempted to include the best sites available at the time we are producing this book.

Good luck in all your international endeavors.

Contents

PART ONE

INTERNATIONAL CREDIT

The importance of credit when dealing in the international arena cannot be overstated. It is an area that many overlook until this neglect comes back to hit them in the face. Some companies start selling internationally with no one taking responsibility for the credit aspect until a disaster occurs. Then things change and change rapidly.

The first thing that credit professionals need to understand is that they cannot take their domestic credit policy and credit application and use it internationally and expect everything to work just fine—it will not happen. For starters, terms offered in the rest of the world are typically much longer than what domestic credit managers are accustomed to. Yet 60 days will seem short to most international customers. And as most credit professionals are painfully aware, the longer the credit terms, the higher the risk.

Thus, credit analysis on international customers needs to be thorough. The dimension of country risk also needs to be addressed.

Finally, the quality of the information is often not as good as domestic credit professionals are used to. Information may be outdated, is likely to be unaudited, and it can be sketchy. Many credit professionals get quite a shock when they find out the prices of international credit reports. They are not cheap. Neither are country reports. Yet both are important to obtain, as both issues will radically affect the ability to get paid—the goal of every credit and collections professional.

1

International Credit Policy

Mary S. Schaeffer

IOMA

A workable international credit policy is the first step to ensuring the collection of international receivables. Although most companies have a formal credit policy for domestic sales, many do not have one for international transactions. They either use the domestic policy to cover international sales or, in shocking disregard of credit managers' ingrained common sense, fly by the seat of their pants. The result is granting credit, often on open-account terms, to international companies whose ratings would earn them a quick and automatic pass if they were domestic. Even those companies that have a formal policy have not reviewed it in eons. Given the ever-changing international landscape and technology innovations, international credit policies should be updated periodically—in any event no less frequently than every two or three years. Thus, establishing and enforcing a strict credit policy for international sales is a challenge facing many international credit professionals today.

GETTING STARTED

Just getting an international credit policy written down and accepted by management can be a big undertaking at many companies. Some start out trying to use the same policy they use for their local customers, only to find it does not work. For starters, financial statements in other countries do not generally conform to generally accepted accounting principles (GAAP). Then there is the issue of longer terms used in most countries.

Finally, U.S. companies are often competing with companies from other countries willing to sell on what at first appears to be more lenient terms. Only after a little analysis do managers discover that their competition might be selling on open account, having purchased credit insurance to handle the risk.

3

Often, a big selling job needs to be done internally just to establish a policy. "I had to convince management that the credit department was not only reviewing the customers' status but also analyzing the risk involved with our exposure" is not an uncommon complaint.

Management is not always the stumbling block. Sometimes the lack of a policy causes the apprehension. To alleviate this concern, write an international credit and collection policy.

ESTABLISHING THE POLICY

Once there is agreement that the policy needs to be established, the next debate typically revolves around what goes in the policy. Often, it is the same old credit-versus-sales debate. Many successful international credit policies work because they contain a number of options. Potential risk and the exposure to bad debt are just two typical concerns. Formulating a policy for establishing sound credit limits addresses these issues. Incorporate certain techniques not typically used with domestic sales. These might include credit insurance, the sale of certain receivables, the use of export factoring, forfaiting, and everybody's favorite: letters of credit.

Country focus also can be an issue depending on where sales are occurring. Companies might use more liberal credit terms in countries where they feel more comfortable. Of course, this approach may have problems, as customers in riskier countries typically are in greater need of more liberal terms.

Occasionally, a company will become concerned about one particular country and will establish a separate policy for sales in that locale. For example, one company, concerned about bad debts in China, established a separate policy for sales to companies in that country. The credit professional reports that normal terms are cash in advance. Based on time and finances, the company moves customers to net 15 as warranted.

ENFORCING THE POLICY

Getting a policy set down is one thing. As credit professionals are only too well aware, getting the sales force to live with it is another. The job is only half done until it becomes crystal clear to everyone within the company that the policy must be adhered to. "Protecting our assets," says one international credit manager of a consumer manufacturing company, "means not being too lenient with terms for customers that sales wants to sell." To make sure the policy is understood, this resolute credit manager says he states the company's credit position and function and ensures there is a clear understanding. While this is a little difficult in the beginning, the net result is a smoother-running operation.

Getting control is often easier said than done. The director of credit of another consumer manufacturing company devised a solution. "I put a form together," he says, "that [guaranteed] no shipments could be made from our factories abroad without my signature." Since he controlled shipments, he also controlled orders and, indirectly, collections—he would not ship if there was an outstanding invoice that had not been paid.

POINTS COVERED BY POLICY

When establishing an international credit policy, take into account the following general considerations:

- The longer time period for delivery, fund transfer (payment), and the credit extension period
- The need for terms that provide for security for the risks of time and distance
- The competition created by credit terms from the domestic market and other foreign competitors
- The competition from other countries having different costs and governmental policies
- The correct use of international terminology such as shipping and payment terms, especially the use of INCOTERMs
- The assessment of political transfer and event risk, including: identifying sources of information, establishing procedures for assessing and spreading the risk, and evaluating and verifying the sources and reliability of information obtained
- The assessment of customer risk

CUSTOMER RISK

The crux of any credit analysis is, of course, the ability and willingness of the customer ultimately to pay for the goods shipped to it by the company. This is difficult enough in the case of a domestic transaction. In the case of a company in another country, the process of analyzing credit becomes more difficult. Additional considerations are:

- *Identify, verify, and understand the customer's financial condition.* Establish customer categories for assessing their ability and intention to meet obligations. Determine the volume of credit and payment terms, credit limits, and the need for on-site assessment. Rarely are international credit professionals offered financial statements that are as thorough as those prepared according to GAAP.
- *Compare current performance with past performance.* To do this effectively, international credit professionals must understand and interpret foreign financial information, including balance sheets,

profit-and-loss statements, notes to the statements, auditor reports, and chairman statements. The move toward one international accounting standard should help with this.

- *Compare performance with other customers from the same country or region.*
- *Assess the customer's ability to pay.* The initial information gathering should include verification of information and references. Credit professionals should review and update these on a regular basis so that they will begin to understand the payment behavior and be in a position to identify warning signals of financial distress. Unfortunately, by the time these trends show in financial statements, the customer is in much worse financial condition and supplier chances of being repaid have plummeted.

EARLY WARNING SIGNS

The ability to recognize the indications of financial difficulty as early as possible is key to successfully limiting losses. Doing so is especially difficult when dealing with companies in other countries, as "normal" behavior patterns often are quite different from what credit professionals might be accustomed to when dealing with their domestic customers. Focus on the following when monitoring accounts for signs of trouble:

- Changes in the general behavior of the account
- Changes in the payment patterns
- News reports
- Financial ratio analysis
- Increase in the number of disputed transactions

Whether the last item is the result of financial difficulty or simply difficulty in the relationship may be irrelevant to the collection issue, and credit professionals need to hone in on this aspect as soon as possible. A good relationship with the sales staff will pay off in these instances, as they may be able to determine whether the problem with the customer can be fixed or not. The Internet also helps international credit professionals stay on top of the news. Newspaper summaries from papers in the local country may be available online. Some international credit executives have been able to spot bad news quite early in this manner.

REVAMP EXISTING INTERNATIONAL CREDIT POLICY

As mentioned, just having a policy is only half the battle. If it is not revised every few years—or more, under certain circumstances—it will become stale and outdated and possibly even worse than having no policy. "How is this possible?" you ask. A policy that works in a country when there are no economic or political uncertainties would be a disaster once the political or economic arena worsened. Thus, a devaluation, an unexpected government overthrow, or a serious financial deterioration as occurred in the Far East in the late 1990s should trigger a review of the international credit policy.

WRITTEN POLICIES

A number of companies are establishing formal written international credit policies. They are requiring the sales force to adhere to these policies when selling internationally. Once a policy is put down in writing and management approves it, the credit professionals have some teeth when attempting to get it adhered to.

A number of respondents indicated that they got buy-in from the sales department when establishing their policies. Not only does this avoid friction when trying to implement the policy at a later date, it also is a good step toward building a stronger relationship with the sales department.

However, after a few years, pull out the policy, and make the changes to it as appropriate. Before going to senior management for approval, discuss the changes with those who will be affected. Also ask for input from those who might be affected and who should have some say. This would include the financial executives responsible for the area or products, the sales force, perhaps the export manager, and any other party touched by the policy. By asking their opinion, you are increasing the odds of their buy-in later on.

If you are making changes that are likely to cause some dissent, discuss these changes in advance with the affected parties and explain the reasons for the changes.

WHAT TO DO WHEN THERE IS NO POLICY

Despite all that has been written on the topic, a number of credit professionals find that their companies still do not have a formal international credit policy. Lack of such a policy not only causes confusion but also conflict. It also gives a manipulative sales force the ammunition it needs to jam questionable sales down the throats of the credit department. Credit professionals in these companies must do what they can to insist on a policy.

At a minimum, international companies should conform to domestic requirements. Even this provision is difficult to enforce, as other countries do not require financial statements that conform to GAAP. Additionally, often long time lags exist before such statements are available; once they are, they may or may not be audited and they may be written in a foreign language.

By insisting on a written approved international credit policy, credit managers will be in a position to establish some reasonable guidelines for all to adhere to. If all members of the sales force are given a copy, no one can say that he or she did not know what the policy was.

It will not be an easy or quick process to get an international credit policy established and approved, but once the policy is written and approved it will be easier, but not easy, to enforce. Keep track of all transactions that are approved against the advice of the credit department. Track those sales to see if and when they are paid. Any time a large international debt is written off, make management and sales aware of the write-off and that this was not a transaction that credit approved. If this is done in a nonoffensive manner, eventually the point will be made and those who prefer no policy will cooperate. Strike while the iron is hot and have the policy written down.

INTERNATIONAL CREDIT POLICY TIPS

Based on conversations with hundreds of international credit professionals, here are the techniques that work best.

- Produce a coherent credit policy for selling international accounts and make sure the sales force and sales reps, if they are used, understand it.
- Begin accepting corporate procurement cards for international sales. Be aware, however, of the fees charged by most service providers and make sure prices cover these fees. Otherwise, you may be giving away all your profits. Procurement cards are a particularly attractive option for smaller sales and allow companies to sell to customers who might not meet ordinary credit standards. Most salespeople love this option.
- Develop a simple, but complete, credit application that can be faxed. Leave adequate space for the customer to fill in needed information. Then accept signed applications that are faxed back. Doing so will make you a hero with the sales department.
- For smaller accounts, use a scoring system to determine which method of account to use for each sale: letters of credit, open account, documentary collections, and so on. Some report success using this technique on larger sales as well. However, you may want to review large sales individually.
- Document your policies and procedures in a manual. Doing so will help the credit staff implement them. Give a copy to the sales department, if that is appropriate.
- Require letters of credit only when absolutely necessary. Companies that have demanded all customers provide letters of credit are beginning to rethink that requirement. Such requirements often lose sales as letters of credit are expensive for customers and a hassle for everyone involved. While proper in many cases, they are not always needed. By eliminating this requirement on small orders, some companies have garnered additional business with little additional risk.

- Within limits, let the selling unit closest to the market set terms. After all, these are the individuals in the best position to know what is typical for that country. The companies that have had the best success with this approach are those requiring these same units to follow up on late payments and those that pay commissions only after the company collects its money. Salespeople who have to wait for their money are going to think very carefully about extended terms.

- Limit export credit to companies with ties in the continental United States. While not everyone will agree with this approach, the few companies that do use it report they have better control over marketing conflicts. This might work for those firms that are just starting to export.

- Have the international credit policy formalized and approved by senior management. While this may take a bit of time in the beginning, it will save time and aggravation in the long run. More than one salesperson has tried to make an end run around credit by going straight to senior management about a credit decision. Doing so is more difficult if the credit policy has been preapproved. If your sales force is apt to try such a maneuver, make sure they understand the formal credit policy.

- Ship goods to a bonded warehouse for release to distributors in countries where international sales are to be made. (Only if the distributor's account is current, of course.) This approach offers freight payment savings as well.

- Upgrade credit policies when key personnel turn over. Several firms have reported stumbling blocks in the form of employees (some of them quite senior) who insist on doing things "the way we always have." Strike while the iron is hot and before newcomers get too entrenched in the old way.

- Rewrite the credit policy as simply as possible. One flexible credit pro reports that he "broke down rules of thumb, which confused everyone, into a few simple categories and then educated everyone involved." The old KISS (Keep It Simple, Stupid) approach really works.

- Get sales involved in the establishment of the new credit policy. Find out what gives them difficulty and see if they can be accommodated. Sometimes a simple adjustment in the credit policy can make their lives much easier. Often what is needed becomes clear if the credit manager goes on some sales calls with the sales force. The old aphorism about "walking a mile in someone else's shoes" certainly fits in this case. Many international credit managers who have done this come back with a new respect for sales.

- Hire agents who will get paid only after the company is paid. This will prevent reps from selling to companies that they know either will not pay or will pay only after a good deal of follow-up and trouble. No one wants to waste his or her time.

- Use a matrix that employs third-party credit reports to evaluate international customers' credit risk.

- Ship to new accounts only on cash-in-advance or letter-of-credit terms.
- Standardize guidelines regarding which companies you will sell to on open account. This will stop the ongoing conflict between sales and credit.
- Use letters of credit designed to meet established seller criteria.
- Incorporate into every international sales contract the letter-of-credit requirements, terms, and conditions of sale. Doing so saves both time and money at the negotiation stage.
- Begin using international accounts receivable insurance. Doing so generally permits companies to offer their customers longer terms and larger credit limits.
- Use credit insurance for marginal customers and those in high-risk countries. Doing so allows sales expansion when selling under standard credit terms would not.
- Begin to communicate consistently and on a timely basis with international customers when payments are late. By doing this with the consensus and agreement of the sales department, you will reduce conflicts and customers will begin to realize that they cannot play one department against the other.
- Develop a comprehensive handbook for the sales force that contains all necessary information, so they can quote accurately. Include matters such as letter-of-credit terms, lists of customers they may sell to on open-account terms, INCOTERMs to use, wire transfer information, and credit card use.
- Rewrite any old, staid policies so they are more user friendly. This does not necessarily mean loosening terms but rather rewriting the policy in a manner that is easy for the end user to understand.
- Do not let the sales force establish terms of sale. The credit department or someone who fully understands and appreciates the ramifications of such policies should handle this. One company that implemented such a policy was able to reduce its Days Sales Outstanding (DSO) by 20 days.
- Create a credit risk model to score customers' audited financial statement figures. Use this to ascertain whether specific customers can be offered open-account terms. Customers who do not meet the open-account standards can be offered secured terms.
- In order to give operating units more latitude in the decision-making process, involve the unit heads in determining whether to accept or reject "unusual" terms and conditions of sale.
- Develop innovative international financing programs to help the sales force meet goals without increasing credit risk. Some credit managers have used receivables discounting in order to offer extended terms. Doing so is especially important to those selling in the Far East.
- Identify customers who also work with other units of the company. Involve upper management in developing a unified approach to establishing credit limits for such entities so that reasonable amounts of credit are extended in total. The goal is not to overextend without realizing it.

ONGOING MONITORING

Luckily for international credit managers, the world is a continually changing place. We say "luckily," because continual movement translates into an ongoing need for international credit professionals. Here is what should be done regularly:

- Don't assume: "It's a big company, nothing can hurt it."
- Obtain updated information from trading partners to ascertain their liquidity and to determine whether they will have trouble meeting their obligations during the course of the next year. If you are having trouble getting new information, go back to the balance sheet statements that you already possess to ascertain the company's debt position when you last reviewed its account.
- Divide accounts by country. Not all countries are in the same position; do not treat the entire Pacific Rim equally.
- Divide the companies into public and private and then look at their payment history with the company and with others, if available. Doing so may allow you to attribute risk appropriately in a market that has risk written all over it.
- Continue to ask for letters of credit if this was the practice in the past. Be careful about the issuing bank and the confirming bank. Analyze, or at least review, the position of the customer's bank if it is involved in the transaction. Do not assume that banks cannot fail. The best protection is to use the services of an American or established European bank for letter-of-credit needs unless you have reviewed the local bank's financial and political situation.
- Monitor the political situation in each of the countries where you are doing business. Many recent troubles stem from internal political and economic inefficiencies. The reaction to economic strife can be the reaction of one individual or family, thus, making it difficult to predict a stable pattern of behavior. This is especially true in the case of dictatorships.

An international credit policy is an integral part of a successful international credit operation. It is the first step toward avoiding bad debt write-offs and late-paying customers. Without an international credit policy, international credit executives will fight an uphill battle.

2

International Credit Information

Lewis Flax

Graydon America

Evaluating the creditworthiness of customers is never an easy task. When the customer is located in another country, the issue becomes more complicated. International credit professionals must deal with the fact that accounting standards in other countries are not the same as generally accepted accounting procedures (GAAP) and are typically less rigorous. Additionally, information available from credit agencies may not be as complete or as up-to-date as one would like.

The country risk issue must be evaluated, separate and apart from customer risk. Customers could be of the highest quality but if it is impossible to get good funds out of a country, then international credit professionals are back at square one. Some companies establish not only credit lines for individual companies but overall credit exposure credit limits by country. These country limits are raised or lowered depending on the economic outlook of the country in question.

INTERNATIONAL CREDIT REPORTS

Most credit executives begin their credit evaluations by requesting an international credit report from one of the agencies offering this information. This information is often simply pulled from a database. While this allows the credit report company to provide a report quickly, the information in the report is dated, sometimes by as much as two or three years. Additional factors to be considered when using international credit reports include:

- Database versus updated information. Do you need current data or will information two to three years old suffice?
- When should reports be ordered—at the time of shipment, for the annual review, or when a new customer is being considered?

- Does the annual review coincide with the financial statement filing requirements within the country?
- The lead time required between ordering the report and receiving it, especially if updated information is required. Remember, the customer is not in Peoria—getting the report will take time.
- Financial statement filing requirements within the country.
- Does the country (or province) maintain requirements for filing financial statements?
- What is the timing of the requirements—quarterly/annually?
- What is the quality of the information? Are the statements audited or prepared internally?
- What information is available through court registries and public filings? This can include:
  — bankruptcies
  — date established
  — ownership and organizational/legal structure
  — liens/suits/judgments/charges
  — authorization to sign
  — other

OTHER SOURCES OF CREDIT INFORMATION

Bank Reference Information

International credit professionals often get references from banks for customers' international banks as part of their credit investigation. When obtaining such information, the first step is to ascertain whether it is available. Before requesting the reference, get permission in writing from customers to do so. Otherwise, bankers may refuse to provide the information requested.

Trade Reference Information

While not as common as with domestic accounts, international trade groups do exist. Membership and participation in the international trade groups can be invaluable. Both the FCIB (an association of executives in Finance, Credit and International Business) and the Riemer organization have international groups.

Management/Ownership

Information about the individuals who own the customer is invaluable. Often, these same individuals own other companies, and it is possible to check on those other entities. Subsidiary, affiliate, and parent information is useful as well. Innovative credit professionals have been able to structure transactions with customers located in countries deemed to be financial unstable by arranging payments from an affiliate located in a more stable country.

IMPACT OF EXCHANGE RATE FLUCTUATIONS

When analyzing financial statements from customers in other countries, note the currency used in the report. Fluctuations in that currency and the impact this may have on financial information should be noted. This is especially important if customers are paying in U.S. dollars. On the face of it, payment in U.S. dollars may seem to protect the U.S. seller, but this is not always the case. If the home currency plunges, a customer may have difficulty getting enough funds to pay for the goods. Imagine what would happen if your monthly mortgage payment suddenly went up 50 percent, especially if the value of the house did not go up. This is effectively what happens to the customer. The price it pays for goods goes up, but the price the goods are sold at cannot be increased enough to offset the additional unexpected cost.

LACK OF GOOD FINANCIAL INFORMATION

Often, international credit executives simply do not have adequate information. The problem may be due to the unwillingness of companies to release information, or the information just may not be available. Many companies keep more than one set of books—one for the taxing authorities and another for the owners. Also, some customers are vaguely connected with other companies, making it difficult to get an accurate financial picture. These factors should be factored into the ultimate credit evaluation and the decision as to whether to ask for a letter of credit or other security.

QUALITY OF INFORMATION

It is not uncommon to hear that credit information in the rest of the world is not as good as it is in the United States. Is this true, or is this boasting just another case of Americans believing that they do everything better than the rest of the world? The "quality issue" in the international arena definitely warrants discussion. These remarks are generalizations, and there are country-by-country variations in the quality of information available. In general, the farther north one goes in Europe, the better the information becomes. Conversely, the data becomes sketchier the farther south a country is located.

The most important thing to realize is that, while the data in the rest of the world is not up to U.S. standards, it is getting better. Some information from other countries is just as good as what you could get in the United States. In a number of cases, information that was not possible to obtain just a few years ago is now available or will be in the next few years.

FINANCIAL INFORMATION

Europe

Most countries require that financial information be filed six to eight months after the end of a company's fiscal year. Companies that miss the filing date are fined. Unfortunately, in many countries, it is possible to pay the fine and never file the reports—and that is what some companies do intentionally. Even when financial statements are filed, the information included may be minimal, as many file on the old English system, which lets a company show sales, expenses, and a net profit without the accompanying details and footnotes. However, many companies are providing more information now. Statements from Belgian companies are quite good. Information from German companies varies, because each province has its own requirements. Italian requirements are not stringent, making the data mediocre.

Asia and Australia

Once again, in most countries companies are required to file limited financial information. The quality varies from country to country, but the information from Australian and Japanese companies is particularly good.

Latin America

The most important thing to realize is that most Latin Americans have a cultural reluctance to share financial information with vendors. For whatever reason, many Latin Americans believe that if their financial statements show they are profitable, North American vendors will charge higher prices. Thus, they would rather show a loss or minimal profit in the hope of getting a better price. Of course, this thinking contradicts what U.S. credit professionals believe. There are no filing requirements in Latin American countries. Companies in Brazil, Argentina, Mexico, and Chile provide the best information.

COURT RECORDS AND PUBLIC FILINGS

Europe

For the most part, the information available from public records is good. Government offices do not compile all information available from public records. In many instances the task has been subcontracted out to private enterprises. In another exciting development for creditors, trade tapes are beginning to be used extensively. Database listings of all companies are also available.

Latin America

The likelihood of getting accurate information from public records is much better in large industrialized regions than it is in rural areas. For the most part, trade tape data does not exist, and database information is a hit-or-miss affair, although database information usually can be found about most large companies. Mexican banks have recently announced the adoption of credit reporting practices similar to those used in the United States. With many loans tied to an inflation rate that occasionally has approached 100 percent, this information is critical in Mexico. Trans Union is a large investor in a joint venture with BC Buro de Credito and has compiled information about 25 million loans, while Exquifax says it has information about 8 million loans and hopes to have the information on 20 million loans in less than one year.

Asia

The only requirements in most Asian countries is that there be a corporate registration. Information about public filings and bankruptcy is not available. At this time, trade tapes do not exist, and database information is limited mostly to larger companies.

OTHER DIFFERENCES

Cultural differences should have an impact on the way financial data is viewed regarding nonsufficient funds (NSF). In this country most creditors do not see the notation of an NSF check in a credit file as a big deal, as long as the payment was made. In most of Latin America, especially Brazil, it is considered a serious problem. Therefore, most companies will go to great lengths to avoid a situation that would give rise to an NSF check. So, credit professionals who run into one should be aware that it could indicate serious financial problems because the debtor would have avoided it if possible.

With ever-improving financial information available about their international customers, credit executives are now in a better position than ever to get that data and make intelligent credit decisions. However, the data available is limited; international credit professionals still need to rely not only on the data but on other sources of information.

OTHER FACTORS AFFECTING THE CREDIT PROCESS

Even if international credit professionals do everything correctly, the company may still not collect all that it is owed because other factors, beyond the control of the credit professionals, affect the eventual outcome. These factors need to be considered when making the final credit decision.

Even after making the perfect credit evaluation, the sale can still be derailed by others in the company who do not handle their functions effectively. While this is true in all sales, it is many times more important with international sales simply because there are so many things that can go wrong. By asking "Do we have internal staff capable of handling these responsibilities?" and "Are we working with other companies that can manage these tasks?" international credit professionals will be able to determine if any adjustments need to be made. Specifically, the areas of concern include:

- Logistics/Transportation
  — Air/ocean shipments
  — Warehouse/storage
- Documentation
  — Contract or purchase order
  — Payment method
  — Evidence of shipment
  — Collection efforts
  — Government requirements—Both United States and buyer's country
- Insurance
  — Marine/cargo policy
  — Risk management
- Sales Representatives/Agents/Distributors
  — Location
  — Coordination

Amazingly enough, many companies with strong domestic credit standards have no international credit policy. On an international basis they extend credit on open-account terms to a company that would qualify only for cash in advance were it a domestic company. Similarly, at these firms, international collection efforts are much weaker and start much later than with domestic accounts. Thus, it is important to establish separate international credit policies and procedures.

COLLECTION EXPERIENCE AND CONDITIONS

Each country has its own rules and regulations surrounding collection activity, especially as it relates to third-party collectors. Some countries permit interest on late payments and others do not. Specifically, when setting a collection policy, the following issues should be considered:

- Jurisdiction
- Legal system
- Documentation requirements
- Standard terms
- Interest provisions

3

International Credit Applications

Mary S. Schaeffer

IOMA

Devising an effective international credit application is not as easy as it might seem. Many companies either do not have an international credit application or use their domestic application for international accounts. However, as international trade grows and becomes a larger part of any firm's sales, the need for a separate application for international sales becomes greater. The information here came from applications currently in use at half a dozen companies and interviews with knowledgeable credit professionals.

DEVELOPING ONE'S OWN APPLICATION

The following list details information that could be incorporated into an international credit application. International credit professionals should assess the list to find items that are applicable to their own organizations. In designing the actual form, information should be arranged in such a fashion that customers have space to provide the information requested. The following information is to be requested of potential customers:

- Name of company
- Date application is completed
- Company address
- Telephone number
- Fax number
- Billing address
- Company web site (if available)

- Name, title, e-mail address, and phone number of person responsible for accounts payable
- Web address where status of payments can be checked (if available)
- Type of business
- Type of operation
- Date of incorporation
- Amount of credit line desired
- Nature of business
- List of primary countries where customer does business
- Name and title of person in charge of buying
- Buyer's primary shipping documentation instructions
- Total annual sales
- Full names of principals
- Kind of business
- Number of employees
- Major products
- Approximate square footage
- Plant capacity
- Project manager
- Name of any parent, subsidiary, or affiliate securing the payment obligations
- Preferred freight forwarder
- Contact information for preferred freight forwarder
- Availability of an international credit report
- International DUNS (Dun and Bradstreet's) number
- One to three bank references with account numbers, addresses, contact names, e-mail addresses, and phone numbers
- Two to six vendor references with account numbers, addresses, contact names, e-mail addresses, and phone numbers
- Statement about truthfulness and accuracy of information provided
- Signature of officer with title

The latest audited financial statements should supplement all international credit applications. Most applications ask for one or more attachments. These could include:

- The most recent fiscal year's financial statements, preferably audited
- A recent credit agency report
- Descriptive company brochures
- Financial statements for the last year or two

Some companies include a list of their own requirements, including fees and acceptable methods of payment, with their credit applications. Doing so helps prevent trouble down the road and avoids confusion when customers justifiably claim that the salesperson never provided a particular piece of data. That list is not quite as long as what is required on the credit application and is included in the next section.

INFORMATION PROVIDED TO POTENTIAL CUSTOMERS

To prevent problems before they occur, many international credit and collection executives provide their customers with the information they will need to make payment within terms and to fill out needed documentation. This information can include some or all of the following:

- Selling terms in detail using INCOTERMs
- Explanation of methods of payment and what is required for each (open account, cash, wiring instructions, credit card, letter of credit)
- Name and relevant information for advising bank for letters of credit
- Document preparation fee
- Freight forwarder fees
- Bank fees
- Special instructions regarding
  — insurance
  — partial shipments
  — transhipment
  — freight collect
  — grace period for letters of credit
  — other special requirements
- Freight forwarder's name, address, and phone number
- Beneficiary's name, address, and phone number
- Any other information customers should have regarding your company's purchase orders

Not all information pertaining to a company's policies should be incorporated into the credit application. Items such as whether arbitration will be used and which courts will prevail should there be a legal dispute are more appropriate for the sales contract.

GETTING STARTED

Any company that has not reviewed its current international credit and sales application and procedures in the last three years is overdue for an evaluation. Three years ago use of e-mail was minimal, and virtually no company made payment-timing information available over the Internet. Now these approaches are commonplace.

If, upon review of the current application, it becomes apparent that a new application is advisable, credit professionals should draft a new one based on the information suggested in this chapter and their company's own special requirements. However, before implementing, get management support. Before sending the new application along for approval, review it to see if you can identify any points that are likely to cause controversy either in your own organization or with potential customers.

Having identified these trigger points, devise a winning line of reasoning that can be used when you are called on to defend your recommendation.

Once you have the approval from management to proceed with the new application, work with the sales staff to make sure they understand it and will have no problem getting potential customers to fill it out.

CREDIT APPLICATIONS FOR EXISTING CUSTOMERS

Many credit professionals will face the question of what to do about existing customers with little or no information in their files. In an ideal world, the simple approach would be to send each customer an application and ask that it be completed. But this is not an ideal world and this approach will not fly at many companies.

Before undertaking any action, get management support for your plan. Once you have obtained management approval you are ready to proceed with a plan to update the credit files. Although what is to be suggested is likely to set off some complaints, it is better than simply sending the requests for updated credit information directly to customers. Inform sales staff before contacting customers. Yes, they will complain, but you will have a chance to diffuse any inappropriate actions before customers call the individual salespeople demanding to know what is going on.

It is not necessary to involve sales on an ongoing basis. However, the credit application and whatever other documentary requirements you may have should be part of the sales call. If salespeople understand that the credit application must be filled out and financial information obtained before any order is released, they are more likely to work with the international credit department than to try to go around the international credit manager.

4

Country Risk and Its Effect on Credit and Collections

Aloysius J. Carl

Dealing with country turbulence is one of the most fundamental differences between international and domestic credit. Therefore, it is vitally important that a company monitors and evaluates a country's risk factors and understands its various components. Country risk has an effect even when working with industrialized economies. When dealing with developing nations, this hazard can be a major contributor to delinquencies and write-offs for exporters. U.S. businesses have a long history of making credit decisions without regard to country risk, much to their detriment.

International credit managers must evaluate a given country's economic and political situation when establishing credit lines, either by utilizing one of the several country risk services or conducting their own research. Evaluating country risk involves assessing elements such as a country's economy, legal system, political stability, social conditions, and trade-related matters in the present as well as from a historical perspective. Each of these categories has several areas where problems can arise and cause creditors havoc in managing and collecting accounts.

POLITICAL RISK

At the heart of the matter is the political system, since the political risk category seems to be the root cause for most ills. When considering a country's political system, a number of questions should be addressed.

- Is the current regime pro-business?
- Are the other political parties?
- How likely is the current regime to remain in control?

- Is the military under control?
- If the military is not, how likely is an insurrection?
- How effectively does the government manage its economy?
- Is it willing to make tough calls?

Political upheaval will forever cause exporters problems. Even a would-be happy event, such as the collapse of the Soviet Union, can cause severe problems for creditors. Profound change does not happen without leaving problems in its wake.

Example 1. Political Changes

Seemingly positive changes can have a detrimental effect.

A Western U.S. seed company had a major crisis as a by-product of communism's demise in the Soviet Union. The company had been dealing for many years with a Soviet seed distributor that had been supported by the state-run economic system. When the downfall occurred, the Soviet company had an outstanding balance of more than U.S. $1 million. The American firm felt there was no cause for concern because, though historically slow in payments over the years, the company had always cleared its account.

No one at the U.S. business considered how the Soviet company would handle the new conditions thrust upon it. The account was handled as it had been in the past and was allowed to go considerably past normal terms. The U.S. company became worried only when the account was well over a year past due. At this point an international collection firm was brought in to help resolve the matter. Collection agents were sent out to Russia to meet with the company's senior management. Upon arrival, they discovered that the business had changed ownership. Worse yet, the old business had closed under enormous debt problems after crucial governmental financial support had ceased, and the assets had been sold to a newly formed concern. There was nothing to be done. The American company was out of luck and over $1 million.

Understanding the potentially serious impact that the change of the economic system could bring and moving faster in efforts to collect on the account may not have resulted in a better outcome. But it certainly would have increased the chances for a quicker, more positive resolution. Another aspect to be learned from this case is there are times when one must simply take some lumps and walk away.

Example 2. Effects of a Weakening Currency

Another example of how political events can cause credit nightmares was in Brazil. During the late 1990s the country's legislature, in a panic move to control its weakening currency, elected to place severe restrictions on foreign exporters' credit terms. The new controls required exporters to extend terms of net 360 days when granting open credit of U.S. $10,000 or more to Brazilian companies, rather than take more rational measures to control its currency. This change wrought havoc on companies shipping into the country. Accounts had to be immediately reevaluated, credit terms reset, and contracts reworked. It severely confined exporters' abilities to conduct business.

One Eastern U.S. office supply manufacturer elected to break up their shipments into smaller loads and to absorb the higher shipping charges. Doing so enabled the company to continue to sell on open terms with some control over the outstanding balances. By utilizing this strategy, the company not only was able to maintain but actually increased its market share in Brazil, which is a highly competitive market. Companies that did not have that luxury simply lost business.

Many U.S. companies elected to conduct business by various kinds of secured terms. These decisions also caused lost sales and credit problems. Brazilian companies, which previously were receiving fairly generous credit terms from foreign businesses, suddenly saw a major source of capitol dry up. Exacerbating the matter was the fact that the local Brazilian interest rates were in the mid-20 percent. Many Brazilian businesses simply could not meet their financial obligations. When evaluating Brazil, always remember that the government tried this radical measure to solve its internal problems. Rather than making some hard decisions internally, it elected to pass the problem onto the international business community.

LEGAL ISSUES

In resolving collections, a nation's legal system and its view of foreign creditors come into play. Credit managers must know how and if the debt recovery system works. Unfortunately, legal terms and conditions vary throughout the world. Quite a few countries simply do not have a legal process in which foreign creditors are dealt with fairly. The problem may be a lack of opportunity to have the case heard, the presence of severe bias toward foreign creditors, or merely a lack of a working legal system to handle credit issues. Many African countries, among others, simply do not have a structured set of laws for debt. All of these situations can and will happen to firms that deal extensively around the world.

Example 1. Timing

In other countries it can take many years for the case to be heard in court if at all. For example, a U.S. manufacturer was attempting to collect an account in India. The Indian collection agents did their best but were unable to collect any of the money, and they strongly recommended that the case be closed. The U.S. client engaged an attorney, who personally made several unsuccessful attempts to collect the account. The attorney also suggested that the case be closed. When the Americans inquired about going to court, the attorney stated that everyone personally involved with the situation would more than likely be retired before the case was ever heard.

Example 2. Bias against U.S. Companies

Another example of legal system problems is a southern U.S. fish company experiencing severe court delays in its efforts to collect an $11,000 claim from a St. Thomas (U.S. Virgin Islands) debtor. The company began pursuing the account in August 1998. The case quickly "went legal," where it still sits at this writing. The creditor's attorney attempted to get a judge to hear the case. After a number of requests, the judge angrily stated that if the attorney asked about the matter again he would put it at the bottom of the stack. In other words, it would not see the light of day. As of the summer of 2000, the sun has still yet to rise on the case.

Various conditions and requirements must be met in order to proceed legally against a debtor. For example:

- Some countries require a power of attorney to be granted to the attorney suing on the creditor's behalf.
- Many Latin American countries require all of the paperwork to be translated into Spanish and notarized by the country's consulate in order for it to be recognized by the courts.
- Others have statutes of limitations for credit matters.

It is not all bad news, however. In some countries the laws benefit a creditor. For example:

- German law recognizes the creditor's right to charge interest of 4 to 5 percent on overdue accounts if the due date is clearly noted on the invoice.
- Spain recognizes a fixed rate of 10 percent if there is not a previously agreed-upon rate for past due amounts.

Knowing the intricacies of a country's legal system is vital prior to extending open credit.

FOREIGN EXCHANGE

As for currency issues and their impact, the Southeast Asian crises and the Brazilian devaluation are still reasonably fresh. Severe currency devaluations present an extreme challenge to credit executives since many currency "experts" fail to predict these catastrophes. Since everyone seems to be short on prediction capabilities, it is imperative to possess contingency plans. Having strategies for dealing with the crashes will return many benefits to the creditor; first and foremost among them, no panicked decisions.

Example 1. Currency Devaluations

During the Mexican peso crisis of 1994 to 1995, many companies ran scared and played hardball with Mexican debtors. Some companies insisted on placing accounts for collection and pushing the matter quickly into the courts for judgments. Others merely stopped selling on open account to Mexican clients. Both choices were the result of a shortsighted overreaction. These companies had spent a considerable amount of time, effort, and money to establish their customer base, believing that Mexico was a key place to conduct business. At the first series of major problems, they elected a payment strategy that hurt both their clients and future business. It told the Mexican business community that these American businesses were not committed to them and their market.

The more thoughtful American firms, realizing that the crises would not last forever (especially with U.S. government assistance), chose to work out repayment plans with their Mexican counterparts. These decisions enabled business to continue and market share to be retained.

One U.S. company elected such a strategy. A midwestern manufacturing firm had a sizable amount of its extensive Mexican portfolio on open account. The credit manager opted to utilize a strategy designed to, first, keep distributors operational and then to collect money. He continued to sell on open account but at smaller increments, while extending terms from 180 days and to anywhere from 300 to 720 days with installment payments and nominal interest charges. Using this system, he was able to collect all of his outstanding balances and develop some extremely loyal customers.

One of his southern Mexican accounts, which owed U.S. $2.5 million, went to the extreme measure of accepting payment in sugar from its clients at 30 cents on the dollar. Ironically, this company then sold the sugar to companies in the Caribbean basin, which then sold the sugar at a handsome markup to the United States. This account has now become the American company's second largest distributor in all of Mexico.

USE OF DERIVATIVES

Another way to help avoid currency exchange problems is to employ derivatives, which have received quite a bit of bad press. Foreign exchange derivatives are commonly used by larger multinational U.S. businesses, but the percentage of practitioners drops off with the size of the business. Derivatives are an extremely effective tool to hedge against currency exchange risk.

Derivatives transfer the currency risk to a third party, thus enabling the creditor to sell the product in local currency and compete more effectively with domestic firms. Additionally, the costs of the derivative are fixed, which eliminates currency fluctuations and attendant problems. Foreign exchange derivatives are used much more commonly in Europe and should be utilized more by U.S. concerns.

Meteoric rises in a nation's interest rates also severely impact a client's ability to pay. In the United States the interest rate system is relatively stable. Other countries are not so fortunate. What would your company do if short-term rates shot up to 23 percent overnight? How would the company handle its outstanding debt, its accounts payable, and future sales? How would the business finance sales? The impact of this rate increase is also indirect. Domestic suppliers would no longer be able to offer standard credit terms. All readily available short-term finance options would be crippled. Businesses would be in an emergency mode, sitting on payables as long as possible. Only those items absolutely essential to keeping the doors open would be paid. At the same time, the company is attempting to collect from businesses doing the same thing it is. Finally, foreign suppliers want their money as well. Everyone would like to avoid this scenario.

Happily, the United States has not had to deal with this scenario for a long time. Unfortunately, Argentineans cannot make the same statement. They experienced this situation in 1999, when their short-term interest rates soared after Brazil devalued its currency. At the time, the Argentine peso was very stable because it was (and still is) pegged to the U.S. dollar. But that did not help lessen the skyrocketing of interest rates and the dramatic impact on business.

ECONOMIC FACTORS

When assessing a country's economy, look at the currency exchange rate, short- and long-term interest rates, gross domestic product (GDP), the Consumer Price Index (CPI), and recent foreign investment activity. The machinations of the international financial communities, the International Monetary Fund (IMF), and the World Bank and their reactions to recent political events have caused quite a bit of turmoil in developing countries over the past six years. When evaluating these items, it is important to gain historical perspective for a number of years to get a feel for a country's stability.

A country's GDP and CPI should be monitored for acceptable growth and unacceptable inflation. A popular economic school of thought believes that a developing nation requires a GDP of 7 percent or more and a CPI and unemployment rate under double digits in order to have a viable economy. Taking a historical view will reveal the stability of an economy and the government's ability and willingness to manage it. Troubled GDP and CPI numbers usually precede currency and interest rate problems. By watching the GDP and CPI, you should be somewhat forewarned of the potential for rising interest rates and declines in currency value. It is possible to overemphasize these two benchmarks and lose sight of the variables that make up a given nation, as previously discussed.

The economic condition of a country and its social stability are in a symbiotic state. If the people can make a decent living and support their families there will likely be stability even if they are not politically free. It bears out the theory that the better off financially the people are, the more willing they will be to trade away personal freedoms. In turn, the more stability a country has the better the ground for economic growth.

The more destitute the populace the less stable the entire system. People will not tolerate squalor forever. As they lose hope for their economic vitality they turn to more dramatic and severe expressions of displeasure such as riots, looting, armed rebellion, and anticapitalist ideologies.

Example 1. Political Unrest

During the late 1990s, with the Indonesian economy hitting bottom, the government was telling its people that it would address their concerns and fix the situation. It did nothing for months. The people were left to scramble for food while seeing rampant corruption throughout the government, which had robbed the country of billions of dollars. First the students rebelled, an initial sign of growing civilian unrest. General rioting followed shortly. The local population, looking for someone to blame, chose ethnic Chinese businesspeople, who make up a large percentage of the commercial economy. Violence and strikes virtually shut down the country.

A U.S. manufacturer with operations in Indonesia had much of its overseas business impacted when their representative for all of Southeast Asia, an ethnic Chinese, was killed. A U.S. midwestern international business service was also affected when its local agent had his office burned down; the U.S. firm did not learn about the problem for three weeks. The company's dealings in Indonesia were severely disrupted for a number of months, and the Indonesian economy was in tatters for years.

Example 2. Kidnapping Problems

Economic bad times do not always precede civil unrest, although generally they do. The relationship can sometimes be reversed. In 2000, there appeared to be growing unrest in Mexico, despite renewed economic vitality and the first genuinely contested presidential race in the country's history. Mexico gained infamy for the kidnapping of foreign business executives and a rising tide of crime, both petty and organized. In many cases the police are directly involved in the criminal activity. This situation, originally exacerbated by the economic distress of 1994 to 1995, could negatively impact the economy.

The head of Sony Mexico met with President Zedillo in May 2000 and instructed him that if the Mexican government did not immediately improve the crime situation, Sony would seriously consider moving its plants out of the country. If this were to happen, a possible domino effect could take place with other major companies doing the same.

TRADE ISSUES

The last area is trade-related matters, a broad category covering major trading partners, trade agreements, and trade sanctions. We have already seen the effect the devaluation of the Brazilian real had on Argentina's economy, especially on short-term interest rates. What actually led up to this was the two countries' successful participation in the Mercosur trade accord. At the time of the devaluation, Brazil accounted for over 40 percent of Argentina's exports. The real devaluation caused a substantial price increase for Argentina's goods, which effectively smothered its export business. This pushed an already troubled Argentinean economy into turmoil.

Other trade situations that result in creditors feeling the pinch are trade embargoes. In 1999, the U.S. government placed sanctions against India and Pakistan for their war, accompanying a worldwide fear of nuclear exchange. The embargo caused serious problems for U.S. exporters conducting business there. Many firms were no longer able to ship product. Some were in the middle of multistage projects, which were effectively shut down with little hope for payment until the sanctions were lifted.

INTERNATIONAL CREDIT INFORMATION SERVICES

Conducting a risk evaluation can seem a daunting task. First the information must be gathered, then there are numerous category ratings. The easiest (and quickest) method is to rely on one of the readily available country risk services. Some of the more recognized providers are:

Company	*Address*	*Phone*
The Kreller Group	Cincinnati, OH *www.kreller.com*	800-444-6361
PRS Group	East Syracuse, NY *www.prsgroup.com*	315-431-0511
S.J. Rundt & Associates, Inc.	New York, NY *www.rundtsintelligence.com*	212-838-0141
Graydon America	New York, NY *www.creditriskmonitor.com*	

The Economist
    Intelligence Unit
    Veritas
	New York, NY
	www.eiu.com
		212-554-0600

Control Risks Group Limited	New York, NY *www.crg.com*	212-967-3955
Intrum Justitia	Amsterdam, the Netherlands *www.intrum.com*	31 20 677 6666
Credit Reports Latin America	New York, NY *www.crla.com*	718-729-4906

These risk services typically supply free samples of the information and countries covered in their web sites. Their reports are very extensive and detailed, giving current information as well as historical data. Upon reading one of them, credit managers will have a better understanding of the country's history and political climate.

INFORMATION AVAILABLE ON THE INTERNET

If your company's exports are small or you have a tight budget, a do-it-yourself appraisal may be in order. There are a wide variety of sources available over the Internet, some of which are listed below.

Web Site	Information Provided
www.kreller.com/k20.htm	List of international information sites
www.dis.strath.ac.uk/business/index.html	Information arranged by categories (company, financial, country, etc.); focuses on UK resources plus others
www.ceoexpress.com/#top	Comprehensive site offering links to many information sources, free and fee based
http://lanic.utexas.edu	Comprehensive site for Latin America
www.pitt.edu/~cjp/rees.html	Russia and East European information
www.coba.wright.edu/bie/bie.htm	Provides links with various international information links
http://ciber.bus.msu.edu	International business resources
www.ibrc.bschool.ukans.edu	International business resources
www.cia.gov	Country background information
http://travel.state.gov/travel_warnings.html	U.S. State Department travel alerts
www.realworldrescue.com	Information concerning volatile situations around the world
www.onlinenewspapers.com	Listing of worldwide newspapers
http://emedia1.mediainfo.com/emedia	Listing of worldwide newspapers
www.ioma.com	Comprehensive business information site with links to over 500 related sites

Many of the available search engines also contain economic and political information on countries, and they are oftentimes a good place to start your exploration.

SAMPLE CORPORATE DO-IT-YOURSELF
COUNTRY REPORT

Do-it-yourself appraisals are usually unscientific reviews. Usually, the person conducting the assessment is looking for a feeling or tempo for the country's situation. After conducting a few reviews, you will develop a skill as to when you should have some concern and why for a given country. As an example, let's look at Peru.

From a brief investigation conducted through Yahoo! searching under "Peru economy" and "Peru politics" and following the chain of web pages, the following information was learned.

Political

- Peru's government is listed as a republic, although many argue that it is more authoritarian. One party controls the presidency but does not maintain a majority in Congress.
- The other significant party is Peru Posible, which is lead by Alejandro Toledo. President Fujimori is pro-business and has gained recognition for opening Peru to foreign investment. Toledo's business stance is not easily understood.
- The present regime's stability is in question. Many analysts feel that the recent elections were rigged. It is generally believed that the Organization of American States (OAS) will declare the elections invalid and call for new ones. The U.S. government has said that it will follow the lead of the OAS. Off the record, State Department officials have already called the vote and Fujimori's presidency illegitimate. The U.S. Congress passed Resolution 43, signed by President Clinton, calling for a thorough revision of U.S. relations with Peru if the elections are shown to be fraudulent. The OAS may call for the international community to pressure Fujimori into calling for new elections by using trade sanctions.
- Fujimori originally came into power in April 1992 by way of an auto-coup. He gained recognition for courting foreign investment and effectively defeating the Maoist's Shining Path and the smaller Tupac Amaru Revolutionary Movement, made famous by their siege of the Japanese embassy residence in December 1996.
- The military has publicly supported Fujimori and has not shown signs of breaking ranks. There are still some reports of the military torturing Peruvians.

Economy

- The reported figures for the first quarter of 2000 indicated a strong performance. GDP increased at an annual rate of 8.5 percent for that period, greatly exceeding previous forecasts. Inflation continues to be low, reaching an annualized rate of 3.8 percent in April 2000. The currency exchange rate is projected to continue its slow decline to reach 3.67 soles per U.S. $1 at year's end. The "soft landing" of the sol helps keep it from overvaluation and speculation.

• Overall, in mid-2000, the economy appeared to be growing with inflation and unemployment was under control. Short-term interest rates are somewhat high but appear to be within historical patterns. The currency is relatively stable but has slowly weakened in the past six years. Trade sanctions or social unrest could dampen the economy if the present situation continues to escalate.

• Annual average currency exchange rates:

1999	3.51
1998	3.15
1997	2.72
1996	2.59
1995	2.33

• Financial information:

	1996	1997	1998	1999
Interest rates	16.0%	13.9%	16.9%	16.8%
GDP	2.4%	6.9%	0.3%	3.8%
CPI	11.8%	6.5%	6.0%	3.7%
Unemployment	8.0%	7.5%	7.6%	7.7%

Social Conditions

There have been reports of frequent and sizable protests since the presidential election, some of them violent. Alejandro Toledo called for continued protests and civil strike. He also requested the other political parties of the congress to boycott the swearing-in of new members. This would cause a lack of a quorum and make it impossible for Fujimori to be sworn in as president. If Toledo is successful, an unprecedented action such as this could quickly bring things to a head, the army out of its barracks, and economic growth to a halt.

Trade Issues

The threat of intervention by the OAS gives rise to the possibility of trade sanctions due to the questions over Fujimora's reelection as Peru's president. In addition, a U.S. State Department official said that the U.S. government reserves the right to impose unilateral sanctions if Peru resists the OAS's efforts. Since America is Peru's largest trading partner, any action taken by the United States would severely disrupt trade between the two countries.

Summary

Due to the history of rebellion, social unrest, and the present instability of the presidency, Peru represents a fairly high level of risk. Things could deteriorate rather quickly and events could get beyond control of Peru's leadership. When assessing credit risk in Peru, whether open or secured, factor the country's high risk to your decision. On the other hand, the competition may have less stringent terms than what you are considering—one more factor to take into account.

It took approximately 45 minutes to review the information available on Peru over the Internet and to print out those items deemed important. The total review took approximately one hour.

This chapter is not suggesting here that companies refrain from conducting business in developing countries, merely that they should do so with open eyes and a clear understanding of the risks involved. Conducting business in developing nations can be a boom/bust proposition. There will be times of great expansion and there will also be times of economic turbulence and upheaval. To expect anything less would be naive. Having a country assessment and monitoring system is as essential as having contingency plans for dealing with a nation's sudden catastrophe.

PART TWO

COLLECTIONS

One of the biggest surprises many collections professionals face when they first start trying to collect from their international customers is customers' attitudes toward payment. Credit professionals who extended 90-day terms to a company may be astounded to learn that the customer will only begin to think about paying on the ninetieth day. Chapter 5 takes a look at collection basics in the international arena and then offers suggestions on what can be done to get customers to write and mail the check a little more quickly.

Chapter 6 considers international factoring, sometimes referred to as invoice discounting. These are techniques some use to get the money in the door just a little bit quicker.

One of the mechanisms that can be used in Latin America is protesting, as discussed in Chapter 7. Now before you start thinking that you protest to your customers all the time and it only helps a little, note that I am referring to a formal legal protest. Many say that they would never protest, as doing so will ruin the relationship with the customer, just as turning an account over to a collection agency might do so domestically. We present the advantages and disadvantages of this approach. We have talked to a number of credit professionals who have used protesting successfully and share the results.

In Chapter 8, the final chapter in this section, a seasoned collection professional shares war stories about her collection successes. The tales show how effort and due diligence can result in collection success where failure seemed guaranteed.

5

International Collection Basics

Mary S. Schaeffer

IOMA

Collecting from international customers presents a whole new array of challenges for the international credit and collection executive. Those accustomed to dealing with domestic customers are often surprised at the lack of concern many of their international customers exhibit regarding payment. Not only are the payment terms negotiated typically longer, in some cases much longer, than many are accustomed to, but many customers do not even begin to think about paying until after the agreed-to terms have expired and the vendor begins looking for payment. This is just one of the reasons many use letters of credit, documentary collections, and other security/collection/financing alternatives.

The other unspoken issue for many international customers is their cost of funding and their ability to obtain it. In some countries interest rates are quite a bit higher than they are in the United States. In others the availability of funds, especially to midsize companies, is limited. Whether the issue is cultural or availability or both, collection problems in the international arena far exceed domestic problems.

STARTING POINT

The best place to eliminate collection problems is up-front, before the first goods are ever shipped to a customer. Begin by doing a thorough credit investigation and grant credit judiciously. One of the most amazing things about international credit is that some companies do virtually no credit checking. The result of this lack of up-front investigation means that some companies end up extending credit to companies that would never be sold to if they were domestic customers.

Once the credit investigation has been completed and a reasonable amount of credit has been granted, payment expectations should be spelled out to the customer in black and white. This can be difficult to do when the customer is located in a country many miles and time zones away and often does not understand English. Combine these factors with the fact that few salespeople like to be involved in the collection aspects, and you can see why international collections, even in the best of circumstances, can become a major issue.

COMMON MISTAKES

Few domestic credit managers would have granted credit to marginal companies after completing even a basic credit analysis. Yet it happens in international transactions—more than occasionally. Here are some of the more common mistakes made when extending credit in the international arena:

- *Neglecting to carefully check the background before selling.* You may not know the financial stability of the company or the potential lawsuits against it, because you relied on the credit applications (often creatively filled out by the overseas customer) and sales agents' opinions (they want the sale and portray customers in a positive light), or you pull a database credit report that is six months to a year old and thus miss important recent red flags.
- *Going on reputation.* Other credit professionals or salespeople in the industry give a good reference, or the sales agent visits the overseas customer and finds the owner to be wealthy (or seemingly so). Based on this, there is a false comfort level to sell.
- *Ignoring signs of problems.* For a number of reasons, U.S. companies will not take action for a long time when a debt becomes past due and they ignore the debtor's broken promises, missed payment schedules, and lost correspondence. The credit manager is often in a Catch-22 situation, because a lot of money goes into establishing overseas accounts, and neither the overseas sales reps nor high-level executives want the foreign company cut off, as this would hurt future sales. The credit manager knows that the longer the wait, the larger the risk of not getting paid.

SIMPLE SOLUTIONS

When a customer does not pay, international credit and collection managers can take the following three steps:

1. Attempt to work out a reasonable payment plan and get the debtor to stick to payment dates that are set forth in writing.
2. Send a final demand letter demanding payment in full by a certain date (no more than 10 days) if the debtor misses payments, ignores phone calls and written correspondence, or flat-out refuses to pay.

3. Place the debtor for collections if there is no response. State in the final demand letter that you will place the account for collections if it is not paid, and promptly do so when there is no response. This way the debtor feels that the creditor and the collection agency are in sync and that the creditor is serious and not merely issuing idle threats.

AVOIDING THE PROBLEM

Obviously, the best way to avoid collection problems completely is to take the appropriate steps up front. These steps might include:

- Ordering a current credit report (investigated fresh in country when ordered).
- Getting a personal guarantee up front especially when selling to individuals or very small proprietorships. Doing so can help collection/legal efforts later. However, in order for the guarantee to be enforced at a later date, the documents must be drawn up in conformity with the laws of the country where it will be enforced. Otherwise, it will not be worth the paper it is written on. Keep in mind that this probably means that the documents will need to be written in the official language of the enforcing country.
- Asking the salespeople to allow enough time for the credit manager to research and investigate the customer, rather than alerting the international credit department about new accounts two days before the shipment has to go out.
- Using current information. Never base a decision on dated credit information, even if other information (trade references, credit application) is available, because you need to verify through a third party that the company is valid and that it checks out legally.
- Keeping the originals of invoices, purchase orders, and bills of lading, and sending only copies to the customer. In certain countries, winning a lawsuit can come down to whether the creditor holds original documents.

HOW TO MINIMIZE COMMON COLLECTION DELAYS

One of the most frustrating aspects of international collections are the seemingly inherent interminable delays. Many managers assume they can do nothing about these delays, but this is not always the case. Next, we offer the eight workable solutions to eliminating these interminable delays.

1. *Eliminate misunderstandings.* Delays are often caused by the simple fact that the seller has one set of understandings and the buyer another. To rectify this problem, simply spell out every detail. For example, if you sell on terms of net 60 days, indicate exactly when you expect the clock to start ticking for that 60 days. If you are sending an invoice, print the due date on the invoice. Make everything as clear as possible.

2. *Give clear payment instructions.* Occasionally, the exporter is actually responsible for the lateness of the payment. Again, it is imperative to let the buyer know exactly how payment is expected. If a wire transfer is to be used, include full wire instructions. Include a complete remit-to address in the instructions and on any invoice that is mailed. Make sure it is printed prominently in large type, not in tiny light gray print on the back.

3. *Start the collection effort early.* As soon as a due date is missed, get on the phone and find out why. Do not rely on letters that can take forever to arrive and might not be in a language understood by the recipient.

4. *Be knowledgeable about payment practices in the buyer's country.* Do not assume that what works in the United States will work elsewhere. It is not uncommon for companies in other countries to pay months after the due date. By knowing what is common practice in the buyer's country, the collection manager will know when to expect payment. This information should be factored into the pricing of the goods. Otherwise, all the profits are effectively lost.

5. *Monitor collections closely.* This is another instance where exporters are sometimes their own worst enemy. If the collection manager cannot readily identify which receipts are late, it is impossible to begin collection activity promptly. Accurate and frequent aging reports are crucial to such an effort.

6. *Perform a thorough credit analysis before shipping goods.* Difficult collection issues sometimes can be avoided simply by doing the necessary homework up front. Those companies that analyze international credits thoroughly before granting credit have many fewer collection problems. It is amazing how many companies still ship to international customers whose credit standards would require cash-in-advance terms in the United States.

7. *Poor coordination with foreign sales reps.* Many who export use foreign sales reps. Cooperation between credit and sales is often nonexistent in these situations. As with a domestic sales force, the goals of the reps are not quite in sync with those of the credit and collection department. By fostering a spirit of cooperation with the reps, the international collection manager will be able to get the changes needed to speed up collections.

8. *Letters-of-credit delays.* Many exporters think that delays and discrepancies are unavoidable when letters of credit are used. This is not necessarily true. By implementing controls to limit discrepancies, exporters can improve their hit rate and thus speed along their collections. They also can try to have letters of credit issued through banks where their company is a significant player. In these instances, the collection manager will be able to get better cooperation from the bank. These banks are also more likely to turn key customers' letters of credit around faster—especially if a fuss is raised every time the bank messes up!

QUICK HIT STRATEGIES TO SPEED UP COLLECTIONS

Improving collection rates is often the result of many small steps rather than one large change. International credit and collection professionals can both speed up collections and minimize bad-debt write-offs by implementing one or more of the following suggestions:

- Develop and implement strong credit and collection procedures that focus on getting the funds collected as swiftly as possible. Once these tactics are in place, insist that the guidelines be strictly followed.
- Significant accounts should be contacted personally to determine if the delayed payment is due to a dispute in the invoice or material shipped. If it is not, the customer needs to be reminded in a friendly but firm manner that payment is expected consistent with the terms agreed on at the time of the sale.
- Have all wire payments made via Clearing House Interbank Payment System (CHIPS) to cut several days off international wire payments.
- Do an extensive up-front credit analysis before granting credit. By weeding out marginal credits, collection times for the entire portfolio should increase.
- Try to understand your customers' needs and how they do business in their country. This knowledge will help you devise a payment plan that customers can meet and that you can live with.
- Use faxes and e-mail to "remind" customers of their payment obligations.
- Concentrate on getting letter-of-credit documentation as discrepancy-free as possible. By not having letters of credit returned to have discrepancies fixed, you will reduce your letter-of-credit collection time by several days.
- Follow up immediately on all aspects of letters of credit. Delays of a day or two at each step of the process can add up quickly.
- Contact delinquent customers on a daily basis to inquire about the status of payment.
- Work with international sales and operations and show them the financial impact on the company's bottom line of granting extended payment terms.
- Become a "very pleasant squeaky wheel" by phone and fax when following up on late payments.
- Review all accounts and terms and the methods of payment utilized with each. Consider adding any terms and conditions that will get the funds into the company's hands more quickly.
- Send advance invoices when you know a shipment will be going out. Domestically, some companies use advance shipping notices for similar purposes.
- Begin collection procedures on the day the invoice is due, not 10 or more days later.

- Have the sales department verify that all paperwork is complete when shipments leave so merchandise does not get held up in customs.
- Take a customer-service approach and try to improve the entire order process so that problems, and therefore the reason for nonpayment, are eliminated.
- Implement proactive procedures to involve finance, logistics, and sales promptly when an account becomes past due.
- Set guidelines for the sales force regarding which terms to offer—and then get them to stick to it.
- Hold future shipments until all payment promises are kept.
- Use international sales reps located overseas to help with difficult collection accounts.
- Identify those letters of credit that are most likely to have discrepancies and scrutinize them closely to cut down on the number of errors.
- Wherever possible, have customers prepay through use of a wire.
- Eliminate pricing errors wherever possible. Have a front-end control verification of invoices prior to billing. Insist that all price exception forms be signed and authorized prior to order entry.
- Hire full-time collection staff if the sales volume warrants it. Otherwise, the collection function will not get the attention it deserves.
- Move the collection responsibilities of lesser-concern accounts to lower-level employees, allowing more experienced personnel to handle the accounts of greater concern.
- Use electronic data interchange (EDI) wherever feasible.
- Reduce discrepancies, not only on letters of credit but in all other documentation.
- Lure customers with more attractive terms. Offer small discounts to those willing to pay by wire transfer.
- If appropriate, take credit cards for low-dollar orders.
- Emphasize customer contact and a proactive, consistent collection approach.
- By having management put a greater emphasis on collection times, the international credit and collection manager will be in a position to demand compliance from sales and others whose actions impede a timely collection effort.
- Minimize bad-debt write-offs by aggressively collecting laggard accounts and aggressively enforcing credit standards.
- Tighten controls on approving credit to marginal accounts.
- Reporting accounts receivable based on the terms in the account's contract provides a more accurate picture of the firm's exposure. Doing so will also identify which accounts need aggressive follow-up.
- Let the sales force handle most of the collections efforts and contact the customer yourself only as a last resort.
- Learn as much as possible about the customer's business to understand what might impact his or her cash flow—and, consequently, payment to you.

- Use e-mail to contact those customers with online capabilities.
- If payment is prolonged, visit the customer personally.
- Review credit frequently to make sure the customer has not had any adverse changes that will cause delayed payments.
- Use payment schedules and monitor them closely to make sure terms are being met.
- Require payment be made by wire transfer, preferably via SWIFT.
- Call periodically to obtain updated financial information about the customer.
- Use software that will automatically generate letters following up on late payments—and then fax or e-mail the correspondence.
- If there is a problem, arrange a conference call among the sales rep, the customer, and a representative from the credit department. Time differences usually mean such meetings have to be scheduled a day or two in advance.
- Negotiate terms at the time of contract, and make sure the customer understands exactly what is expected.
- When a sales rep is used, constant communication with the rep will ensure that the rep knows what is expected. This information should then be transmitted to the customer.
- If the sales rep is supposed to resolve discrepancies, make sure he or she has all the necessary documentation, including copies of statements, invoices, and, most important, proof of delivery. If there have been any conversations with the customer, pass that information along as well.
- Require cash in advance with risky customers, realizing, of course, that sometimes this might foil the sale.
- Develop a good understanding of the various types of letters of credit and use the right type for each customer. By understanding the risk profile of each customer, it is possible to identify the best vehicle to use for each sale. Once the letter of credit is obtained, check the documentation thoroughly for discrepancies that would cause a bank to reject the letter. Using letters of credit not only reduces risk but guarantees timely collections.
- Prepare a report by country showing the due dates. Send reminder notices when the items first become due. Also, list a dozen target accounts to go after aggressively each month when attempting to reduce receivables.
- Set up periodic meetings with sales reps to determine what problems they are encountering and discuss with them the best ways to speed up collection of their accounts. By understanding the problems the reps are encountering, credit managers sometimes can kill two birds with one stone and resolve collection issues. After all, if customers are not satisfied with something, most will retaliate by paying late or taking unauthorized deductions—two actions that directly affect collections.
- Hire a collector who speaks the same language as the customer. This person contacts the customer by phone instead of fax or letter. Also

provide a weekly list of accounts that are under consideration for credit hold due to nonpayment. A report of this type is often all that is needed to light a fire under a sales rep who is reluctant to help with collections.

- Make European customers understand the importance of adhering to open-account terms. Explain that companies will be put on credit hold or will be dealt with on a secured basis in the future if payments are not received. When they understand that you are serious about this, they will begin to comply.
- Obtain an in-depth understanding of the way the customer conducts business before terms are offered. Incorporate this knowledge into the offer when trying to determine what terms are appropriate for a particular customer. Once a history is developed with a given customer, share the information with sales and have it incorporated into future sales offers. Those who pay well should be rewarded with more lenient terms. Those who have not paid within a reasonable time frame should be penalized.
- Begin using export credit insurance for international transactions. This can be expensive, but often the cost can be incorporated into the sales offer. This approach will take cooperation from the sales force. However, if they understand that credit insurance can be used in instances where the credit manager is not comfortable with the credit quality in question and a sale might be refused, they are likely to be receptive.
- Offer training to the international credit and collection staff regarding the most effective ways to handle collections of international receivables.
- Devise a detailed collection-dunning report and letter program for all customers. Send dunning letters to any and all customers who are late. Put any company that goes more than 60 days (or whatever is appropriate for your industry) past due on credit hold.
- Keep a payment history for existing customers and share this information with sales. When this is combined with an education program for sales or when commissions are tied to collections, the sales force is apt to be more willing to helping with collections and insisting on secured terms for those customers who flagrantly ignore the terms under which they agreed to pay.

TURNING AN ACCOUNT OVER FOR COLLECTION

When all else fails, accounts should be turned over for collection. As with domestic transactions, turning an account over to a collection is a serious step. However, the longer you wait, the less likely you are to collect. Thus, most experts recommend that a delinquent account be turned over as soon as the final deadline for the demand letter has passed. It is a mistake to sit on an account and hope the debtor will come around. Payment will not be forthcoming. If the final demand letter is ignored, take it as a hostile response.

International credit and collection professionals need to do whatever they can to improve the odds of collection should they find themselves in the unenviable position of having to place an account. To improve the likelihood of collecting the money:

- *Turn over the file quickly.* Many U.S. companies wait a long time before placing an international account for collection. This may be due to the extended terms (120 to 240 days) offered to foreign companies. If an account goes 60 days past term, it is in trouble. This is the ideal time to turn the account over for collections. If for some reason this is not feasible, make sure to place the debt before it becomes a year old from the date of sale. Debts more than a year old are very difficult to pursue.
- *Provide the agency with invoices, purchase orders, and written correspondence with the debtor.*
- *Tell the agency the history of the account,* so it knows the best way to approach the debtor and avoids the problems you have already encountered.

SELECTING INTERNATIONAL COLLECTION AGENCIES

When looking for an international collection agency, many international credit professionals turn to U.S. companies with alliances in other countries. These agencies coordinate the efforts and deal directly with the agency in the debtor's country. The benefits of such an arrangement include:

- Use of in-country collection associates, not just an American calling from the United States. Many have contacts in virtually every country who speak the language and know the customs. They are also working during the hours that the debtor is.
- The account and the overseas reps are both managed from the United States, so the response time and service is what American companies expect.
- Volume the agency places with each overseas agent results in better response time and service.
- The agency is experienced in dealing overseas, and can prepare customers and help them through the potential paperwork so they know what to expect in certain countries.
- Agencies offer relatively attractive pricing with no requirement for a commitment of all business.

6

Export Factoring and Invoice Discounting

Mary S. Schaeffer

IOMA

Export factoring, sometimes called international factoring, lets companies reduce risk and collect funds immediately—at a price, of course. Export factoring is sometimes referred to as invoice discounting. This relates to the practice of "discounting" the face value of the invoice and giving the seller its money up-front rather than at the end of the previously agreed-to terms. Export factoring can be an attractive alternative for customers who need or are accustomed to extended terms.

HOW IT WORKS

The factor typically preapproves customers and then collects the payments once the goods have been delivered. There is no deductible and coverage is for 100 percent of the sale. Companies using this technique can sell on open account and compete on a more level playing field.

Most of the activity is done through a two-factor system, with one factor representing the seller (the export factor) and the other the buyer (the import factor). This enables cross-border transactions. Typically, the import factor will be responsible for the credit analysis, and if something goes wrong, the purchaser does not pay. For example, the import factor is responsible for making the export factor whole. In no event do factors get involved in disputes.

The factor may belong to a larger group through which transactions are cleared. Several of these groups are listed at the end of the chapter along with contact information. An Internet search will uncover others. Some groups work on a one-country, one-member approach, while others allow more than one member from each country to join the group.

LOCATING AN EXPORT FACTOR

Once the decision is made to use an export factor, international credit and collection professionals will have to find one to handle the business. Some companies that have a domestic factoring unit also handle international business. Even if your domestic factor does not have an international arm, it may be able to refer you to a company that does. NationsBank Commercial Corporation, CIT, Heller, and Bank of New York all have international factoring units.

FINDING THE RIGHT FACTOR

Numerous companies offer factoring services in Europe. Many are unaffiliated but others belong to loosely amalgamated groups. Once you decide to use these services, it is important to choose the right factor, as these agreements generally have a notification period before they can be terminated. But first you should determine what features are important given the circumstances of the company and the reasons for turning to such a service in the first place.

Features

Before evaluating individual service providers, international credit professionals need to understand why the factor is being used. Are the considerations financial, in that the company needs to get the funds in as quickly as possible, or are they credit driven? Is the company looking for protection against bad-debt write-offs but uncomfortable with making credit decisions about a potential customer located in another country subject to different laws and market constraints?

Big or Small?

Once companies decide which features are important, most interview several service providers before selecting one. One of the most basic considerations is whether to use a large factor or a small one. With a small factor, you will be in a much stronger bargaining position, especially if you have a sizable amount of business with the factor. Additionally, you probably will get more personalized service. The drawback to small factors is that they sometimes go out of business. While this can happen with a large business as well, the likelihood is much greater with small factors. When this happens, there is a greater chance that the factor will just close up shop, not attempting to place accounts with another factor.

Factor Groups

Factors Chain International
Keizersgracht 559
1017 DR Amsterdam
The Netherlands
Phone: 31 20 6270306
Web site: *www.factors-chain.com*

Commercial Finance Association's European Chapter
225 West 34th Street
New York, NY 10122
Phone: 212-594-3490
Web site: *www.cfa.com*

Factors and Discounters Association
Boston House, 2nd floor
The Little Green
Richmond
Surrey TW9 1QE
England
Phone: 020 8332 9955
Web site: *www.factors.org.uk*

Association of British Factors and Discounters
1 Northumberland Avenue
London
WC2N 5BW
England
Phone: 0171 930 9112

International Factors Group
Aenue Paul Hymans, 127/3
B-1200 Brussels
Belgium
Phone: 32 2 772 6969
Web site: *www.ifgroup.com*

7

Documentary Collections and Protesting

Mary S. Schaeffer

IOMA

Documentary collections are one of the safest collection techniques used by U.S. exporters. Should the customer not pay for, or not accept, the goods, the exporter has a definite recourse: The goods are simply not released to the importer. This recourse, unfortunately, is not quite as wonderful as it sounds. Sure the product is not gone, but in most instances it is sitting on a ship hundreds, if not thousands, of miles away from home. And the clock is ticking.

At this point the exporter can call the shipment back, attempt to sell the merchandise to another buyer in the same locale (often easier said than done), or move the goods to another market for resale if a customer is available. All of these responses effectively reduce the profit from the sale. However, there is another option. The exporter can protest—and not just to the person sitting at the next desk. Protesting is a legal process used in many Latin American countries. It can have serious business repercussions for the purchaser, and sometimes just the threat of filing a protest is enough to elicit payment.

CAVEAT

While documentary collections are typically used for safety reasons, nothing is 100 percent secure. There have been instances where documents have mysteriously ended up in the buyer's hands and the seller was left, effectively, with an open-account sale.

REASONS FOR REFUSAL

Before determining whether to protest the importer's action, the international credit manager should ascertain why the customers took the action they did. When clients do not meet their obligations, the collecting bank will not give the documents of title to the drawee. The seller continues as the owner of the cargo but faces additional costs for warehousing the merchandise or shipping it home.

Banks have no obligation pertaining to these goods other than their advisory function. The collecting bank must advise the remitting bank of the situation on a timely basis, and the remitting bank should give instructions as to the course of action. In reality, the collecting bank may take the actions it deems necessary to protect the merchandise, although it has no obligation to do so and assumes no liability.

The failure to accept either the goods or the documents can be due to justifiable reasons or unethical ones. If the price of the goods falls between the time they were ordered and they are received, some people will try to find any excuse to refuse the goods. Price fluctuations of this type are most typical when dealing with commodities, although it can happen with other merchandise as well.

However, when dealing with scrupulous customers, the reasons for refusal may include:

- The condition to release documents is not what was agreed on.
- The amount invoiced is higher than agreed.
- The description of the goods does not match what was ordered.
- The import license is not released.
- The shipment is made earlier than agreed.
- The shipment is made later than agreed or was delayed in transit.
- Certain documents are missing and as a result the merchandise cannot clear customs.

By determining the true reason for the refusal to pay, credit managers can decide what course of action to take.

LIMITING FACTORS TO A COURSE OF ACTION

Even after determining the cause for the nonpayment or nonacceptance of documents, international credit executives must take into account certain limiting factors before deciding on a course of action. These factors include:

- Manner in which the bill of lading is issued. If, for example, it is to the order of the importer, the customer is the only one who can endorse it. In this case, selling the goods to a third party will be difficult.
- Local regulations, which sometimes limit the exporter's options, especially in countries with strict import license laws. Countries with strict license laws also may not allow documents to be transferred to a third party.

- Overall relationship with the customer and the prospects for future business. If, for example, a long-standing customer refuses a shipment claiming that the shipment arrived later than had been agreed on, a company might decide to swallow its pride and not protest. This might be deemed as the price for doing future business.
- Chances of winning the protest. There is little sense in protesting in a country that does not allow such actions. Protesting will only further aggravate an already tense situation.
- Wording. While a bill of exchange that contains phrasing such as "no costs, no protest" might appear ironclad, it is contestable.
- Timing. Some countries require a limited time frame. If you have not protested within that limit, do not assume all is lost. In many countries a protest can be made at a later date. The information may not be published, but the protest will serve as legal evidence of the nonpayment.
- Collecting bank's customers. If the importer is a customer of the collecting bank, the bank may be reluctant to enforce protest instructions.

Thus, credit managers need not only to determine the reason for the nonacceptance but also any special circumstances that might affect the protesting decision. Once all the information is gathered, it is possible to decide whether to protest or not.

WHY PROTESTING IS ADVISABLE

There are only a few arguments in favor of protesting. As noted, it is not permissible in certain jurisdictions. However, presentation of documents for payment is a step in the natural course of business, a process that the buyer has agreed to in advance. Changing circumstances, usually prices, are not sufficient reason for customers to renege on the agreement.

Additionally, the protest is the one way that exporters have to let customers know that they expect to be paid and to be compensated on a timely basis.

WHY PROTESTING IS INADVISABLE

While each situation must be evaluated case by case, the issues against protesting are more numerous. As mentioned, protesting is sometimes not allowed. Some additional reasons why a protest can be ill advised include:

- Unless an aval (an unconditional and irrevocable guarantee securing the bill of exchange) has been given, there is no third party contingently liable and the protest is not likely to be useful. There is no threat to hold over the importer's head.

- When there is a protest, the information is usually published. This simple act can unnecessarily alarm other creditors and effectively cause a "run" on the debtor. This may have unintended consequences.
- The negative impact may adversely affect the debtor's creditworthiness, as discussed above, and negatively affect the ultimate chance for collection.
- The act of a protest is a drastic collection action. Is this something you want to do?
- Protesting in certain countries can be quite costly. Make sure the costs are more than offset by the proceeds collected.
- If it turns out that the seller was responsible for the problem that caused the nonpayment, the relationship with that customer could be permanently damaged. Make sure your own house is in order first.
- Protesting can result in foreign exchange implications detrimental to the seller. Since a protest is the first step in potential legal action, the debt will be converted to the local currency at the time of the protest. If this is not what was required in the bill of exchange, the eventual settlement may be for much less than the original invoice. (Yes, it could also be higher, but is it ever?)

International credit and collection managers should be aware that certain presenting banks do not protest as a general matter of policy and will notify the remitting bank of this should it be required. Those professionals who are aware of all the intricacies of protesting nonpayments or nonacceptances of documentary collections will be best able to deal with the situation should it arise.

PREPARING TO PROTEST

In order for protesting to be a viable option for those selling to Latin America, everything must be in order. The following information was gathered from several international credit professionals who have successfully used protesting with delinquent customers in Latin America. Here are four guidelines.

1. Investigate the protesting rules for the country where the customer is located. Each country seems to have its own rules, which makes the task of protesting a bit cumbersome. In Peru, a supplier must protest within seven days after a draft matures or executory rights in court are lost. But seven days is much too short a time to know whether the situation truly deserves protesting. In Brazil and El Salvador, the time period for protesting is up to one year. This time frame seems more reasonable.
2. Give the customer a chance. Realizing the serious implications of a protest, most savvy executives do not take protesting action without giving notice. Assuming time allows, always inform delinquent customers in Latin America several times that you intend to protest their past-due debt if they fail to pay or reschedule it fairly. As a last resort, file a protest.

3. Check out the fees. The first formal or legal step in all payment defaults in most every Latin American country is to formally protest a draft, an invoice itself, or a *pagare* (promissory note) via a notary public, who might be employed at a local bank or might work independently. Generally, the fees to protest are not high and average about U.S. $50 per instrument.

4. The language of the documentation, as many learn the hard way, is important. In most Latin American countries, drafts in English are almost self-defeating once you start a protest action. The local language is usually required.

COUNTRY-BY-COUNTRY TIPS

What follows is some country-specific information from several international credit executives based on personal experiences. Before proceeding, international credit executives are advised to check with legal counsel to determine current rules pertaining to the given country.

Argentina and Chile

In these two countries, company drafts (no U.S. bank in the picture) can be used and forwarded with documents attached to the local company office. The draft is presented for acceptance, and the local rep turns over the original shipping documents to the customer. At maturity, the local office collects from the customer.

Some Argentine clients are very slow to pay, and in one case a credit executive insisted that the local manager give some of the defaulted drafts to a local law firm to formally protest them. Unfortunately, this action did not result in payment to the company because other suppliers were doing the same thing and the debtor was quickly forced into *concordata* (bankruptcy) and eventually liquidated with recovery for suppliers.

Brazil

In Brazil, direct collection letters, a fancy term that U.S. banks now use for drafts, are forwarded with the original documents to the customer's local bank for presentation and then collection at maturity. Always check the box on the bank's form to "protest for nonpayment" but be aware that Brazilian banks are notorious for refusing to protest such drafts.

In fact, a Brazilian bank once faxed a credit executive saying that it was the bank's policy not to protest drafts. The bank said it would either return the unpaid drafts to his company or release them to the company's local representative if he continued to press the matter. But since the customer had defaulted and not paid the draft, the credit executive had his local office retrieve the draft from the bank and give it to a local notary who did protest. Eventually, he collected all the money owed.

Despite most Latin American banks' acceptance of the uniform banking rules for direct collection letters, in many Latin American countries the normal banking practice is to ignore protest requests. Thus, if international credit professionals want to protest, they may have to take the same steps as the above-mentioned executive did. Remember that the local bank represents the customer, not your company, and for that reason may be reluctant to protest because the "public notice" will make the customer look bad in the local business community.

Guatemala

Most drafts used by U.S. exporters are written in English, which immediately puts the supplier in a weak or negative position with local courts and judges throughout Latin America. When one international credit executive's company formally protested a delinquent draft in Guatemala recently, the court refused to even consider the matter when the protested draft was presented to the judge for executive action. The judge said it was not in Spanish and not properly endorsed by the company or by the local customer. No clear explanation was given in this case, and the customer went out of business before any money was recovered. Unfortunately, the experience in this case is not atypical. Many feel that U.S. companies are not treated fairly by other legal systems.

El Salvador

Some international credit executives insists that all risky customers in El Salvador execute a *"pagare sin protesto"* for each shipment. This works, although not without hassle. Many will still pay at the last second when the local attorney is preparing the formal protest, while a few marginal risks do pay the *pagares* at or close to maturity.

Dominican Republic

Personal guarantees also help. One international credit executive reports that a former distributor in the Dominican Republic became seriously delinquent on open-account invoices. The credit executive agreed to a one-year payback with interest and personal guarantees from the two owners. They executed a *pagare notario* in front of a local lawyer. The fact that the *pagare* was executed in front of a local notary public and a lawyer gives added powers in the event the customer defaulted. Some installments were paid slowly, but the final payment of principal and interest was received recently—after the executive served the owners with a protest action.

International credit professionals will find protesting a useful tool when used carefully. Protesting may be an appropriate action with delinquent Latin American debtors.

8

International Collection Case Studies

Jennifer Hudgens

Kreller Business Information Group, Inc.

Years ago, when I first started helping clients pursue debtors domestically and overseas, I had no idea of the pitfalls involved in the collections process. Prior to that time, our company had focused on providing information on international companies, and due to requests from some clients, we began to offer collections services as well. Now I had people calling me asking for help with their claims and for advice on the best way to collect, their chances of collecting, and so on. I realized the only way I could truly learn the collections business and be a real help to my clients was to have them to tell me the whole story of their relationship with debtors, starting from when they actually became customers. I didn't just want to sell collections; I wanted to understand why these accounts went wrong in the first place and where that crucial point was where a great customer changes to a firm's worst nightmare. I wanted to learn this not only to have a high collection rate on my end but to help customers avoid these problems in the future.

As I listened to so many people's experiences, I realized how emotional an issue dealing with collections is. People were angry and felt betrayed. Often, the debtors were not just a one-time sales situation but longtime customers. Most cases I handled, I soon discovered, were long-term relationships that went sour. Often, the dollar exposures had become quite high, as there was an established relationship of trust for such a long period of time. This led me to start reading the notes and paperwork on the cases my customers had sent me. Any credit manager's files can be quite a mess, and I often found myself sitting on the floor of my office going through a box full of bills of lading, statements of accounts, and letters of correspondence between the creditor and debtor, sometimes covering several years. This process was grueling at times, but boy, did I learn some things.

At first, my research yielded more questions than answers. Some of the more frequently raised issues were:

- Why did one department of a company continue selling to the debtor when another department was owed money for over a year?
- Why was the customer not checked out thoroughly *before* the account went open term?
- Why were additional shipments of product sent after the debtor's letter of credit, wire transfer, or check was voided, bounced, or rejected by the creditor's bank?

When I called my customers for answers to these questions, I often found that there were politics involved. The same controller who would not approve a $200 credit report to check firms out originally was now blaming the credit manager for the debt. Sometimes sales continued to debtors for years because there was a false feeling of security. Perhaps the salesperson kept giving reassurances: "Oh, I've been out to visit Mr. So-and-So, and he has a huge office, and is a *really* honorable man. You better not put the kibosh on this deal—it will mean millions for the company!"

Sometimes debtors would be judged on a good relationship they had enjoyed previously, when over the last two years, say, they did not deserve this trust anymore. Of course my customers did not want to be the one to "kill" what was once viewed as a great customer, and I did not blame them. What I did find, however, was that warning signs could have been caught sooner, and there were ways to be more effective in resolving these touchy situations. In this chapter I discuss a few of the lessons I have learned and share some of the stories I have heard over the years from my clients. I hope these tips will be as helpful to you as they were to me.

LOOK BEFORE YOU LEAP

Several years ago I had an interesting case cross my desk. I got a phone call from a panicked credit manager asking for my help pursuing a debtor in Taipei, Taiwan. I asked the man to tell me his story from the beginning of the sale. Apparently, the president of my customer's company (a small citrus grower) had met a Taipei businessman at a Taiwanese trade show. This businessman was very convincing and said that he could buy and sell large quantities of my client's fruit. The now interested president spent the next day with the businessman, riding around town in his luxury automobiles and touring his expansive warehouses. The president even spent several hours in his impressive office, located in a wealthy part of the city. Upon returning to the United States, the president instructed the credit manager to ship $150,000 worth of citrus to the Taiwanese company.

Not wanting to question the president, the credit manager did as he was asked. The Taiwanese Company was late in paying and had multiple excuses:

The bank messed up the wire transfer; they had the wrong account number; and so on. The Taiwanese company owner called the U.S. president and told him they could not keep the fruit on the shelf; send another shipment immediately. The president then instructed his credit manager to send another $100,000 worth. The credit manager reminded the president that the first $150,000 had not been paid. "If we wait for the payment we will loose our window of opportunity" was his response. So now the debt was 120 days past terms. At this point, the credit manager asked our firm to check out the debtor's credit.

When we did this through our in-country agent, we found that this Taiwanese company was a complete sham. The office where the president had met the debtor was rented out for the month. The automobiles were rented for the day. The warehouses that he had toured were actually owned by people who had nothing to do with the subject. The president was now upset and called me directly, saying we were wrong; he had seen all this with his own eyes. Further documentation proved that the debtor had absolutely no assets, except for a joint profit from his brother's market stall stand in Hong Kong. After the debtor was called directly by the now-furious American seller, he realized the jig was up and fled the country.

We were able to arrange payments through the debtor's brother by appealing to his family's sense of honor several days before the Chinese New Year—a time when it is customary to pay all debts. We were lucky to convince the brother to do this, as he was not liable, and the customer really had no legal recourse. It will take years to pay back this debt, which only represented three months of transactions. It was a huge blow to my client's small company.

BASIC PREVENTION TECHNIQUES

What could have been done to prevent this whole mess is actually one of the simplest solutions: Pull a current, in-country credit report prior to shipment. This may sound obvious, but it is amazing how many collection claims pass my desk that were never thoroughly checked out. There is also the political aspect of business (i.e., the president tells the international credit manager to ship immediately). In these cases, I suggest that the international credit manager recommend that the company wait for the credit report. If management refuses to wait, the international credit manager should put the recommendation in writing, as management has a short memory when transactions turn out poorly. Numerous international credit professionals have been blamed for a shipment that went wrong. When asked if they pushed for a credit report, they say something like: "You know, I wanted one, but the president (or sales, marketing) made me ship at the last minute."

I know very well that salespeople often bring orders to your desk with demands for approval in 24 hours. Of course, when you ask them when they got the order, they say "Oh, about three weeks ago." Right? Understand that the salesperson is living in a different world from the one you are, a world where getting the sale at all costs is the rule of the day. You have to educate them on the importance of getting you the order with enough lead time to secure vital information. Perhaps your boss can help you coordinate this in writing, so people are more bound to follow it. In addition to having enough lead time, it is also important when requesting the report to use a source who obtains the information in the country of origin. I am sure you have been in a situation where you need information right away and pull one of those database reports only to find that it is two years old, or not even available. I cannot stress this enough: Do not base credit decisions on old information.

Some credit professionals tell me that they do not pull credit reports but check trade references that are on the credit application. This is a helpful part of the process but is *not* a substitute for a credit report. Very few people will send you a bad reference. Often, overseas companies that are having financial problems will pay a few accounts well and use them as references when, in reality, they are on the verge of bankruptcy. Do not be lulled into a false sense of security. A credit report should always show you whether debtors are being sued, have collection claims against them, have liens on their property, or have any pending lawsuits.

One customer had us check a potential client in Brazil. Apparently, his credit application and references (even the banks) checked out. But my customer was a smart lady, and she would not release the $1 million order until she had pulled the credit report. She wanted it fast because she had two salespeople breathing down her neck for that deal to be approved. They expressed great irritation that she was "holding up a big sale." When we checked the company out, we found it had a debt of $2 million with another local bank, one that was not on the credit application. Soon after receiving this report, my customer called me to say that the sales reps had gone to the president of the company and told him she did not know what she was doing.

I had my in-country agents get the tax ID number for the Brazilian company and a statement from the bank in question that also had the same tax ID number. Faced with the evidence that the credit manger did the right thing, the president made the sales reps apologize to her publicly. She called and thanked me for "saving her job," but I told her *she* had saved her job by following her instincts and holding out for complete information. You can bet when raise time came, she did not let the management forget she prevented a $1 million loss! Follow her example and always hold out for the information you need. If things go wrong, it is not the salesperson that gets the blame.

PERSONAL DEBT AND PERSONAL GUARANTEE

A couple years ago a regular customer came to me about a debtor located on a small island in the Caribbean who had really left the customer in the lurch. Apparently, the customer had sold about $60,000 worth of dry food goods to a small food distributor. My customer had done her homework and pulled the credit report first, finding that this small company was really only as financially strong as the owner himself. The location was rented, but the owner appeared wealthy and did a large amount of trading with several large, well-known grocery stores. My customer made the debtor sign a personal guarantee drawn up by her legal department. This way, she figured, if the sale went bust, she could pursue him individually.

The debtor told her company when his payment was 60 days past term that he was declaring bankruptcy, as the companies he sold to did not pay him. My customer called me right away; we got a collection attorney in the country to check the debtor out the next day. The debtor had closed his doors and we could not see into the warehouse to see if the goods were still there. The attorney then went to the debtor's home address, but he was not at the location. Apparently, he had given a false address. After multiple searches, the lawyer could not locate the debtor. She assured us she would ask around a lot. As a precaution, the attorney filed a motion with the courts indicating that this man was not dealing with his debts and that we wanted legal recourse (a judgment) if he could be found. She also pulled the legal records and found that he owed over $300,000 to other companies, all about the same age as my customer's debt. He had run up debts with multiple U.S. suppliers and, when he got the goods, took the money and declared bankruptcy.

It was amazing to find that no one had filed a legal action against him. This made our attorney more determined, as we would be first in line to get paid if we found him. About a week later, the attorney went to a cocktail party thrown by some friends. Another attendee was regaling the crowd with a story of how that day she had bought several expensive items, brand new, at a garage sale. "They were even selling their TVs and all the furniture, and the cars and house were for sale too!" the woman continued. Our attorney asked the name of the people having the garage sale and, to her shock, the woman gave the name of our debtor! Our attorney rushed out of the party, ran home to change into casual clothes, and hightailed it to the debtor's home address.

The garage sale was winding down but the debtor and his wife were still there. The lawyer played dumb and asked a lot of questions. "Turns out we have to leave the island very quickly," the debtor's wife stated, "so we are selling everything." The attorney asked to see the inside of the house, and she walked through and wrote down every item of value, including the license plate numbers on the cars. Within 24 hours, we had a Mareva injunction, which froze the debtor's assets and insured that he would be arrested if he sold any goods or left the island.

We liquidated the property and got all of my client's money back. The important thing was that we had an original, notarized personal guarantee. This document gave us claim to the debtor's assets. Although this debtor had stolen money from several other creditors, we were the only one with a personal guarantee and lawsuit, and thus the only ones that got paid. I cannot stress enough how important it is to get a personal guarantee in cases where the financial stability rests on the owner's personal assets. My customer's initial credit report showed that the debtor was a rich man, and he was! Of course, he got rich by stealing shipments from multiple companies, closing shop, and moving from island to island. Unfortunately, this is quite common in the Caribbean and Florida, as well as in many other areas of the world, where tax shelters and laws make it very easy for lawbreakers to flourish.

The homestead law in Florida prohibits the attachment of liens to a resident's property for any reason. This law was originally set up to protect senior citizens from having their property taken from them prematurely by their children. Unfortunately, it makes it easy for con men to get a number of shipments, close their company, and wait six months and start over. Their house is in their name, and all the other assets—bank accounts, cars, and the like—under the wife's name or located in offshore accounts. This makes these con men virtually untouchable. It is important to know the laws in the areas you sell, especially overseas. I have one customer who sells to small medical clinics throughout South America. The products cost in the $100,000 range plus. So the company gets a personal guarantee from each doctor who owns each clinic. It is my understanding that the company rarely has a problem getting paid. With small companies such as this, personal guarantees are a *must*.

NEVER GIVE UP ORIGINALS

A customer of mine came to me to pursue a case in Mexico. The debtor resisted at every turn with my client's efforts and ours as well. Our collection agency in Mexico even approached the debtor directly, when phone calls were not getting anywhere, and the debtor ran our agent off at gunpoint. We immediately filed suit against the debtor, and my customer carefully prepared and provided every document imaginable, from the shipping documents to every last invoice, including correspondence with the debtor. The attorney called me and said this is really great but of course she would need the originals of everything. I went back to the customer; she had sent all the original invoices to the debtor but carefully kept copies of all the documents. Could she have the copies notarized? she asked.

The attorney told us that copies would not be accepted in the courts, we had no chance to collect, and to close the file. Needless to say, my customer was very upset. This is common procedure for courts all over the world. Many debtors will claim they never got the goods. When only copies are provided to prove otherwise, courts feel that these could be fraudulent. (Indeed, many people do draw up false invoices to try to press payment for goods or services never rendered.) Although some countries accept notarized copies, it is becoming much more prevalent for court systems to demand originals. In Latin America, especially, this holds true. Always keep the originals and send customers copies. Pink and yellow carbon copies often do not count as originals, either.

One side comment. Always have special terms, such as "interest due on late payments," or "the debtor must pay all collection and legal fees," printed at the bottom of your invoices. It is also acceptable to print the terms of doing business with your company on the back of the invoice. A signed contact between the two parties of the companies' terms is ideal.

To collect interest or other fees, if it is not on the invoice in a lot of countries, it cannot be added to the debt in a court of law. Asking to have this added to the bottom of all your invoices can save you a lot of grief in court later! I had a gentleman recently tell me, "But they knew the terms of the sale and fees, because it was in our sales literature." It may have been, but if it is not on the invoice or in signed contract form, you cannot make it stick. Some people say "Well, it is our company's policy to send the original." On these large international dollar deals, do you want to forfeit your chance to sue? Having the originals can make a difference in court!

SALESPEOPLE ARE NOT COLLECTORS

So many times I have had customers tell me about terrible collection account problems—large exposures owed, over a year past due, and so on. When I ask them what they are doing to collect, they say, "Oh, we have a great salesperson who travels there all the time, who said he is going to talk to them about it." When I ask when the salesperson last said he would follow up, it was usually several months ago. It is important to look at things from the salesperson's point of view. Salespeople are great at what they do and do travel overseas and have direct contact with the debtor. No one questions that this is a benefit. In regard to handling servicing issues and working out initial payment plans, the salesperson is well equipped to help you.

However, the salespeople have a very different mind-set from yours, and different objectives. Salespeople are under constant pressure to sell, sell, sell. Salespeople do not want to do anything that will lose a customer. Oh, sure, they will ask to get paid, but it is done very casually. No salesperson is going to risk angering a long-time customer. Often, sales reps tell the credit manager who presses for payment to hold off calling the debtor and let them handle it. They do not want the credit manager upsetting a source of future business. The problem with this scenario in regard to collections is that often claims become dangerously old and the chance to collect is extremely low or lost. I have had credit managers tell me that sales reps will not release a file to them to collect, vehemently arguing that they are handling it. Not only do they not want to lose future business, but also they do not want to lose the commission from that sale. If *they* collect it, it is better for them.

I highly recommend putting a plan in place that if a debtor is *x* days old, the account automatically goes to the credit manager. Files have crossed my desk where the account was on hold two years, due to sales not wanting to let it go. By the time we were able to pursue the company, it was bankrupt. Also, the advantage of having a third-party source pursuing the debtor is that a collection agency has no emotional stake in the case and can be a lot tougher. Debtors are much more likely to take notice of a collection agency, which has the ability to sue them and destroy their credit rating and local reputation, than their good friend the sales agent, whom they know wants to keep them as a customer. I speak from experience, as I am in sales for a living. The other important thing to keep in mind is setting deadlines on when debts will be pursued and sticking to them. I have been to countless credit manager's offices over the years and personally seen the three-feet-high stacks of accounts they were trying to pursue.

It is easy to hand off the international accounts to the in-country agents and leave it up to them. Salespeople are great for those initial contacts to retrieve money; many are quite effective. Just do not let them sit on it for months and months. Some salespeople get paid their commission only if the account is paid in full. These sales reps are much more motivated to get the money back. But even they should be given deadlines; otherwise, you lose control of the collection. Also, once a file is placed for collections with an agency, make sure to tell the sales reps to stop pursuing the debtor. Many times debtors will get that first demand letter/call from the collection agency and, to stall payments and stop being pursued, they call the sales rep, saying, "Let's work something out." Of course, it is tempting for sales reps to do this, as getting their commission is the most important thing to them.

The problem is, if the sales rep starts working with debtors after the account has been placed with an agency, the agency loses control to collect and debtors play the same games they have for the past year, and you are back to square one. Not to mention you now have an angry collection agency that has rights to the claim. It is important to set up boundaries with sales reps before the collection gets to this point. I would also recommend that once you pull an account from a sales rep to be collected, send a final demand letter to the debtors yourself, with a specific date of when you expect to be paid. They may pay, but if not, and if that date comes and goes, then place the account with a collection agency immediately. Remember, if debtors have any intention of paying and want to continue doing business with you, they will not ignore a final demand letter. In closing, boundaries set up front between sales and credit can provide much better results. International credit managers should sit down with the head of sales, hear that person's side, explain theirs, and then if possible set a policy. Sales reps will have a policy to refer to as the standard when emotions are running high.

GO TO THE SOURCE

It is very important to use a collection agency that has local attorneys that specialize in collection law based in the debtor's country. Many collection agencies claim that they collect overseas, but when you place the file, all they do is send a letter from the United States (in English) demanding to be paid. Now, if debtors have ignored you, why would they pay someone who sends them a letter from the United States? This is no threat. However, having someone based in that country who speaks the language, knows the customs and laws, and can virtually show up on the debtors' doorstep, is much more compelling. Not only do debtors feel intimidated that you have followed them to their turf, but they are also concerned that their local reputation will be harmed. In the United States, use an agency that has a collection attorney in every state, as each state's laws vary.

Let me close with an amusing case that illustrates my point. I had a customer who sold frozen fish and seafood. He came to me with a collection case in Germany, where the debtor was refusing to pay for a large shipment of red snapper. When our collection agency asked him why he would not pay, he explained that his end user was an Asian seafood chain that did not want the fish, as they "were the wrong gender." Our agent was quite confused and asked for the debtor to explain. Apparently, Asians want female fish, as they are more tender. The males are "too tough." The debtor insisted he wanted this cleared up as much as the creditor and that he had the entire shipment sitting deep frozen in dry ice in his warehouse. We relayed this to our customer, who said this was all a ridiculous story to avoid payment, and to sue. We involved our local attorney, who, per procedure, approached the debtor to see if an amicable settlement could be reached. When the attorney got to the debtor's warehouse, he saw the shipment for himself and saw that it was all there, as the debtor had said. We shipped the goods back and my client resold his (male) red snapper to his less discriminating American clients. If we had not had an in-country representative, the case could have been a long, drawn-out battle from the United States. Instead, it was all cleared up on site in one afternoon. Be choosy in the firm you select. Ask a lot of questions, including:

- How many phone calls will be made versus letters sent?
- How often will you receive status reports?
- Does the agency have people who work the debtors' hours, speak their language, and know their laws?

These things are all important to know up front.

I hope these tips are of help to you in your business dealings overseas. Always remember to thank the powers that be for all those deadbeats out there—they keep all of us in business.

PART THREE

CULTURAL AWARENESS

Without a thorough understanding of the differences in how people operate, think, and feel, those operating in the international arena will fail and fail miserably. Simply reading the information and learning it is only half the battle. Incorporating it into your everyday activities is much harder.

I, Mary Schaeffer, was a speaker at an international conference several years ago. A big issue was made about the proper way to handle business cards in the Pacific Rim. Take the card respectfully with both hands, study it for a minute, and then put it on the table or away carefully. After the talk, a Japanese gentleman who had shared a panel with me came over and introduced himself. He offered me his card. What did I do? Grabbed the card and stuck it, without looking at it, into my pocket. Clearly I knew what to do—I had just been told. But incorporating proper manners into my routine was not so easy. Reflecting on the incident afterward, I realized how hard it is to incorporate other people's customs. To put it more colloquially, "You can't teach an old dog new tricks." Always the optimist, I believe that, with a little effort, most international credit professionals can learn new manners.

What is particularly interesting is the fact that each country within a region is different. Thinking that you, the credit professional, will treat all Latin Americans or all Asians the same is likely to land you in hot water. This section contains chapters written by credit veterans who have spent much time in the areas on which they write. Their stories are fascinating.

9

Cultural Awareness

Cynthia Wieme

Jeppessen

While communication skills are often touted as the critical underpinning of every successful executive, cultural sensitivity and awareness are also required for the success of an international professional. That said, let us explore the specific preparation and skills that will facilitate this process.

With a decision and commitment to work in the international business arena, each manager has affirmed the belief in ongoing personal and professional development. Regardless of the level of expertise in the industry or credit profession at the time this decision is made, additional skills are necessary for the successful transition from domestic operations to international operations.

Also, creating global contracts and relationships requires that a sufficient amount of energy be exerted toward creating these connections. Particularly within the United States, cultural-awareness programs are in demand. Few companies have created programs to educate employees in the cultures of the clients and potential clients. Fewer still recognize the critical nature of bi- and multilingual employees when walking into new business relationships.

Curiosity and research skills, already second nature to successful credit executives, will become more integral to the daily decision-making process. Additional facets of successful international relationships include complete comprehension of the company's risk profile and parameters, internal politics, and culture. Customer relationships are created and maintained within the scope of the organization's culture. Therefore, identification and acknowledgment of the company and industry culture are the starting points in the awareness process for international relationships.

RECOGNIZE THE COSTS OF
INTERNATIONAL BUSINESS TRAVEL

All companies are quick to see the expense of sending sales reps to see customers in relation to the revenue attached to the trip. However, when credit executives travel to work with customers, there are many less obvious financial aspects of the travel and business relationship. Virtually all customers will immediately understand the significance attached to the business relationship when someone from the company's finance department shows up at their office. Being able to convey the message of the value of the relationship is a wonderful tool and opportunity for every credit professional.

Another factor to take into consideration is the cost of not traveling. Relationships with external customers and internal colleagues are critical in the evaluation of the decision. When the preliminary conversations begin, include discussion of all concerns and/or risks to your organization. Personal relationships are always an excellent tool in negotiations. If a trip to the customer or country is not made or is canceled, review the company's position on the decision.

While the trip itself can be lengthy and expensive, the cost of not being prepared is significantly higher and will result in damaged relationships. Recovery of the relationship is not guaranteed.

BUSINESS RELATIONSHIPS

Working with the sales and marketing teams will greatly enhance your opportunities in bringing your first international trip to fruition. The support of your colleagues will weigh heavily with the chief financial officer or controller when authorizing the travel expenses.

Typically, the first visit should be all about creating a relationship with customers and becoming more familiar with their culture and country. Therefore, the strength of your internal relationships continues to be a significant contributor to customer relationships. Reviewing all aspects of the anticipated trip requires some very candid conversations in most organizations. Be prepared to state and restate the goals and expectations of the visit. Help establish and review the measurements of success after the trip has been completed. For example, does management expect you to return with a payment? To receive a payment before you return? To have a security tool in hand? Are these expectations realistic? In addition to the tangible measurements of success, what will you bring back to the office in the way of intangible success?

Your organization should identify overall success for the trip before departure. The overall understanding of these concepts and plans for specific levels of success may be the responsibility of the credit professional. The length, scope, and depth of the discussions and decisions vary from company to company and often between departments. Be ready for the internal negotiation and communication requirements. Again, this is where you will rely on previously established relationships.

PREPARATION FOR INTERNATIONAL
TRAVEL AND CUSTOMER VISITS

To ensure a well-planned customer visit, start preparing yourself long before a specific customer or country is targeted for a visit. Assuming this trip preparation is the least of your concerns will result in the complete failure of the trip and, potentially, the business relationship. Begin by studying the countries assigned. The history of each country, its relationship with the United States, and its current events will enlighten you to the logic behind the current relationships. Sources of information include country profiles available through various vendors and your business travel agent (not to be confused with a travel agent specializing in vacation plans). Do pick up some sightseeing information, in the event you will have the luxury of a bit of time. And familiarity with the locations of interest can be helpful in making conversation. Here are some additional pointers:

- If no company-wide, published, or established travel guidelines exist, visit with your supervisor. If this is the first international trip for your organization, an experienced business travel agent can be helpful. The World Trade Center (WTC) office, the United States Export Assistance Center (USEAC), and the U.S. Embassy offices are great sources of country and cultural information.
- Search out seminars and classes offered by various organizations. The National Association of Credit Management (NACM) affiliate offices and the WTC often have seminars and industry groups for international activities and training. Check with the local mayor's office; more and more cities have sister relationships with communities in other countries. In addition, many large cities have established an office of international affairs within their local government structure. Teams of people in these offices are at the ready to assist their local businesses in many ways.

    The various chambers of commerce throughout your community are also terrific sources of information. Examples of the names you can research are German American, European affiliate chambers, and so on. The community chamber office and the mayor's office are good starting points for these contacts. Get involved in the local chapters! Certainly do not overlook the network available in your own organization. Start talking to others who have already visited the customer or country under consideration.
- When the opportunity arises for the customer or country visit, your familiarity with the culture, customs, people, and language will significantly impact your ability to navigate and negotiate. If you are feeling at all concerned, a quick call to your recently created network can calm your fears, help you prepare the finer details of the trip, and subsequently enhance your chances for a successful adventure.
- Other information sources include the American Automobile Agency (more commonly known as AAA), the Internet, your local library, and

bookstores. The NACM Bookstore has several publications available that address specific aspects of international travel and business relationships.

- Be sure to include some basic language skills. Start by picking up a dictionary that shows the translation of individual words from English to the other language and vice versa. Then contact the local university or community college language department and local businesses offering language training. Review with them your needs and time frame, for the services available. If your company will not pay for these classes, remember that most nonreimbursed, work-related expenses are tax deductible. Keep your receipts and check with your tax consultant about this option.

    Keep in mind that English is not the same the world over. Minimize your use of acronyms, slang, and contractions. Also, be aware of standard industry words and verbiage. Often, these are also specific to use in America. Terminology for credit and banking also can be quite different. Be ready to define or describe your documents and contractual arrangements in a couple of different ways, using different words.

- Specific travel tips are available in many of the same resources noted above. Travel agents, the WTC, NACM, the Internet, AAA, USEAC, and chamber organizations have a wealth of information. People frequently overlook the time required to acquire your passport and any required visas and be familiar with the local currency. A short summary: Be sure to allow plenty of time for passport processing; take an appropriate amount of the destination's currency for meals, tips, and ground travel; and be familiar with the exchange rates. Understand the local acceptance and use of credit cards. Credit card usage is restricted in many locations due to the extreme expense for the merchants. Small communities and countries with economic hardship or political unrest are frequently reluctant to accept credit cards.

    You may find that certain types of purchases (consumables) are discouraged overseas; many merchants will also require a minimum purchase value. Credit cards typically are accepted without problem for major travel (airfare) and hotel expenses. Your credit card company and your bank's international business department can provide information. Ask if the card you carry will be accepted in the countries you plan to visit. As a precautionary measure, take at least two different cards (e.g., American Express and MasterCard).

    Considerations for your first international trip can include traveling with a business partner or colleague. It is often helpful to travel with a seasoned traveler, especially if you are fortunate enough to be traveling prior to a serious problem with a customer. A sales or technical support person is familiar with the customer's location, country, and culture. Take advantage of these opportunities.

PREPARING FOR THE CUSTOMER VISIT

When you start to think about visiting a country or client, thoroughly review the goals and expectations. You must consider the requirements of your organization and the credit department. List the driving force of the need for the trip. Identify the desired outcome. Review the amount of time you anticipate you can be available and the amount of time you feel is necessary for adequate visits and travel time. If at all possible, allow for delays once you are traveling.

After all of the preparation and internal groundwork have been laid for the trip, it is important to begin talking to your customer(s) about the possibility of the trip. Matters to take into consideration include country holidays; your customer's production schedules; climate conditions and seasonal, weather-related impacts to the travel plans; and any impact on your own organization affected by the trip and/or your availability at critical periods. Within your organization, be aware of any contract negotiations, delivery problems, system issues, and so on. While the United States has a short list of trade restrictions, it is very important to be aware of these and any connections you may encounter while traveling.

As soon as you are able to confirm an appointment with a customer, begin making contact with other customers in the region or country. While this may seem an obvious statement, there is risk of offending customers or potential customers if you omit them from a strategic opportunity. Make your plans carefully; understand the travel times and distances between customer locations. Be prepared with ground transportation and any necessary security precautions. Certainly, it is appropriate to consider letting your customers know who else you are visiting. The decision to communicate this is heavily reliant on the industry, the market competition, and specific cultures. Once a comfortable rapport has been established with the customer, you are in a better position to decide if it is appropriate to mention visits with other customers in the area.

LOCATION

The location for the meeting is a serious consideration in setting up a customer visit. It is terrific for the credit professional to tour the customer's operations and facilities. However, the customer may or may not be able to host a meeting in the facility. Be ready to suggest neutral locations for a meeting.

U.S. embassies are available for neutral meeting locations. USEAC can facilitate these meetings. The overall assistance can include the location, transportation, security, catering, and gifts. Certainly, embassy staff can make appropriate recommendations and arrangements, taking into consideration all of the cultures involved. These services are frequently available at no charge; nominal fees tied to the specific expenses of the meeting or reception may be assessed. The assistance of the USEAC and embassy staff is particularly helpful if you are interacting with a culture that is significantly different from that of your company and yourself.

Another neutral location can be meeting facilities at an airport or hotel close to the airport. When you choose a more "public" location, it is recommended that agents or colleagues familiar with the location assist with the arrangements. Anticipating the needs of the client is critical when choosing the meeting location. These neutral locations are also helpful if you have a limited amount of time and need to meet with more than one client in one city.

One last detail: Before leaving the office, spend the last business day confirming appointments with the clients. By this point, this should be your third or fourth contact with the customer about the visit. The confirmation will include the date, time, an agenda (if appropriate), and the parties who will be participating in the meeting, as well as the roles and titles of each individual. Spontaneous or unconfirmed appointments are generally not received.

APPOINTMENT IS CONFIRMED

Every traveler will warn you to "expect the unexpected." Any number of circumstances and events can cause delays. Some will be within your control but most will not be. To be ready for such events, hand carry telephone numbers and names as well as directions to the meeting site. The various time zones may create challenges in being alert and calm in all circumstances. So get plenty of rest, avoid alcohol, and drink bottled water. As challenges and changes occur, your ability to be creative and flexible according to the circumstances will greatly enhance your ability to successfully manage the new time lines.

Shortly after you arrive in the country, contact the customer(s) to confirm the appointment. Solidify any preliminary details at this time. Again, get some rest and drink more water in order to be alert and in top form for this very important first meeting.

AFTER THE FIRST MEETING

It is very important to follow-up the meeting with direct customer contact. A note of thanks, hand-written or via e-mail, addressed to each individual is necessary. If it is too cumbersome to address a note to each individual, consider sending a gift for the group to acknowledge their time and effort. A basket of snacks, specific to your state, or a box of chocolates never fails to please any crowd. It is important to include only things made in your state or in the United States. Be sure to acknowledge the customer for taking the time and opportunity for the meeting.

Review the list of commitments made to your employer. Complete any reports or communications established as part of the success measurements as soon as possible after the meeting. Remember to check in with your office and colleagues as scheduled. Take note of specific "learning experiences" for the next trip. Be ready to make appropriate recommendations for future meetings and travels.

MOVING FORWARD WITH
THE CUSTOMER RELATIONSHIP

After the first visit, there is a virtual guarantee of an enhanced relationship with your customer. While taking advantage of this new commitment to mutual success, be sensitive to taking care of the relationship. Maintaining contact and planning for future visits are important aspects of the ongoing health of the initial face-to-face contact.

Now is the time to pursue new contracts and negotiate terms and conditions for future transactions. Review the internal concerns and aspects of the need for negotiation. If it is appropriate, reevaluate the perceived risk for the organization with the "new" information from the actual meeting. This is the time to consider the customer's facility and operations, the economic conditions witnessed while traveling, the relationships between the various people you met at the customer site, and many other tangible and intangible aspects of a business relationship. All of your casual observations during the trip will help to enlighten your negotiations with internal and external customers. Being the resident expert on a country or customer will also dovetail nicely into opportunities within your organization and for professional development.

10

Cultural Differences: Latin America

David I. Marsh

Novis International, Inc.

Let us begin by asking "What is your attitude toward time?" A few more questions will help you focus on a major cultural difference between Latin Americans and those who live outside the continent. Consider the following scenarios:

- Do you remain relaxed and comfortable in business meetings or negotiating sessions that last more than two hours? And then do you go directly to a local restaurant for a two- to three-hour lunch that may end by 6 P.M. at the earliest?
- Is your Argentine customer upset when you arrive at his office for a scheduled business meeting about one hour late?
- Is your customer in Mexico surprised (and probably unprepared or not available) if you arrive at his office less than thirty minutes late?

If any one of these situations frustrates or bothers you, it is a good bet that you should not pursue the role of international credit professional in Latin America.

This chapter does not attempt to analyze human behavior in Latin society or perform a deep study of their social structure or the influence of religion on business success. Instead, it will demonstrate cultural differences by showing examples of how Latin values and norms directly affect a credit professional's role across the continent.

We will look at the importance of cross-cultural literacy, how the culture of a country affects business practice. Without such literacy, businesspeople can jeopardize relationships and long-term sales opportunities. Global managers must realize that all of the countries and people south of the U.S. border are not basically the same.

CULTURE: WHAT IS IT?

Culture has been defined as that complex whole which includes knowledge, beliefs, morals, law, custom, art, religion, and other capabilities acquired by people as members of a society. Culture gradually forms our individual behavior by pointing out appropriate and inappropriate types of human behavior. This learning process begins at an early age and stays with us for the rest of our life.

The fundamental building blocks of any culture are its value system and its norms. Values are society's ideas, views, morals, and attitudes about what it believes to be right, good, and desirable. They provide the context within which a society's norms are created and justified. Norms are the social rules and guidelines that define appropriate behavior in particular situations. They shape the actions of people toward one another and include routine conventions of everyday life as well as the laws that provide order in a functioning society. They are influenced by political and economic philosophy, social structure, religion, language, and education.

The value systems and norms that have evolved over the years throughout Latin countries reflect important differences that directly affect business activity and the credit professional's degree of success at all levels. Let us now explore several norms that all credit people must accept and deal with if they expect to have a positive impact in Latin markets.

HOW IMPORTANT IS TIME?

Now that your "attitude toward time" has carried you this far, your patience will surely be tested as we focus on several seemingly routine credit situations. The concept of time is most complex (and boring) and is obviously viewed differently in all Latin countries. In the United States, we believe that neither the past nor the future even exists . . . and the present is experienced only momentarily. Thus, we tend to hurry through all phases of our daily tasks; we tend to be very time conscious. This "requirement" to be prompt will limit a credit person's patience in collecting payments at maturity, in getting to know customers, and in resolving debt obligations realistically and fairly for all parties.

Payments

Payment at maturity is virtually unthinkable throughout Latin America. This attitude, coupled with historically long and generous payment terms, leaves most foreign businesspeople with the idea that Latins are unreliable (or very clever) and basically marginal credit risks. Not so, in most instances. The pace in Latin America is traditionally slow, especially when payment negotiations are under way. Unfortunately for foreign suppliers, some Latins take full advantage of this "tradition" and simply expect us to live with often-extreme delays in payment, in keeping a business appointment, or just in having a meal together. In all fairness, many people in Latin America do honor their word and do pay at maturity.

Meetings

This slower pace, this relaxed attitude toward time exists to various degrees in every Latin country. It can be especially bothersome when personal visits are needed to reverse unacceptably long payment trends or to avoid a looming bad debt or just to agree on the "rules" that both parties will live by in a new relationship.

You may feel embarrassed or believe you are rude when you arrive at your Argentine customer's business almost one hour after the scheduled time. The guilt will quickly subside when you learn your host has not yet arrived, is already in a meeting that may last another hour, or has totally forgotten your appointment and will try to receive you before going out to lunch. For you to arrive with no appointment and totally unexpected is indeed rude and will do nothing to enhance your position.

Farther north, in Mexico, even the most serious companies expect you to arrive for an appointment about 30 minutes late. This is very normal and offends no one. Last-minute cell phone calls to explain "We are running a little late and are just a few blocks away" are part of the procedure. Certainly, in every Latin country there are businesses that expect you to arrive punctually or very close to the agreed time. These typically are customers who pretend to be extremely busy and probably see little benefit in your visit anyway.

Once a meeting begins in any Latin country, be prepared to choose between a glass of cold water (*agua sin gas o con gas*) or a coffee (*cafecito con azucar* but probably no *leche*). The meeting can easily last one hour with less than 50 percent of the time devoted to business issues. A credit person, accompanying his or her regional manager on an introductory visit, should be delighted when the meeting exceeds two hours. Whether firm commitments or detailed payment arrangements are promised carries little meaning unless you have reciprocated with a price reduction, longer terms, or another compromise in which your host realizes some tangible value. Lunch and drinks and dinner may follow such meetings with only a "banjo" break in between. This can easily devour another two to three hours, which should not be taken lightly. Again, stay relaxed, attentive, and sociable and accept the premise that all this time has not been misused or unproductive.

WHEN CAN YOU EXPECT TO BE PAID?

Perhaps you already know the answer. Payment terms in Latin America seem to take on meanings that are surprisingly different from the words printed in a "terms" box on an invoice. In Brazil, the official prenumbered local invoice forms request both the payment terms and the due date(s). Five or six due dates spaced seven days apart and starting with 28 days is very common. This practice is a carryover from many years of high inflation when the currency devalued daily.

Although "normal" terms may be 60 days in Mexico and Guatemala or 120 days in Chile and El Salvador or 150 to 180 days in Argentina, most Latin customers only begin to think about settling a routine invoice on or soon after it matures. Another 15 to 30 days may easily evaporate before payment reaches you. Foreign suppliers who have not yet persuaded their Latin clients to remit abroad via wire transfer must understand the importance of having a local office or agent who will either pick up the customer's check or send a messenger to wait an hour before learning if the check will be ready today. Electronic banking has been perfected in Brazil, and local banks in other countries are now well equipped to arrange payment transfers within and outside the country on a same-day basis.

Third-Party Checks

In Argentina, it is especially important that a credit person is willing to accept partial payments in the form of postdated checks and third-party checks. At one time or another, most Latin countries have imposed a financial tax on all types of banking transactions. Accepting third-party checks to settle a trade receivable and then passing them on to pay a supplier can often avoid these taxes. A rudimentary system of pencil codes in the check's corners helps identify the involved parties in the event such a check fails to clear the issuer's bank. Credit professionals are urged to accept such checks when payment is in doubt. Many companies do not maintain sufficient bank balances to pay a U.S. $50,000 invoice all at one time. Their accounts payable system does allow for a number of smaller remittances at regular intervals. Accept this practice and relax your attitude toward time.

Rescheduling

In situations where an overdue debt is substantial, your customer's financial capacity—and attitude toward time—may require a credit person to reschedule payment over long periods. Six months is normal, with serious cases requiring up to two years with minimal or no late interest. Such negotiations can only be handled in person, face to face. Deals are never concluded over the phone and usually not even by letter. This entire process can be quite torturous for credit professionals who are accustomed to having clients keep their word, who promise with all certainty that they will honor the payment agreement, and who even appear delighted to receive your follow-up letter confirming the details.

Gringos love detailed written agreements to cover themselves against all legal ramifications and contingencies. They must realize that written agreements hold little importance in resolving most Latin credit problems. Latins prefer to rely more on their word, even though they might not do as they have promised. Always be mindful of the mañana concept, which means an indefinite future to a Latin. It is common and to be expected that your "deal" will break down sooner rather than later and have to be rescheduled more than once. Latins require more flexibility in adhering to agreements. An Argentine sees a contract as an ideal scheme in the best of worlds. But we do not live in the best of worlds, and we should expect the outcome to fall somewhere short of the agreed terms. Payment will be late, there may be heated exchanges of faxes, but things will not be so bad that further deals are completely out of the question. I suppose a customer who pays six months late is better than one who does not pay at all.

Promises

So why do overdue customers make such promises knowing that they may not pay you as agreed? Who knows? A miracle may happen and the payment will be remitted. Meanwhile, you are happy. This is important. To make people happy is to exercise power and appear honorable. Argentines especially dislike being told when a payment is required. They will decide when to pay you, regardless of the terms.

These dilemmas are all the more troublesome if you stop delivering product during a period of slow payment or nonpayment. Then you are perceived as being nonsupportive, not a friend, or, worse, as a pretend admirer not really committed to a long-term relationship. Latins will always remind you when you were not standing with them in difficult times past. This brings us to the true measure of success in Latin America or in life everywhere: your relationships with other people.

GET TO KNOW EACH OTHER, THEN DO BUSINESS

Universally, Latins strive to conduct business in a friendly atmosphere. They view a supplier as a friend or even a family member who will support the relationship during rough times as well as in good times.

Nobody rushes into business in Latin countries. Local sales representatives are well advised to make return visits to fallen away and prospective clients even if their prices, terms, or technical support is inferior. Business meetings are viewed as social occasions where everybody is to show respect, discuss grand outlines as opposed to petty details, and show sincerity of intent. Negotiating is often just a brainstorming session. Gringos tend to be very businesslike and straightforward in addressing issues. They think getting to the point early in a business meeting helps both parties clarify the issues and thoroughly discuss alternative solutions before closing with a firm agreement.

In Mexico, Salvador, Brazil, Colombia, and Argentina, such an approach will usually be unsuccessful and do little more than frustrate you. Americans must learn to take our time, talk about our family or compliment the weather, the city, or the local soccer team. Be prepared to share experiences about family and to offer an informed opinion of the local political climate, stock market, and industry conditions. Resist the American habit of getting to know people by asking a lot of questions. To reach a Latin businessman, relate everything in terms of his family, his town, his country, and, above all, his personal pride. Personalize everything for him.

Be careful not to oversimplify reality or feel that you must replicate business customs that have become efficient and effective outside Latin America. Some of these customs may not be practical or applicable in Latin cultures. If you fail to adapt your strategy to local practices, the results can be just the opposite of what is desired.

CREATIVITY

In Brazil, people have developed an uncanny ability to come up with clever, unorthodox, and creative solutions for just about any business, legal, bureaucratic, or financial problem. These solutions are what is known in Portuguese as the *jeito* or its diminutive, *jeitinho*. It provides more space for negotiating. Dr. Robert da Matta, an authority on the subject and anthropologist at Notre Dame University, calls it a bridge between two worlds, one in which old ways and common sense hold firm and another in which the new framework of society is not just or rational. In traumatic times, many companies use the *jeitinho* as their only means of survival. Most are within the law but appear to be roundabout ways of reaching a desired conclusion.

For instance, you might give a distressed client 28 days longer terms but then allow them an extra week to actually remit their payment. In effect, you are granting an interest-free loan, which allows smaller customers to cover immediate expenses while customers on more solid financial ground can use the money to invest in high-yield government bonds. Most *jeitinhos* are more complicated mechanisms for creating win-win solutions that give one supplier a distinct advantage over a competitor without adding significantly to the credit risk.

OTHER CULTURAL DIFFERENCES

This discussion would not be complete unless we also talk briefly about the influence of language on Latin cultures. The Roman Catholic Church is also an important cultural force, but its influence in credit matters is difficult to ascertain. Formal education is another factor, which is too complex to be introduced here.

Language does far more than enable people to communicate with each other. It structures the way the world is perceived. Although English is the language of international business, there are considerable advantages for an English-speaking person who learns Spanish and Portuguese. Naturally, most people prefer to converse in their own language. Being able to speak even a little Spanish or Portuguese will help in building rapport and in completing a business deal.

Nonverbal cues and body language differences in Latin America are the most apparent and important elements of communications. To convey their ideas fully, Latins, especially Mexicans and Brazilians, use their hands, arms, and facial expressions and make maximum use of tone and pitch. They are not necessarily being dramatic or overemotional. They just want you to know how they feel. They will appeal, directly and strongly, to your good sense, warm heart, or generosity if they want something from you. Be prepared to decide, on the spot, whether to say yes or no to a business proposal.

A normal distance between parties standing in a business discussion in Latin America is two to four feet, which is "too close for comfort" for most foreigners. As a result, Americans often back away from customers during conversations. Hosts may construe this as rejection or aloofness, ending in a regrettable lack of rapport. Credit professionals should overcome these tendencies and be willing to negotiate shoulder to shoulder if that is what it takes to achieve results. Do not object or back away when men embrace instead of shaking hands.

IMPLICATIONS FOR BUSINESS

An important implication that flows from the cultural differences in Latin America is the need to develop a cross-cultural literacy. One of the more serious dangers facing a company that wants to expand into Latin America is the danger of being ill-informed. Any business that lacks sound knowledge about practices in Latin countries is unlikely to succeed. Foreigners must adapt to and embrace all aspects of a firm's operation: the way deals are negotiated, pricing and volume strategies, organizational structure, incentive pay for local salespeople, criteria for granting unsecured credit, methods of collecting open debts, and so on. All of these are sensitive to cultural differences. What works in Mexico might not work in Argentina but will work in Brazil.

To build cross-cultural literacy, a company must employ local citizens and ensure that home-country businesspeople are cosmopolitan and understand how cultural differences will impact their success in Latin countries. Local employees, conversely, should have an idea of the "gringo way of doing business" and know what is expected from the Latin customers. He or she is a mediator between two business cultures. Latin employees must understand certain "basics" in order to conduct business in a mature manner, one that is globally acceptable. Finally, credit professionals must always be alert to the dangers of ethnocentrism—the belief that one's ethnic group or culture is superior and a disregard for the culture and people of other countries.

11

Cultural Differences: Pacific Rim

Paul Beretz

Pacific Business Solutions

The classic understanding of a credit manager's primary responsibilities include the approval of the creditworthiness of customers and insuring that the company's accounts receivable are paid in a timely manner while always keeping bad debts to a minimum. These characteristics are bundled together in support of the company's overall goals, whether the business exists only in North America or in a global environment. So if proper credit analysis and effective collection techniques are the ground stakes, why should an international credit manager really care about country culture?

Doing business in any place in the world, including regions within the United States, means understanding the people. A comprehensive understanding of the country's culture maximizes an opportunity to achieve results. Whether the goal is to secure a sales contract, approve a credit application, or collect money, possessing a cultural awareness of the geographical part of the world is critical.

PACIFIC RIM AREA

The Asian market is generally considered to be composed of 29 nations from Afghanistan to Vietnam, and is located in Asia, Central Asia, Eurasia, Southeast Asia, and the Indian continent. Many U.S. companies concentrate on developing trade to the Pacific Rim, especially China, Hong Kong, India, Indonesia, Japan, South Korea, Malaysia, the Philippines, Singapore, Taiwan, Thailand, and Vietnam. The typical person from the Americas will think of the Pacific Rim as "one culture"; however, many Asian cultures coexist within the same country. (For example, in Singapore, the majority of the population is Chinese, with the balance Malay and Indian. Various other groups in Singapore include (Europeans, North Americans, Australians, and Japanese.) Within the country of China, many people perceive the "business" culture to be different: The traditional, state-owned businesses continue to flourish in the country seat of Beijing (although that is beginning to change) while in Shanghai there is a more Western influence (i.e., privatized companies and joint ventures began to develop in the mid-1990s). The seasoned businessperson recognizes the differences in cultural nuances even within these two major areas of China and understands that the country of China possesses a history and tradition consistent with one of the world's oldest continuous civilizations spanning over 5,000 years.

RISK AND THE CREDIT MANAGER

As "risk" executives responsible for protecting accounts receivable, often the first or second largest asset on a company's balance sheet, credit managers may call on the Cs of credit risk management in order to evaluate the risk elements of a customer's creditworthiness. These risk assessment traits include character (the background and experience of the owners), capacity (the ability to generate cash flow), capital (the level of net worth or capital funding), and conditions (the market—competitive, seasonal—that impacts the business today and in the future).

In the Pacific Rim—or in any international risk assessment situation—there are three more Cs: currency, country, and culture. Knowledge of currency relates to understanding currency issues within the country, an area critical to the credit manager who expects payment to leave the country and wind up in his or her company's bank account. Knowledge of country requires a grasp of political happenings and issues that could impact the international credit manager's company from doing business or, worse yet, result in funds being frozen because of political changes. It is the C of culture that this chapter addresses, for the credit manager doing business in and with the Pacific Rim. Some seasoned, battle-worn credit managers claim that another C exists in many high-risk evaluations, whether it is North American–centric or international in scope—the C known as candle: When all else fails, go to your local place of worship, light a candle, and pray and pray some more.

STOP, LOOK, AND LISTEN

Awareness, attitude, anticipation: In the Pacific Rim business environment, observant credit managers will remember the sign they may have seen at railroad crossings: "STOP, LOOK, and LISTEN!" This admonition includes not only dealing with customers offshore but with a company's own "internal" customer, the branch office in the country of business. It is critical for credit mangers to ensure that a smooth relationship exists and is constantly maintained with their own overseas company employees. Those who travel from the United States to Asian nations in particular need to stop promoting the United States (by saying such things as "That may be the way you write a contract here in China, but that's not the way we do it at home" or "Can't I find American food anywhere around this place?"). We are visitors in their land, not the other way around. Americans in particular need to *stop* comparing local practices to the way business is done at home.

The *"look"* caution means that astute business visitors to a Pacific Rim country will study behavior, learn about verbal and nonverbal differences that exist, and probably use a "go-between" (a *shokaijo* in Japan) to help develop the desired relationship. Credit managers should understand how important the go-between is in the Pacific Rim country. The person may be the firm's own country manager, or it could be a banker, accountant, or individual in a key position in the country who understands how to help achieve the objective.

To *"listen"* is a concept difficult for many Westerners. The Japanese saying "Hollow drums make the most noise" recognizes this fact. Why do Americans think they have to restate questions because someone takes time to answer? Why are Americans not more conscious of the use of idioms? Idiomatic phrases are extremely difficult for non-Americans to understand. For example, Americans are fond of saying such things as "better late than never," "in the long run," "put it on the back burner," "get the ball rolling," "get to first base," "quick on the trigger," and "beat around the bush." Just think how a customer sitting across the table in a Pacific Rim country may react when one of these phrases is used.

In considering specific cultural profiles and how the concept of "stop, look, and listen" should be part of credit managers' business goals, consider Japan and Korea. In Japan, the concept of *wa* (meaning peace and harmony) is the basis for a working relationship. Japan's crowded island condition has driven that society to value conformity. As a culture, the highest priority is placed on *wa*. In a small place, one has to work for smooth relationships. The Japanese person with closed eyes sitting opposite the credit manager is not necessarily being rude, he or she may be working toward inner harmony. In the Japanese culture, "Speech is silver, but silence is golden."

In Korea, the priorities are family, respect for authority, formality, and class. Koreans are aggressive, hardworking, friendly, and hospitable. A driving force in Korean relationships (and significant to a degree in all Pacific Rim countries) is "saving face." Most Asian cultures are keen on "saving face." As long as no one points out any errors to the people responsible, it is possible for them to assume there are no errors, so no "face" is lost. Will credit managers recognize the level of people they are dealing with and understand that an immediate decision—in the expected, American way—may not be forthcoming in a Pacific Rim culture? Open conflict is counter to the Pacific Rim cultures, even if public emotional displays are expected in America.

Do Westerners stop to appreciate the significance of use of the "name" (business) card in Pacific Rim countries? It is amazing how many visitors to

Asian nations do not have separate cards printed in the country language (especially if they do extensive, repeat business, for example, in Japan or China). The card is presented with both hands, with a slight bow, or *ojigi* in Japanese. A card recipient looks closely at the name of the other person's company, and does not write on the card or put it away during the meeting. An insult tendered at the beginning of the meeting—even an unintentional slight—can destroy the chance for any successful outcome.

Japan's cultural roots have a strong middle management, deep working relationships, seniority in rank; seniors look after subordinates. Management is participative, with consensus problem solving. Open expression of conflict is avoided. If credit managers are aware and anticipate these cultural nuances, they have a better chance to succeed.

TRUST

Any person-to-person relationship, especially in the business world, has a better chance of succeeding when trust is both understood and established. In the Pacific Rim, cultures depend on trust, or *amae* (the "oil of life"), in Japan. In any relationship in this region, a feeling of complete trust and confidence must exist. People must feel not only that the other party will not take advantage of them but also that they can presume upon the indulgence of the other. A study of cultural history in this region will show that those most qualified to leadership positions are perceived as being dependent on the people beneath them. This is the purest form of egoless relationship; it contrasts to Western societies that foster the need to repress trust.

In Japan, a humble attitude, by public figures especially, is still considered an essential virtue. Westerners should realize that apologies in this culture may be real as well as "pretended," often the same as Americans bragging about their imagined skills. The purpose of the Japanese apology is to avoid ill will, friction, and anything else that may be seen as wrong. If Western credit managers are not aware of these nuances, they will not be able to gain the confidence of the Pacific Rim businessperson, or doing so will be difficult.

USING AN INTERPRETER

While English has truly become the international language, there are areas within the Pacific Rim where top executives have not mastered (or care not to) the language of the Anglo. In these cases, using an interpreter can help. However, certain caveats should be considered.

- The presenter (the credit manager visiting a customer, for example) needs to find his or her own interpreter, usually through a go-between in the country.
- The interpreter must be given a written text of the presentation (or at least the gist of the notes for the meeting).

- The English speaker should speak slowly around a single topic, avoid slang and puns, and use metaphors and analogies with care. For example, would the speaker expect an interpreter to translate "What's good for the goose is good for the gander" into an Asian language?
- Charts and visuals should be used whenever possible.
- The English speaker should monitor facial and nonverbal expressions and talk to the person, not the interpreter.

BRIDGING THE CULTURAL GAP

Unfortunately, it is human nature—some say a Western trait—to stereotype. Before I made my first trip to the Pacific Rim countries of South Korea, Japan, Taiwan, and Singapore, I felt that I was going to "Asia." I felt individual country customs might be different but that the real difference would be between "Asian culture" versus Western lifestyle. Americans in other countries have the tendency to treat the natives as foreigners and to forget that they themselves are the foreigners. Stereotyping constrains our ability to work with people, is a lazy way of categorizing people, and uses group categories while ignoring individual differences.

Harmful examples are often subconscious, evaluative, and certainly inaccurate. Such an example might be the idea that "All Chinese are submissive and passive and don't make good managers. Mr. Yu, therefore, will not make a good manager." Direct and immediate information can result in positive conclusions. One would learn, for example, that "Many Chinese value group efforts and are reserved in how they express themselves. Mr. Yu might make a good manager."

NEGOTIATING IN THE PACIFIC RIM

Negotiating skills are vital to effective credit executives. Some immediate cultural differences in negotiating in the Pacific Rim include:

- Silence (*wa* in Japan)
- Tone of voice—no talking loudly
- Cleanliness (especially in China)
- Orderliness/punctuality (although you may have to wait in Singapore)
- Trust
- Eye contact
- Gestures—It is okay to smile but rude to wink; it is impolite to point a finger (point with the open hand)
- Touching—Avoid pats on the back or any touching; however, it is acceptable for men to hold hands

Use of humor is frowned on. Even though humor may be an "icebreaker" in Western negotiating circumstances, it can be seen as disrespectful during negotiation sessions in the Pacific Rim. Never assume that the person doing the most speaking is the boss. During a negotiating session in a remote area outside of Beijing, it took me two hours to realize that the woman at the end of the table who had said nothing during the discussion of open-account versus letter-of-credit terms was the director of the other eight people in the room.

In Thailand, when making a major point in a negotiating session, perhaps one that would make the credit manager angry (perhaps rightfully so), be as quiet as possible. In that country, the lower the voice, the more emphatic the atmosphere and the point to be made. The technique really works!

Japanese seek flexible relationships. Do not expect snap decisions; they must retreat, confer, and reach a consensus.

Remember that affirmative words or even nods of the head do not mean agreement. "Yes" does not mean the "yes" that Westerners know; it really means that the question is understood but that it is not acknowledged in the affirmative. "Yes" often means that listeners will go back to their management group and attempt to reach a consensus decision. Many American negotiators have gone back home thinking that an agreement was reached simply because they did not understand the use of the affirmative in a particular culture.

And please, negotiators, leave lawyers at home. Koreans negotiate with Americans from a position of strength. Compared to the Japanese, they have a straightforward, American negotiating style. Koreans respect stature in Seoul, so Westerners should hire a chauffeur and emphasize their link with *Fortune* 100 companies.

Remember that in Korea (as well as Japan and many other Asian locales), there are expectations to drink alcohol, although in recent years it has become understood that some people simply do not drink. If possible, negotiators should pace themselves over an evening by nursing one or two beers.

Negotiating with the Chinese involves detail—they expect detail about product characteristics and specific contractual terms and conditions. Research has shown that the Chinese negotiating process is greatly affected by their ingrained politeness and restraint, their emphasis on social obligations, and their belief in the interconnection of work, family, and friendship. Appealing to individual members of the Chinese negotiating team rather than directing the benefits to the group as a whole will probably backfire.

Harmony is very important in the Chinese culture. After the Chinese establish a cordial relationship with foreign negotiators, they use this relationship as a basis for the give-and-take of business discussion. This attitude of *guanxi* means "Before we can deal, you must be hooked into my friendship circle." The Chinese are among the toughest negotiators in the world. American managers must anticipate various tactics—delaying techniques—and the Chinese avoidance of direct, specific answers. Where Westerners negotiate with specific goals in mind and are willing to compromise, the Chinese are reluctant to negotiate deals. Most of all, remember that in China negotiations usually begin *after* the contract or agreement has been signed.

NEGOTIATING TIPS SPECIFIC TO THE PACIFIC RIM

When negotiating in the Pacific Rim environment, *do not:*

- Plunge immediately into business
- Insist on "all or nothing"
- Use "I" excessively
- Touch people
- Believe that walls have no ears

When negotiating, *do:*

- Build relationships
- Work for trust
- Listen to innuendo
- Respect elders
- Protect intellectual property
- Bargain for tight terms

Effective international credit managers in the negotiating process will "Stop, look, and listen." They must study the facts, when possible, with attention to priorities depending on the significance of the deal. Americans probably will never get it all right unless they live in the country. Learn silence, keep an open heart, and change the "always win!" attitude with which you were raised.

CONCLUSION

It is not possible to be culturally correct all the time. Astute American businesspeople, even those well traveled in the Pacific Rim, will learn to "expect the unexpected." We must attempt to understand and relate to local customs and practices. We must maintain awareness, keep an open attitude, learn to anticipate difficulties, and attempt to appreciate the significance of history and customs when doing business in any part of the world. Credit managers who ignore cultural influences doom their activities—requests for a financial statement, approving credit, negotiating payment terms, collecting money, or developing a relationship with their company people in other countries—to failure or at best to a long, drawn-out process.

In my travels to a variety of countries in the Pacific Rim, I have heard much about "those Americans!" The perceptions about Westerners include:

- We talk too much.
- We interrupt other people and finish their sentences.
- We do not listen enough (do we just "hear" but not absorb?).
- We are too direct in asking questions.
- We give opinions and poke fun.

- We fail to express thanks and appreciation sufficiently.
- We appear reluctant to admit faults or limitations and seldom apologize.
- Our managers and directors give more attention to individuals than to the entire group.
- We do not appreciate the importance of certain formalities.
- We are too time conscious.

Whether we sense that these qualities are applicable in our own behavior or not, in this case perception is really more important than reality.

Understanding customs and practices means integrating the cultural differences into one's own experience. It is not just for courtesy; rather, it reflects a strong business sense and will add to one's success in the international business arena.

12

Cultural Differences: Europe

Cynthia Wieme

Jeppessen

Some people think Europeans are just like North Americans. Why, they even speak the same language in some countries. Such generalizations are likely to get international credit executives into trouble.

Collating credit and trade information specific to European customers remains as difficult as ever. While progress is being made by many "information" agencies, the lack of guidelines and continuity in accounting practices and reporting throughout the world minimizes the value of such information. Fiscal reporting periods, currency devaluations, and taxes are just a few of the areas where the measurements are quite different from standards applied in the United States.

The network of industry group contacts and "current events" awareness continue as the leading sources for decision-making criteria. Successful decisions will rest on every skill and piece of information brought to the table. Therefore, it is reasonable to expect that a resident expert on cultures, law and administration, and the organization's goals and mission will greatly enhance successful trade relationships with customers. Each of these factors must be heavily weighed on the scale of evaluation. In deciding who the "good customers" are and in choosing to continue business relationships, credit managers must balance fact and intangible data.

PUBLICATIONS

Many publications provide direction in evaluating trade conditions and terms. As the European continent is comprised of many different countries and cultures, the only universally applicable factor is that every country is different. Over the years, the viability of the European countries and cultures have been significant factors in any trade decisions. Over the last 10 to 20 years, many changes have occurred in worldwide trade, country alliances, and, in fact, country borders. Languages and cultures impact daily transactions; change is much more obvious than in years and centuries past.

The European Community and conversion to the Euro in many countries are significantly impacting the roles and interaction of countries. Credit professionals should take every opportunity to stay current in the events and issues. Trade journals, newspapers, books, and the Internet all provide information and issues for consideration. Again, the specific requirements of one's organization and industry will predicate the direction of research and decisions. It is also appropriate to review more general business and trade practices to gain perspective on the decisions being made within one's organization. Awareness of credit decisions and trade measurements in other industries will also open doors for creative credit professionals. The challenge to "think, and move, outside the box" continues as a mantra from many chief financial officers. Every new initiative brought to the table enhances the opportunities for all concerned.

COLLECTIONS AND TECHNOLOGY

With the evolution of Internet trade and information, coupled with the conversion to an almost universal currency in the Euro, most European countries are looking closely at "best business practices." Standards have been in place and practice for hundreds of years, and the transitions cannot be expected overnight or even at a pace of less than a decade. While individuals are moving and changing stride, the more established businesses typically move slowly. On a worldwide scale, many companies are beginning to evolve away from ownership established during or after World War II. These changes in ownership and management, often away from family ownership and ties, will open doors for change in business practices.

While Americans use checks and credit cards interchangeably and literally without thought, Europeans are more accustomed to moving funds through the banks. Most European companies operate directly through the banks for currency movement and exchange for all disbursements. Financing tools and instruments considered cumbersome in the United States are quite standard in virtually every European country. The direct banking tools also allow wide parameters for accepting virtually all currencies for payment. These transactions also reduce banking fees, currency exchange costs, and delays in funding. However, they also require a level of expertise in treasury management. Hedging, investment, constant monitoring, and multiple transactions per day are the norm in managing the cash flow of larger European businesses.

Acceptance and familiarity with such transactions allows for greater options in negotiating payment arrangements. Conversely, if an organization is not familiar with currency exchanges and fluctuations, it is appropriate to bring in experts to work through and set up necessary changes to policy and procedure requirements. The international department at one's banking institution can help with these matters.

CURRENCY ISSUES

Most European customers will be able to pay obligations in U.S. dollars. There is little difficulty accessing U.S. dollars, and few countries restrict the movement of currency from their banks or country to the United States. In general, currency value fluctuations are an area of risk. Contractual stipulations of the currency exchange value should be avoided. Few sales will be lost over the refusal to tie in currency valuations. However, being the "resident expert" on such matters will allow for intelligent discussion of these issues with sales and management colleagues.

The most significant aspect of currency valuation risk is tied directly to the economic conditions of the country. This is where travel experience and attention to current events, political issues, social unrest, and economic conditions will factor in to the decision making necessary for successful relationships and payment plans. Negotiating around potential obstacles up front will bring confidence to the business relationships. Known parameters also factor in to one's ability to forecast cash positions and long-range commitments within the organization. Once again, some of the considerations presented in Chapter 9 will be affected by these later decisions. The strength of the relationship will continue to grow with the proven success of decisions.

PART FOUR

DEALING WITH PEOPLE

Establishing relationships, both with customers and with the sales force, is important for credit professionals. Doing so can be especially difficult for those dealing in international waters. First, credit professionals must learn the cultural differences and nuances discussed in Part 3; then they must use that information to build relationships with customers and sales.

Many times credit professionals have a difficult time convincing management that a trip to international customers is necessary. Chapter 13 explains how to convince management, how to prepare for the trip, and how to document afterward what was gained.

Some credit professionals have had a lot of success setting up customer visits at U.S. embassies in their customers' countries. Doing this can be quite impressive and a big help if trying to collect from a delinquent account. Chapter 13 also explains how to arrange an embassy visit. It contains information gained from interviews with many successful credit professionals.

Chapter 14 offers the reader some tips on establishing a sound working relationship with the ever-important sales staff. As annoying as salespeople can sometimes be to some credit professionals, the reality is that most companies are sales (or cash) driven rather than credit driven. Thus, credit managers usually must bend and find ways to make a sale happen when the customer is of less than stellar credit. This chapter contains tips on how to make this happen and how to work well with salespeople.

13

Customer Visits

Mary S. Schaeffer

IOMA

The value of customer visits cannot be overstated, whether they are used to strengthen relationships, compel customers to pay past-due invoices, or perhaps to discuss credit issues.

CULTURAL DIFFERENCES

Many people believe that understanding the cultural nuances of the countries to be visited is critical. Just as no two U.S. states are the same, no two countries are alike. U.S. credit professionals should not be too aggressive. If they go into the first meeting with high hopes, a full agenda, and ready to talk a blue streak around the customer, the meeting will end very abruptly. (This can happen in the United States as well.) People talk about the need for personal relationships and cultural awareness in other countries. Recognition of great customer relationships goes even further than the "partnering" with customers during tough times. All of these aspects are critical to the organization's success and the individual relationships that continue to grow.

The information in this chapter is based on numerous interviews with international credit executives including Paul Beretz, John Chung, Dave Marsh, Donald S. Richmond, Javier Vela, and Cynthia Wieme.

TIMING

There's no way around it: A visit to another country is expensive. The timing of the trips, which can be as infrequent as once a year, will depend on a number of factors, including:

- A request from the sales department (yes, this does occasionally happen)
- Complaints
- Disputes or inquiries from the customer
- Sales level
- Currency devaluations
- Customer carrying an excessive receivable exposure compared with its financial capacity.
- Slowdown in Days Sales Outstanding (DSO) figures
- Length of time since the last visit

LEVEL OF SALES AND OTHER CRITERIA

Sales volume plays an important role in determining when and if customer visits are arranged. If the accounts are small, the costs involved with the trip do not make it worthwhile. However, some executives make trips to build relationships rather than to address special problems. Building a strong business (and personal) relationship with the owners and finance people is a top priority for many.

Others visit customers to show them that they will always treat customers fairly and offer competitive payment terms and credit facilities whenever possible. These visits are a good time for credit professionals to let customers know that they are expected to keep their promises regarding payments. The importance of sharing basic credit information and submitting reliable financials annually or more often can also be addressed at these meetings.

Some credit professionals also let customers know that they will come back again to resolve any misunderstandings and problems.

While collecting past-due money is sometimes the main reason for a visit, many try to make relationship building the primary goal, especially during the initial visit with customers. A sound relationship may eliminate the need for a visit for collection purposes. Many customers are proud of their facilities and will show them off. So, depending on one's business, credit professionals may get to see some pretty unusual sights.

Several executives report that they try to leave these meetings with the most current financial statements, if they have not received them in advance. Postdated checks are sometimes received from past-due Latin American customers.

WHO PARTICIPATES IN INTERNATIONAL VISITS?

Companies that arrange customer visits intend to make the most out of them. Again, depending on the nature of the business and the purpose of the trip, the meeting may include the international credit executive, the customer's finance manager (or chief financial officer), general manager, purchasing manager, and the regional sales manager. Often, the owner will sit in on part of the meetings. Occasionally, legal counsel will also attend. If needed, a translator should be included. Those in need of a translator are strongly urged to hire their own and not rely on someone from the customer's company. In this way, the translations will not be tainted by the customer's viewpoint. Additionally, after the meeting, the translator may be able to provide valuable insights.

The credit executive should bring:

- Current, detailed statement of the customer's account
- Copies of pertinent correspondence since the last visit
- Ratio trend analysis of the customer's financial picture
- A color chart showing the customer's payment trend over the last 12 months (when the trend is not good)
- Notes taken during previous credit visits.

(Note: Some customers do not wish to have the account manager in the meeting because of their "business friendship" and the disclosure of finances.)

When it comes to preparing a formal agenda, the views are divergent. Some believe that a formal written agenda should be prepared in advance and sent along to the customer. At the other end of the spectrum are credit executives who simply bring a short handwritten list of the items they wish to discuss. The choice will depend on the personal style of the credit executive involved and the primary reason for the trip.

CONFIRMING AN UNDERSTANDING

More than one executive—both those in credit and those in other professions— have returned home from a visit to a customer in another country thinking they had an understanding only to learn later that there was no agreement. Part of the cause can be cultural. For example, in Japan, customers might nod their heads in what appears to be an affirmative manner and say "Yes, yes." All this means is that they have heard what is being said and understand it. It does not mean they are agreeing to the terms.

Credit professionals should tell every customer during the meeting that they will fax or express mail them a letter clearly confirming what agreements, "pay plans," and so on were agreed on during the visit as soon as they return to the office in the United States. Then do it. Most professionals prepare such documentation in English, although several successful credit executives report that they sometimes prepare such letters in Spanish for Latin American clients.

In addition to visiting customers, some credit professionals handle a few other tasks on their international trips: They give credit training to local employees and meet with local bank lending officers, other credit professionals, and attorneys who are familiar with local security instruments or have collection litigation practices.

PREPARING FOR AN OVERSEAS TRIP

Overseas trips to visit customers are both time consuming and expensive. Management often views these excursions as waste. Thus, international credit executives need to make sure that they get the most out of the trip and that management realizes the value of the trip. While some of the following advice may seem trivial, the following guidelines are useful for those traveling for the first time or the fiftieth.

- Do not leave preparation for the trip to the plane ride. For starters, unless you are riding in business class, you will be cramped for space and will not get much work done. Even if you are fully relaxed, you will not be able to do anything about missing information and reports while on the plane. Better to stay late in the office a few nights before the trip and get the itinerary, important papers, and reports together. That way you will have time to gather all the information needed.
- When planning the trip, define the objectives. Write down what you are trying to achieve. Be very specific in the details. Your notes will serve as a useful reminder and ensure that you do not forget anything. If management is skeptical about the value of your trip, share your goals.
- Get input from internal customers. These are your own product and country specialists. Find out, beforehand, what your company's competitive position is with the customer in the country you are visiting. This information will help you come across with confidence.
- Use your bankers and accounting firms to develop information on what is going on in the country where you will be doing business. These professionals can help you establish contacts in your customer's country.
- Use the bankers as a firsthand source of information regarding the difficulty of getting funds out of the country to which you are exporting. This may or may not be an issue, but if the currency is blocked or partially blocked, you will want to know this before you ship. In such instances, you may be able to make other arrangements.
- Be realistic about your time. Allow time for delays, layovers, and other transportation difficulties. Do not schedule your first meeting right after you land. If your plane is even a little late, you will be behind before you even get started. Additionally, you may need time to adjust to time

zone differences. Do not fool yourself into thinking that you can operate in a different time zone with no adjustment time.

- Have a contingency plan if the person who is supposed to pick you up is not there when you land. This is especially important if you are going to a country where you do not speak the language and/or have never been there before.
- Always carry with you the local phone number of someone you know in the country. Have your destination address faxed to you in advance. Make sure the fax is in both English and the native language, so if you are forced to rely on a taxi or other means of public transportation, you can show the fax to the driver.
- Be wary of fatigue. A business trip is not the time to experiment with foods you have never eaten before. If your trip includes a weekend, take time off. Do not try to schedule business meetings. Give yourself a break. If you like, do a little sightseeing—with the emphasis on little.
- Get a good country analysis before you go. This way you will have the political lay of the land before you arrive.
- Laptops are great for working on the plane or back in your hotel room at night. But, as anyone who has ever lugged one around can attest, they can get heavy very quickly. If you decide to take one along, make sure to carry the invoice for the machine, particularly if you are traveling to the Pacific Rim. If you have the invoice, when leaving the country you will be able to prove that you did not buy the computer while visiting. It is also advisable to check to see if you will need an adapter to connect the laptop to the electricity. Adapters can be purchased at most electrical supply shops and stores such as Radio Shack.
- If you want to send and receive e-mail, check with the hotel. Those with older wiring may not have the capability to allow you to connect with the Internet. You may also need to purchase a phone adapter. These only cost a few dollars. If you simply want to check e-mail and will not be sending documents, a better solution might be the Internet cafés springing up. Again, check beforehand to make sure they are available.
- Allow for canceled meetings. In order to get the maximum return out of your trip, have some backup plans in case one of your contacts cannot meet with you as originally arranged. These plans can be as simple as visiting with local employees.
- Send along a copy of your written agenda to the local branch of your company before your visit. This should be fairly detailed and should include the names of the people you are planning to see, when you will be seeing them, and what you are going to do. Additionally, it should clearly identify who is supposed to do what. Get the locals' concurrence with your plans and itinerary. Ask them for suggestions. At all costs, avoid the "We're from headquarters and we're here to help" approach.
- Be up-to-date on your company, your products, and the country you are visiting. This education will help you understand the problems of

those you meet while making you appear the informed executive you strive to be.

- While it is almost always more advantageous rate-wise to exchange U.S. currency for local denominations on arrival, consider converting $50 or $100 before you depart the United States. Doing so will allow for situations where offshore airport money exchange centers are closed and provide you with "walk-around money" or taxi fare until you arrive at your hotel. Note that airports typically offer the absolute worst exchange rates.
- Have credit cards appropriate for the destination country by confirming their acceptance with your travel planner.
- Do not depend on overseas ATMs to obtain local currency. You may be disappointed, despite assurances from your travel planner that the ATM card of choice will work in the overseas location.
- While this point seems obvious, remember that you can always learn something, whether you are a novice or a veteran traveler.

A trip overseas can be very worthwhile. Savvy credit managers should plan in advance to get the most out of these visits.

GETTING TO KNOW INTERNATIONAL CUSTOMERS

Credit professionals who know their customers stand a much better chance of providing both the customers and their employers with better credit and collection services. Here are some strategies that have helped successful credit professionals to get to know their customers better.

- *Visit with the company's larger overseas clients.* Those who do report that companies are much more willing to share information when you are there in person. They have gotten information that they would not have if a letter or credit application had been sent.
- *Review the customers' accounts receivable in person.* When visiting customers, ask to see their receivable portfolio. Review what type of credit insurance they have on their customers. In many instances, this may save your company from having to get such insurance, which would, in effect, be double insuring the product. Since most European companies have credit insurance, this can be a big savings when selling in Europe.
- *Visit the customer's banker.* While on overseas trips, if possible, spend time with the banker, who will provide additional information useful when trying to set credit limits. Customers make these introductions.
- *Get trade references.* Insist that these references come from U.S. companies rather than local trade references.
- *Get information from industry groups.* Join an industry group where information is traded freely among members. Doing so will help

evaluate the creditworthiness of a potential customer. It is also a good way to monitor existing customers. Many credit professionals use industry groups for domestic customers but do think about these groups when it comes to international business. These professionals might be missing a good source of data. Both the FCIB (an association of executives in Finance Credit and International Business) and Riemer have international groups.

- *Visit with customers when they are in this country.* By taking out your international customers when they are in the United States, you will cement your personal relationship. This is especially useful when it comes to collecting money. When you pick up the phone to discuss the matter, you will have already established a personal relationship and increase dramatically the odds of collecting quickly.
- *Communicate with everyone involved.* This should include the marketing person, who is often left out of the loop.
- *Use all mediums of communication.* Use phone, fax, and now even e-mail. Many international credit professionals use e-mail on a regular basis with international customers. In many ways, it is even better than a fax because the response can be instantaneous. A few credit executives report that e-mail might not work as well with companies in France, where people love letter writing.
- *Speak the language.* Being able to communicate with customers in their native tongue will give international credit professionals a distinct advantage. For the most part, customers will be impressed with anyone who attempts to speak their language, although fluency, of course, is preferable.
- *Review terms as a relationship develops.* Where credit background is scant, the company might begin a relationship on letter-of-credit terms and, as it becomes more established, switch to credit insurance. Then even more liberal terms may be appropriate.

USING U.S. EMBASSIES FOR MEETINGS

Many international credit executives are not aware that U.S. embassies can be used for meetings with customers in other countries. There are a number of reasons for doing this.

For Collection Issues

The U.S. Embassy (the State Department) is a good "neutral" meeting place to settle problems or disputes with an export customer in which the relationship has deteriorated. The first step to this process is to file a trade complaint with the Commercial Section of the U.S. Embassy in that country. Once this has been done, you can arrange a meeting with the customer at the embassy through an embassy trade specialist, who can assist in making meeting arrangements and translations.

Contact the U.S. Department of Commerce commercial officer to get the name of the trade specialist at a particular embassy. The U.S. Embassy requires a minimum of one month's notice. Better to allow yourself six to eight weeks. The fee to the U.S. Embassy for making these arrangements typically is about $250 to $700.

For Sales Leads

The U.S. Embassy is also an excellent source for seeking out new distributors or agents. Through the U.S. Department of Commerce's Gold Key Service, meetings can be arranged in the embassy to meet potential new distributors or agents that have been prescreened by the embassy. The first step in utilizing this service is to contact the U.S. Department of Commerce commercial officer.

Give him or her a profile of your company, product, and targeted countries, and he or she will forward the information to the embassy in the targeted country. If a potential match is made, the U.S. Embassy's Commercial Section will arrange a one- to two-day meeting with the prospective customer at the embassy. Again, the embassy charges a fee and requires one month's notice to arrange a meeting once a match has been made.

Getting Information

Ask the commercial section of the U.S. Embassy to provide you with a profile of the export customer, outside references, and a summary of economic conditions in that country. However, to make the most of your meeting, it is wise to do your homework—know as much as possible about the customer and the country. The embassy's staff economist can brief you about the local economy prior to a meeting. Many payment issues arise because the customer faces economic problems in the home country, such as currency devaluation or a natural disaster.

OTHER TYPES OF CUSTOMER MEETINGS

One organization sponsors a symposium once every three years. It invites the end users to attend, rather than executives. These symposia are terrific opportunities to talk with customers. The format is "trade show." The company has a captive audience in a nice setting (such as Vail and Colorado Springs, Colorado) and can showcase all of its best products and people. Everyone is relaxed and company executives can network with their customers. The symposia are great opportunities to chat with customers. They are not the time to discuss terms, conditions, or payment schedules. Rather, they are the time to get to know each other and build relationships.

CASE STUDY: USING CUSTOMER VISITS TO RESOLVE A COLLECTION ISSUE

Relationships with companies in other countries often start small and gradually grow into larger ones. If the proper care is taken every step of the way, this can be an ideal way to develop a relationship. Lose control or fail to make needed adjustments in time, though, and you can end up with nothing to show for your efforts. A credit manager for an East Coast producer of poultry feed ingredients selling in the Dominican Republic relates the following story about a collection problem his company had with its distributor, how he solved it, and what could have been done differently to avoid the problems in the first place. He wishes to remain anonymous.

Background

"A small local supplier to the retail food and poultry production industries in the Dominican Republic became our distributor in 1992 at a time when we had only two or three end-user customers there," the credit manager explains. "No formal agreement was executed until early 1997, by which time the distributor had grown our business to include some 43 end users—small feed mills and farmers growing broilers throughout the island. All along, it was verbally agreed that this was not our exclusive distributor even though we never sold to other local distributors.

"Foreign suppliers to the Dominican Republic should become knowledgeable of Law 173, which gives local distributors and agents serious protection provided they register their foreign supplier with the Central Bank within 60 days after the first shipment arrives in the Dominican Republic. The financial penalty can be heavy if the foreign supplier eventually terminates the commercial relationship under almost any circumstances.

"From the beginning, the distributor paid us slow and shared financial statements on a very irregular basis. Payment terms were quasi-consignment in that we shipped large containers full of our drummed liquid product directly to the distributor who was then supposed to remit partial payments in U.S. dollars to us 60 days after it made small, daily deliveries to the individual end users. This became a bookkeeping nightmare for the distributor but its limited financial resources made single large payments to us impossible. Total credit risk and devaluation exposure rested with the distributor who invoiced and collected from end users in Dominican pesos."

Collection Solutions

Not happy with the payment history, this savvy credit professional tried several approaches. Here are two of the strategies he tried:

1. By 1997 he was accepting five or six postdated checks to cover a single invoice with final settlement stretching out four or five months after bill of lading date.

2. The two principals then personally guaranteed four *pagares* due "on demand" totaling U.S. $200,000, which was the approved credit limit.

He also visited with the debtor several times to try to make the relationship work. This credit professional believes that these visits helped promote a personal relationship with the debtor and helped keep the matter from deteriorating further.

"After a few of these checks were returned NSF [nonsufficient funds] by Cayman banks, my company stopped shipping, and the end users were left with no choice but to buy from our competitors," he continues. "Since late 1997 the distributor has complained that our pricing was too high for it to earn a profit. Our knowledge of the local poultry market confirmed this; however, many months passed before a needed price adjustment was seriously considered.

"The distributor's last checks cleared the banks in early 1998, after which a small bank transfer was received in mid-December. Several pay plans were negotiated during 1997 to 1998 but all have ended in default, due in part to our delay with a price adjustment. Now both parties appear anxious to end the relationship and part company without burning bridges.

"Local attorneys are in the picture consulting, and both sides are hopeful a settlement fair to both sides can be negotiated without litigation in the Dominican Republic."

Lessons Learned

"One result of all this has been a realization that you are always better off if you can service and sell directly to your end customers," says this weary credit executive. "Distributors, no doubt, offer many sales and financial advantages, but they quickly become a barrier between you and your customers. In most countries, terminating a distributor usually results in severe financial costs for the foreign suppliers. Take great care in selecting your distributors and try to have more than one in a given country—if just to defend against an eventual claim of exclusivity.

"Personal visits also are important when trying to resolve this mess, versus attempting to solve it with phone calls or with faxes and e-mails. I anticipate a quicker resolution now that I have been there three times in the last five months to meet with him personally, with our local attorney, and with our potential new distributor," the credit manager concludes.

Knowledge of local laws, regardless of the country, will help companies avoid similar problems when entering new markets.

14

Credit and Sales: Solidifying the International Team

H. A. (Hal) Schaeffer Jr.

D&H Credit Services, Inc.

The international arena offers a myriad of opportunities for companies looking to grow sales. With those opportunities come some additional concerns and issues. Since the first contact most customers have is with the sales force, these individuals are often key in establishing the relationship. And if a company wishes to turn a profit on these international transactions, it is vital that sales and credit work well together.

A quick review should be done of the areas that most frequently result in "opportunities" that need to be resolved by the credit function as a result of accepting orders internationally. The first and foremost in every good credit manager's mind is: Will we get paid? The next and also most obvious to most credit managers is: When will we be paid? Will we get the sale and is it profitable are the two most important objectives to the sales and marketing group. If the firm's philosophy is very cash oriented obviously "cash will be king," as in the case of a leveraged buyout firm.

POTENTIAL AREAS OF CONFLICT

The country the goods and services are sold into, the terms of sale that are accepted, and the creditworthiness of the customer all greatly influence what steps must be taken to make the sale a successful and profitable piece of business. With international sales there are three primary additional credit risks associated with the normal extension of credit that is not part of a domestic-only sales operation: political, economic, and monetary risks.

Political risk deals with the stability of the country in relation to the governing powers that rule it. Is the government firmly in power? Have there been any coups lately? Is it a democracy, dictatorship, socialist, or communist country? All these different forms of government can greatly influence the laws, which can hamper or encourage the free flow of goods across borders.

Economic risk deals with the debt structure of the country in which the customer is located. Does the country have a tremendous trade deficit, or is there a solid balance of goods and services in and out of that country?

Monetary risk deals with the comparison of currency between countries and the effects of inflation on it. In some countries three zeroes have to be added to the currency in order to make it keep up with local hyperinflation. In selling internationally to some countries where payments are made in the local currency, it is necessary to buy a hedging contract to make a transaction remain as profitable as when the order was taken.

PAPERWORK ISSUE

The last and sometimes the most overlooked part of the international sale can be whether all paperwork is in order. This is if terms of sales such as documentary letters of credit are used to finalize an international sale. A shipment of valuable goods could contain bricks instead and be paid for in full assuming all documents were in order as reflected on the letter of credit. If what is required to get paid is impossible for a company to comply with and goods are indeed shipped, the vendor may never be able to collect on the document.

THREE-PRONGED APPROACH

How do international credit managers avoid the "opportunities" that present themselves daily to deal with not only the daily risk of domestic "land mines" but also the new and exciting features of global sales? You use the "ICE" method: information, communication, and education.

Information

In order to keep the company always ready to compete, information must be readily shared. The credit function must provide the sales and marketing staff with:

- *Access to customer aging and deduction detailed information.* By having access to this information, sales and marketing can know at a moment's notice the status of their customers. They can reference deduction items and past-due invoices, and discuss any noncredit issues that may be connected to a particular item.
- *Background information* on the customer that can help them to better sell the company's product. This area adds just one more weapon in the company's arsenal to better sell its products or services. Things such as

terms of sale to customers' customers, who are its main suppliers, and any products that they currently promote give the sales staff and agents an edge to use in comparing your products to that of your competitors.

- *Alerts to held orders or limit changes.* It is much better for sales reps to know before walking into the customer's office that there are problems. Knowledge of increases in limits can help sales reps nail down that large order that they have been trying to get. Decreasing the limit can result in sales reps focusing on other more creditworthy customers.
- *Details of the terms of sales* between a particular customer and the seller. In the case of international sales, by keeping sales reps informed, credit can keep a tighter control over the problems with discrepancies, documents, and any situations with accommodating the order as reflected in the customer's purchase order.

Sales agents in foreign countries also need information to stay within the selling parameters set by the firm. This information should be accessible via the Internet, and proper limits to needed data only through password protection should be in place at all times. By having the information available on the Internet, you resolve the age-old problem of time-zone differences. Information is always available when it is needed. The credit professional also has full control and authority over what information is available to them, which leads into the "C" of ICE.

Communication

Without ease of communications between all areas that are directly responsible for keeping the company's sales and cash flow at its peak, the firm will cave in to competition. In the case of a domestic sales, a meeting held with key sales and marketing staff on a weekly basis should be mandatory to:

- *Cover problems with customers* and how they both can work together to resolve them. This open-air discussion helps all areas to work as a team, vent any differences that they may have, and prevent problems before they can occur.
- *Explain any new programs or sales promotions* that are pending. By alerting credit to new sales and marketing strategies, they can be better prepared to adjust to the new opportunities that the company will be open to. These types of presentations can also be made at regional and national sales meetings, which the credit staff should always attend.
- *Review any ways to develop new business for the firm.* By brainstorming together, credit and sales and marketing as well as international reps can focus their attention on the best manner to service their customers, look at pluses and minuses of new business, and concentrate on making every sale more profitable.

Communication also is vital on the international side, although physically holding group meetings is not possible. In this case there can be two possible plans of attack. One is a teleconferencing meeting via the Internet with the sales agent and any company sales staff outside of the United States. The other would be weekly status notes sent on agents' or salespeople's current customers or pending orders. Weekly times could be set for the sending of this information with limits set on response time. Likewise, agents and salespeople will be required to submit information weekly on any new orders or issues that they have pending along with questions that they may have on company credit and sales policies. Using Internet communications allows for faster reaction to "opportunities," such as letter-of-credit discrepancies, delays in getting letters of credit from customers as provided by your local sales representative, and required changes to orders. It also provides for quick updates from sales reps on country conditions, economic and currency changes, and new laws and import restrictions that can greatly impact selling into a country.

Education

Without mutual education between those partners who are directly responsible for the success of your firm, all previous efforts to cooperate will be wasted. No one can make a sound business credit decision without understanding the requirements of the other partners in the team. Likewise, sales reps and agents must fully understand their impact on the firm due to errors that can result in nonpayment of invoices. Many sales agents have relinquished their commissions as a result of bad debts due to uncollectable documents. So what ways can education be handled?

- *Plan regular educational programs* for credit, sales and marketing staffs, and international sales reps to keep all members aware of what is important to each other's area.
- *Always offer a set training program for each new hire in both areas.* (Obviously, this does not mean that each new person from the credit function will visit each agent in every country that your firm does business. Semiannual or annual meetings, however, should be held at a central location.)
- *Present a cohesive front to the customer.* Remember that every employee and representative who has direct contact with the customer must always present a positive and united appearance at all times.

OTHER RELATIONSHIP-BUILDING APPROACHES

While all of the above methods are ideal ways to move the company forward in beating the competition, not all firms share such an enlightened perspective. An alternative to the ICE approach can include gradually building solid relationships with the sales and marketing staffs as well as the international reps. Open communication, being visible to both them and top management, and providing reports that alert all involved of recurring problems helps to strengthen the move toward improved cooperation. Presenting educational credit programs at sales and marketing meetings, making sure that you are available when international reps are in town, and planning visits to meet with major international customers and reps also help to strengthen the relationship.

Some initial efforts to build these bridges include:

- Locating new potential customers for the sales and marketing staff to review. With credit's access to many sources of information, such as credit reporting agencies and Internet web sites, reviews of competitors can be made that can lead to new potential customers or ways to beat the competition. One such source is a database called Dialog, which is listed on the Internet. On a past occasion using this site, I was able to provide 900 distributor leads in six countries using a five digit Standard Industrial Classification (SIC) code. The information that was provided included address/phone, a list of top executives, estimated annual sales, products currently sold, terms of sale, how long they had been in business, and approximate number of employees.
- Prequalifying customers as to creditworthiness helps to save sales staff on time. They can focus their efforts on more profitable customers. Many times, domestic and international sales reps have thanked me for steering them away from some new potential customer. The new and exciting customer who would not buy from them in the past but is now "desperate" to buy may be no bargain. Competitors may have shut off this company and they may be forced now to buy from anyone who has similar product. Most companies charge their salespeople's commission if the account is written off to bad debts; saving a salesperson's commission can make you his or her best friend.
- Offering quick turnaround time on approving new customers and putting forth extra effort to make every sale work for the benefit of the entire company will likewise strengthen this partnership. Working with key sales and marketing staff as well as international reps to design reports that cover all information that they consider valuable from the credit area will help expand the value of credit to them. All of this should be done while maximizing communications between all areas.

To summarize, the ICE approach to both the domestic and the international credit/sales relationship enhances the ability to render sound business credit decisions and will increase the chances for more profitable sales. Success is guaranteed when access to necessary information is facilitated, when communications are free flowing, and when education strengthens the degree of understanding and appreciation of other people's responsibilities and limits.

PART FIVE

CREDIT INSURANCE

Many experts estimate that 30 percent of European transactions use credit insurance while only 1 percent of export sales in the United States are covered by credit insurance. This can put U.S. companies at a disadvantage when it comes to extending terms while competing against their European counterparts.

Chapter 15 provides a look at the basics of credit insurance. Chapter 16 explains how to use it effectively, and Chapter 17 provides case studies.

15

Export Credit and Political Risk Insurance

Thomas M. Rispanti

Creditek Risk Management Group, LLC

When most people think of insurance, they rarely think about the risk of a company not getting paid for its goods or services. But, as those involved in the credit profession are painfully aware, nonpayment happens all the time. In international circles, the matter is complicated even further because nonpayment sometimes occurs for reasons having nothing to do with the creditworthiness of the customer. Europeans have traditionally addressed these nonpayment risks by purchasing credit insurance (policies that cover them in case they do not get paid). The policies work just like other insurance policies with deductibles and certain preestablished criteria for payment. The use of credit insurance for a variety of purposes is slowly spreading to the United States, especially when U.S. firms sell internationally as the insurance lets exporters compete on a level playing field with their European competitors.

Trade credit and political risk insurance is a contract between an insurer and the insured, whereby the insurer agrees to indemnify the insured for foreign receivable losses resulting from the occurrence of specific credit and/or political risk perils.

Traditionally, export credit and political risks insurance is used as a tool to:

- Increase export sales
- Improve financing
- Access debtor information
- Mitigate risk

INCREASE EXPORT SALES

The ability to increase export sales is perhaps the most powerful attribute of export credit and political risk insurance. An insured company could use this feature alone to cost justify the purchase of coverage.

When an exporter requires a foreign buyer to post a letter of credit prior to shipping, the cost to that customer for doing business with the exporter increases for three reasons:

1. The foreign buyer incurs letter-of-credit fees charged by its local bank.
2. The local bank provides lines of credit that are tied up by the issued letters of credit.
3. The buyer incurs administrative costs associated with the letter-of-credit documentation.

Letter-of-credit sales also cost the exporter for three reasons:

1. In order to mitigate foreign bank and political risk, the exporter pays fees to local U.S. banks to confirm foreign bank–issued letters of credit.
2. The exporter ties up its administrative staff to handle the letter-of-credit documentation and all the associated problems.
3. Orders must be held until the letters of credit are processed.

These additional selling expenses erode the exporters' profit margins. Not only is there economic incentive for exporters to sell on open account, in an effort to maximize profit margins, but some foreign buyers require open-account terms from their suppliers. Those exporters relying exclusively on letters of credit to mitigate nonpayment risk will lose sales.

Export credit and political risk insurance enables exporters to sell on open account with the comfort of knowing that they will get paid. Foreign buyers find that they are able to purchase more product than in the past, since their total acquisition cost has been reduced. Customer relationships are enhanced when exporters sell on open account, a sign of increased confidence in the buyer's ability to pay. Orders are released faster, accelerating the order-to-cash cycle and improving working capital for exporters.

The significance of this concept is magnified in today's arena of electronic business-to-business (B2B) commerce, where sellers are matching up with unknown buyers at Internet speed.

IMPROVE FINANCING

Most lenders will exclude foreign receivables from the eligible collateral pool when advancing against accounts receivable. Such restriction on a company's available cash flow can mean lost opportunity to grow its export business.

When a lender is named as loss payee or collateral beneficiary on an export credit insurance policy issued by a U.S.-based insurer, the lender typically acknowledges accounts receivable as eligible collateral. Advance rates that can range from 70 to 85 percent of the foreign accounts receivable can provide exporters with additional "fuel" to run their businesses as a whole.

In theory, the internal rate of return on capital that insured exporters realize will offset the tax-deductible premium expense associated with the credit insurance. The ability to generate and sell more widgets is a win-win for everyone. Here's how.

- Insured exporters grow their business via the additional working capital and new sales generation.
- Lenders realize additional interest income from the secured advance against the foreign accounts receivable, permitting loan balances to grow.
- The insured grows its customer base.

ACCESS DEBTOR INFORMATION

Companies of all sizes selling overseas always need reliable information pertaining to their customers and host countries. The trade credit insurer can be a valuable information resource and can provide the exporter with a competitive advantage in the marketplace.

By tapping into the insurers' trade experience and financial information, sellers use insurers as extensions of their international credit department. For those companies lacking the capacity to build such databases, credit insurers provide turnkey access. For sellers with extensive systems in place designed to track foreign debtors, insurers can serve as additional eyes to monitor foreign customers and sovereign risks.

MITIGATE RISK

The motivation for purchasing domestic or export credit and political risks insurance is often closely aligned to the seller's appetite (or lack thereof) for risk. These risks can include, but are not limited to, commercial and political risks. Insolvency risks are:

- A voluntary or involuntary petition for relief under Title 11 (including Chapters 7, 11, and 13) of the U.S. Bankruptcy Code is filed by or against an entity.
- A buyer's assets shall have been sold under a writ of execution or attachment, or a writ of execution shall have been returned unsatisfied.
- Any buyer who is a sole proprietor shall have absconded.
- Possession shall have been taken of a buyer's assets under an assignment or a deed of trust executed by a purchaser for the benefit of its creditors.

- A buyer who is a sole proprietor shall have been adjudged mentally incompetent.
- The business assets of a buyer shall have died.
- A buyer shall have transferred or sold its stock in trade in bulk.
- Possession shall have been taken under a security agreement or other instrument having like effect given by a buyer on its stock in trade or equipment.
- A purchaser, or third party on its behalf, shall have made a general offer of compromise in writing to its creditors for less than its indebtedness.
- A general meeting of unsecured creditors is called by or on behalf of the buyer, with the date of the first meeting constituting the date of insolvency.
- An insolvency bankruptcy is made against the buyer, or the buyer files for Chapter 11.
- In the course of execution of a judgment, the levy of execution fails to satisfy the debt in full.
- A valid assignment, compromise, or other arrangement is made for the benefit of the buyer's creditors generally.
- An effective arrangement is made for the liquidation of a buyer.
- An administrative or other receiver or manager of any of the buyer's property is appointed.
- Insured demonstrates that the buyer's financial state is such that even partial payment is unlikely and that to enforce judgment or to apply for a bankruptcy or winding-up order would have no foreseeable result other than one disproportionate to the likely cost of the proceedings.
- An event has occurred elsewhere in the United States, which, under the law of court having jurisdiction, is substantially equivalent in effect to any of the events listed above.
- A buyer shall file an assignment or make a proposal to creditors under the Canadian Bankruptcy Act. The filing of the assignment or the date on which the proposal is filed shall constitute the date of insolvency.
- A receiving order is made against the buyer under the Canadian Bankruptcy Act; the date of the receiving order shall constitute the date of insolvency.
- A buyer's assets shall have been sold under the Canadian Bank Act or a winding-up order under the Dominion Winding Up Act of Canada is made against a buyer.

There is also the risk of protracted default. The situation of the insured's buyer if at the expiration of the waiting period (as defined in the credit insurance policy) has not discharged their undisputed debt in full shall be treated as if they were insolvent.

Political risks include:

- *Transfer Risk*
  — Inability of the buyer and/or insured to convert local currency into policy currency or eligible currency in a lawful market of the buyer's country and/or effect the transfer of the policy currency or

eligible currency equivalent of the local currency from the buyer's country to the insured as payment for shipments made to a buyer, provided that the buyer has made a depository of the buyer's country which has been designated by law or administrative regulation for the acquisition and transfer of policy currency or eligible currency.

— Enactment or enforcement of any law, order, decree, or regulation having the force of law occurring no later than the expiration of the maximum claim filing period, which prevents the deposit describing the item from being made.

- *Cancellation of License.* Cancellation of insured's export license or the buyer's import license, or the imposition of restrictions on the export of covered products from insured's country or the import of covered products into the buyer's country, not subject to license or restriction immediately prior to date of shipment.

- *Embargo.* Enactment and enforcement of any law, order decree, regulation, or embargo having the force of law that prevents the export of covered products from insured's country or the import of covered products into the buyer's country.

- *War/Civil Violence.* A state of war, civil war, rebellion, revolution, insurrection, or other civil disturbances pertaining thereto in the buyer's country or relevant foreign country, which directly prevents delivery or payment of the buyer's shipments of covered products.

- *Illegal Foreign Government Intervention*
  — Expropriation or arbitrary intervention in the business of the buyer by the government of the buyer's country occurring no later than the expiration of the maximum claim filing period, which legally prevents the buyer from fulfilling its payment obligations.
  — Confiscation, expropriation, nationalization, seizure, requisitions, or willful destruction by the government of the buyer's country of shipments of covered products within the maximum claim-filing period.

- *Sovereign Buyers.* Nonpayment of a valid trade obligation by a sovereign buyer.

OTHER CONSIDERATIONS

Bad-Debt Reserves

Many companies "purchase" nonpayment protection via their bad-debt reserve. Unfortunately, exclusive dependence on the bad-debt reserve is not an efficient use of capital because:

- There are zero tax benefits to holding bad-debt reserves. (Insurance premium payments are tax deductible.)
- No reserve can adequately address a company's exposure, as no company will fully reserve. (Trade credit insurance can provide capacity to match the insured's exposure.)

The combination of a reduced bad-debt reserves and credit insurance enable the insured company to:

- Budget more accurately for bad-debt expense.
- Smooth out the peaks and valleys of bad-debts.
- Obtain maximum coverage in line with true credit exposure.
- Capture additional tax-deductible operating expense.
- Realize a one-time gain to earnings when the reserve balance is reduced.
- Free up capital for other uses as a reduced bad-debt reserve balance is maintained.

B2B E-Commerce

The explosion of B2B e-commerce, via singleseller web sites and multitrading online exchanges, creates an increasing need for risk mitigation, at Internet speed. While companies increase their sales to anonymous buyers, domestic and export, the need for nonpayment protection becomes paramount. Fortunately, the trade credit insurance community is responding to this need/ opportunity and launching web-enabled products designed to facilitate e-commerce.

Specialist Broker

Trade credit insurance is a specialty line of coverage that should be purchased only with the guidance of a specialist broker. The knowledge and expertise that the broker brings to the purchase decision is invaluable. There is no charge to the insured for this service, as the insurer pays a brokerage commission for new business placed.

16

Changing World of Credit Insurance

Bob Frewen

Coface Holding Company

During the first half of the 1900s, European governments created national export credit agencies (ECAs) to help develop the exports necessary to enable their economies recover from the devastation of the world wars. In the United States, President Roosevelt initiated the Export-Import Bank in 1935 to help this country recover from the depression. These agencies both insured foreign receivables and gave guarantees to banks, or directly provided the loans necessary to facilitate trade. By the 1950s all developed countries had either ECAs or an export-import bank, the latter usually based on the U.S. model.

Despite the economic power of the United States, the European state ECAs always held a dominant position in the credit insurance industry. The diversity of business cultures and languages in Europe probably ensured the need for an expert to assist smaller companies in their cross-border trade. That situation pertained, with a little competition from the private insurance sector, until the last decade of the 1900s. The advent of new European Union legislation, finalized in 1992, rapidly changed the face of the entire credit insurance industry.

SHORT-TERM CREDIT INSURANCE MARKET

In 1998, the size of the world's short-term credit insurance market amounted to premium of U.S. $4.1 billion. Western Europe continues to be the traditional heartland of credit insurance, but other regions, such as Asia and the Americas, now are the fastest-growing markets for this product. (See Exhibit 16.1.)

The views expressed in this chapter are those of the author and do not necessarily reflect those of Coface Holding Company or its partners.

	Premiums	Market Share	y-on-y Growth
Western Europe	3,231	78.9%	5.2%
Asia	349	8.5%	9.3%
North America	**314**	**7.7%**	**10.8%**
Oceania	76	1.9%	25.3%
Africa	57	1.4%	11.0%
Latin America	27	0.7%	31.4%
Middle East	31	0.7%	29.8%
Central Europe	11	0.3%	33.6%
Total	4,096		

Exhibit 16.1   Market Shares in 1998 and Growth of the Worldwide Short-Term Private Credit Insurance Market (millions U.S. $, export and domestic)
Source: Figures compiled by Coface from corporate and OECD data.

The strength of the European insurers (and their partners) is that they can offer a diversity of products—either straightforward excess or catastrophe covers, or those with "value added"—using the benefits of their huge databases and an international clientele whose experience is shared. Other insurers who do not have a strong European connection (i.e., a substantial buyer database) cannot provide the latter category and must rely on the credit control in the insured company. For that reason, the U.S.-based credit insurance underwriters tend to have large deductibles built into their policies. Simply put, European-linked insurers can offer either product while U.S. insurers are limited to the catastrophe-type product.

DEVELOPMENTS IN THE 1990s

The Single European Act, which became law at the end of 1992, allowed financial institutions approved by a member state of the European Union (EU) easy transborder access in other member states, thereby intensifying competition among EU states. In the credit insurance industry, this forced a more level playing field. The short-term business (i.e., trade on terms of less than 360 days) of the British credit insurer ECGD was privatized in the late 1980s. The privatization of other state insurance agencies followed, and reserve requirements became more equitable. International trade itself was changing—new international management practice, resulting from reengineered companies, brought new product requirements to the market and competition intensified for the bigger accounts. This competition was coupled with the recession in the early 1990s, the aftermath of the collapse of the Soviet Union and the economic "fallout" from the unification of Germany.

One of the main costs for the credit insurance industry is credit information. During a recession, or in "difficult" markets or sectors, credit exposures must be reviewed more frequently and constantly monitored. This is both expensive and paradoxical—to avoid large claims credit insurers must constantly review key exposures and spend considerable sums to constantly update credit information.

STRATEGIC ALLIANCES

Credit insurance companies that anticipated the change in their industry and prepared for it by forming strategic alliances have done well primarily because of economies of scale. Smaller insurers could not maintain either costly databases of buyer information or international networks on their own; thus they could not compete effectively. Those companies that operated only in domestic markets also were "closed out," as they never could hope to develop the critical mass necessary to compete effectively.

There are now about five big international credit insurers, all of which are European. Together they account for more than three-quarters of the world's private credit insurance market. The other firms have been taken over, are fighting to retain market share, or operate as "shopfronts" with support from the big specialists. The biggest worldwide export credit insurance network is the Credit Alliance. The 44 partners of this network share a common database with corporate details and payment information on more than 35 million companies.

They also share an international collection system. By doing so the small member ECAs—for example, in Ireland, Thailand, or Oman—have the same immediate access, online, to the database used by the leading insurers and to the same international collection network. Thus, their insured clients are not disadvantaged when competing internationally. The benefits to all from economies of scale are obvious.

CREDIT INSURANCE IN THE UNITED STATES

The biggest European credit insurers arrived in the United States during the final years of the 1900s. Through acquisition, joint venture, or partnership, these companies have shown year-on-year premium growth of more than 50 percent in their export insurance activity, whereas growth of U.S. domestic credit business has been less than spectacular. U.S. exporters now have an excellent choice yet their bankers are slower to accept what has become an essential trading tool. In many cases banks continue to advise their clients to sell on irrevocable letters of credit (ILCs), and most banks will not finance receivables from foreign buyers. In Europe, studies have shown that up to 18 percent of insurable foreign trade is credit insured and more than 80 percent of international trade is conducted on open-account terms. In the United States, less than 2 percent of exports are credit insured and ILCs are a commonplace for exports. U.S. exporters have to learn that ILCs are not appropriate terms for selling overseas.

FINANCE AND CREDIT INSURANCE

Banks and credit insurers had an uneasy relationship for many years. Banks competed actively for the business normally serviced by credit insurers. Products based on forfaiting and ILC discounting grew in popularity. The growth of international factoring is another example, albeit small, where less than 6 percent of U.S. factoring outstandings relate to export factoring. In most European countries, where factoring is seen as a sign of financial weakness, attitudes have been slowly changing and are gradually moving toward acceptance. The big credit insurers have become involved by providing insurance on nonrecourse factoring agreements. Additionally, the insurers have proven that they have better networks for business information and collection. This cooperation will continue to grow as more companies outsource their receivables management to factors, not necessarily just to obtain finance.

Since 1993 there has been a dramatic upsurge in the number of U.S. companies using export credit insurance to raise working capital. Banks are familiar with assessing the worth of U.S.-related debts; however, the value of foreign debt is often beyond their comprehension. For that reason, exporters have difficulty in raising finance on foreign receivables. A credit-insured receivable makes access to finance easier.

Recent developments have shown a trend for credit insurers to work more closely with financial institutions. Much of the developing closeness between bankers and insurers is due to the banking sector's gradual realization that it views risk different from insurers. Banks lend on the basis that there never will be a loss; insurers underwrite on the basis that there will be sustainable losses. This has led to partnerships between banks and credit insurers, whereby the insurers underwrite the debtors and the banks lend on the receivables, secured by an assignment of the credit insurance policy. In some cases this concept has been developed further, with the bank becoming the policyholder and adding end debtors to its policy for insurance protection.

For larger companies, an alternative means of raising finance is the securitization of a block of trade receivables. Under a securitization arrangement, a bank agrees to purchase a company's receivables, sometimes retaining some risk on a portion of the receivables. The balance is placed in the capital markets with institutional investors, such as mutual funds or life insurance companies. The credit insurer takes the buyer credit risk and manages any defaults. The facility usually is a revolving one within a fixed period, as the credit terms of the trade debt—usually less than 180 days—require a longer tenor to be financially worthwhile. The attraction to the borrower is that the paper issued carries the rating of the insurer, thereby making the interest rates payable on the funds raised more attractive.

With minor exceptions this activity has covered only domestic receivables. In addition, to date, it has been done on a deal-by-deal basis on the receivables of individual companies. It is only a matter of time before an insurer pools the receivables of several companies from various sectors—or foreign markets—to enlarge and further enhance the credit valuation.

BIG BANKS ARE LOSING THE MIDSIZE TRADE FINANCE MARKET

Large banks, particularly those with global networks, continue to chase high-ticket export credit deals and the attendant publicity. The creation of separate business units or subsidiaries to capture and manage these transactions often has led to cracks in their business structure. These gaps frequently allow export opportunities in trade finance—particularly for small to midsize companies—to slip through the corporate net. When a potential borrower arrives at the bank, the corporate lending divisions often suggest that trade finance is dealt with by the foreign departments; and foreign departments say the opposite. As a result, exporters face a never-ending circle of frustration, and banks lose their share of the middle-market trade sector. Their competitors, often small regional banks, have developed a strong position in this niche. The rapid growth of bank-based export credit insurance in the United States will continue; it remains to be seen how big a role large banks will play in its success.

Banks always have been slow to innovate. It is no surprise that to date the best package banks have been able to develop for e-commerce is an electronic means of processing letters of credit. It is a commonly accepted fact that more than 75 percent of all ILCs are incorrect on first presentation. The banks' "new" product will allow them to correct these errors online, reduce the eventual amount of paperwork, and, of course, retain their hefty fee income. This response misses both the point and the needs of the market. Back in the 1890s there was little sense in trying to develop a better steam engine for a car when Mr. Daimler had developed his gasoline engine.

Banks need to realize this, depart from a product that is centuries old, and innovate. Other institutions in the secondary finance markets have done this and are making funds available online, primarily by means of trade acceptances. Unfortunately in the United States, banks and these other institutions are confined to buyers/sellers. The U.S. banking community must start to comprehend that the first two Ws of WWW stand for "Worldwide" and that they must act accordingly.

CREDIT CONTROL: WHAT NEXT?

Credit insurance must work in close cooperation with customers' credit control function, although it could be argued that in the United States a better relationship often exists between the credit insurer and the sales department. Either way, whatever is happening to the customer will impact on the relationship with the insurer.

Customers—and the marketplace—are changing dramatically, and credit insurers have had to adapt in line with their customers' requirements. International mergers and Internet activity will have a big impact on the credit control function. Merger and acquisition (M&A) experts believed that 1998 would be the record year, with M&A activity at a record $2.52 trillion. However, 1999 saw the level rise to $3.43 trillion. Already, for the first quarter of 2000, figures given by the Thomson Financial Securities Data Corp. indicate yet another increase, with global activity at $1.12 trillion, surpassing the $1.08 trillion of the preceding quarter. While Europe accounts for about one-third of these figures, it is noteworthy that the M&A rate there has doubled in recent years, and it has tripled in Asia. Add to this the introduction of the Euro and the accession of new countries to the EU. These factors will have a profound impact on credit control as sales on open-account terms will continue to grow and EU standards, particularly in accounting, will become much more widespread.

In recent years, international management methods have shown a preference for "horizontal" structures, with autonomy for local subsidiaries. With increasing frequency this no longer applies to the credit control function, as centralized corporate treasury units have come to the fore. Funding operations, international cash pooling, and investment maximization need to be closely managed. So too does credit exposure need to be monitored at group level. Doing so leads to the development of a single common accounting/customer system and either a shared service center or the outsourcing of activities such as accounts receivable management. As a result, fewer controllers will be employed, particularly at local subsidiary level. However, for those who remain, their work will have an increased responsibility level and they will have a more important role in the management hierarchy.

This broader depth of responsibility poses problems of multinational management. For example, in regard to risk management, it means understanding several different insurance policies, often in foreign languages, and how best to negotiate premium reductions on a group level. To overcome this, insurers must be able to offer their customers local services for overseas subsidiaries and at the same time maintain a global "umbrella" cover for the parent.

INTERNATIONAL CREDIT PRODUCTS

To provide a truly global policy, insurers must have a truly global network. A typical credit insurance product is Globalliance, the international product offered by the Credit Alliance, which allows a multinational to have identical policies, issued in all the main foreign languages, with local service for claims and underwriting, and connection to a common risk assessment system. For example, a U.S. multinational can have a policy in English issued by the Credit Alliance's U.S. partner; the subsidiary in Brazil can have an identical policy in Portuguese; and the distribution company in Tokyo can have the same in Japanese, all with local service. In recent years, many of the bigger international insurers have begun to create international networks through a blend of merger, acquisition, and start-up, although only one has attained truly global reach.

It no longer is possible for insurers to maintain a satellite information-gathering office (or a flag on a map!) in a foreign market. That office must be staffed effectively and in a position to issue and service policies in the local language. Similarly, any database of local information owned by an insurer must be available online to other members of the group. With many recent acquisitions in the credit insurance sector, the subsequent cohesion of information technology systems has not been evident.

E-COMMERCE TRENDS

E-commerce will continue to secure a greater share of international trade. Credit insurers, who are trade service providers, will have to become more involved and develop web-based products for their customers. All companies have to cater to their customers' needs if they are to survive; credit insurers are no different. Although e-commerce is dramatically speeding up every step of the supply chain, it is difficult to estimate with any accuracy what is happening due to the hyperbole surrounding e-commerce activity. Business-to-consumer (B2C) sales account only for about 10 percent of e-commerce, yet it receives nine times more press coverage than business-to-business (B2B) trade.

How can credit insurers become involved and how big will the B2B market become? All the experts agree on the rapid development of e-commerce over the next few years. Estimates tend to indicate B2B trade figures of somewhere between $1.8 and $3.2 trillion by 2004. Prepared by such diverse experts as Morgan Stanley Dean Witter, Forrester Research, and IBM Analysis, there is no consensus with the Jupiter Communications giving a figure of $6 trillion for 2005 and Gartner Group estimating $7.3 trillion, and Goldman Sachs indicating $1.5 trillion for 2004. One thing is certain: There will be huge growth in online B2B commerce. To put this growth in perspective, Gartner estimates that Latin America's B2B commerce in 2004 will equal today's *global* B2B market.

Of all the indicators or estimates, a demonstrable one that truly reflects the potential of the "Internet revolution" is the growth of Internet users. Between 1995 and 1999, the number of Internet users more than tripled to reach 130 million worldwide. The Computer Industry Almanac forecasts the number will reach 350 million by the end of 2000 and 770 million by 2005. (See Exhibit 16.2.)

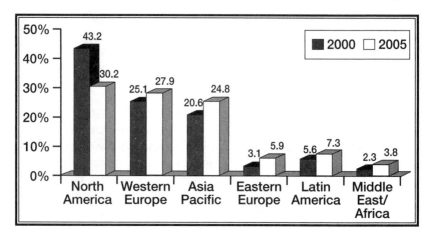

Exhibit 16.2   Internet Users by Region
Source: Computer Industry Almanac.

Until companies realize that the Internet has changed the face of commerce forever, they cannot partake of its benefits and they risk losing the business they already have. The opportunities being created for web-smart companies, regardless of size, do not contain new business, they merely are a redistribution of what already is being traded elsewhere. Furthermore, currently much of the business conducted online between corporate suppliers/buyers is an electronic version of existing business and is not "new business" per se. U.S. businesses will conduct about $400 billion in B2B e-commerce in 2000 but an estimated 87 percent of this is "replacement" business (carried out between companies that already have an existing relationship). This business can easily be covered under existing credit insurance mechanisms.

The resharing of business opportunities is brought about by greater competition, for example, negative auction sites, and by cutting out the middleman. The majority of people, including even those who do not buy online, use the web for product and price research. This use will continue to drive down margins and facilitate migration of customers. For that reason, the land-grab era analogy is inappropriate. In the land-grab era, once the stakes were driven in, the property was owned. A property in California could not suddenly disappear and reappear in Michigan. Today, Internet customers who supposedly represent the "available land" can leave a business partner with the click of a mouse. Many Internet banks have discovered this to their cost.

Classic distribution channels no longer have the importance they once had. Ten years ago who would have believed that a computer manufacturer could tailor-make a product to individual order and distribute it? Yet Dell has achieved this; by cutting out the middlemen, it has been able to pass the savings back to the purchaser, along with a better product. Why should insurance companies and their intermediaries believe that they are different?

B2B: THE CHALLENGE FOR CORPORATE SELLERS

A growing number of companies are online, advertising their products, finding new buyers and suppliers, and trading online. As a result, two key questions have to be answered in a marketplace where any business can deal instantly with another, even if they are on opposite sides of the world: (1) Who are my potential clients? and (2) Is it safe to deal with them? Those questions are not new. What is new is the rapidity of response required. If the response is not immediate, e-commerce cannot work. Additionally, the success of e-commerce depends on trusting several other participants in the transaction chain. The participants and questions are:

- *The Internet service provider (ISP):* Can I access when I need to? Is access secure?
- *The portal:* Can I find what I am looking for?
- *The counterpart:* Are they really who they say they are? Are the products really what they offer?
- *The logistics:* Will I receive what I ordered on time and in good condition?
- *The payment:* Is my transaction financially secure? Will I receive payment?

Already many e-businesses have solved the reliability and system security issues. Also, they have resolved some major issues regarding identity and on-line signature through powerful PKI certificates (public key infrastructure) and the formation of "communities." However, one gap remains to be filled: the financial security of transactions.

The Internet does not solve the problem of financial security or risk assessment. On the contrary, it makes the problem more complex as companies must decide instantly how and with whom to do business. In a business model where transactions are instantaneous, companies cannot afford to lose time in taking days or weeks to assess a potential client's creditworthiness. If the amounts of B2B transactions are above credit card limits—and they usually are—decisions still must be immediate and if necessary new formats must be developed to process the transactions.

The banks are, at the time of this writing, unable to respond to this demand. They have created business enablers—for example, companies such as Bolero and Identrus—but these essentially replicate existing paper systems and convert the paper to an electronic format. No bankers seem to have done market research and asked the basic question of "What buyer wants to trade on a letter of credit?" Had they done so, the answer would have suggested that they find something more creative.

B2B: THE CHALLENGE FOR THE INSURANCE INDUSTRY

E-commerce is not new to the larger European credit insurers. Most have been processing and delivering online credit limits to their clients since the 1980s and some since before that date. Additionally, they have been big purchasers of products online for years. For example, Coface spends more than $35 million a year buying business information. In 1992, Coface decided that it required its 46 percent online information delivery increased to 100 percent by the year 2000 and in a specific format.

For those markets where that target was estimated as being unlikely, the decision supported a plan to create a business information company to satisfy the objective. The result: 1998 saw about 98 percent electronic delivery level, and by 2000 99.8 percent had been achieved. A new business information network—the InfoAlliance—was located in 66 strategic countries, and all members shared a common platform. With this type of experience, Coface is in a much better competitive position than its rivals. There is a well-known brand name, synergies within the InfoAlliance, familiarity, and most important of all, trust in the product.

Due to what most outsiders regard as archaic legislation, U.S. insurers have a major marketing disadvantage. Consequently, U.S. traders will suffer. U.S. legislation in general is against online insurance. For example, direct (online) insurance is farcical in many U.S. states. Applicants are able to complete their proposal forms online and, after hitting the "send" button, are told either to wait for an agent to contact them or that they will receive a quote in "a couple of days." The Internet is about instant decision, whether acceptance, rejection, or gratification. Two days will not do. While in some states this situation is due to the reluctance of insurers to disintermediarize, it generally is due to legislation.

In the leading industrial nations (the old "G7"), an estimated average of 36 percent of the 18.6 million small businesses are online. This figure is 44 percent in North America (according to Cyber Dialogue); about 38 percent have their own web sites elsewhere. Another survey, conducted recently by the Maryland-based Association of Financial Professionals, indicates that more than 50 percent of the risk managers/insurance buyers surveyed state they expect to purchase insurance online within the next year and nearly two-thirds say they will do so within two years. This estimate is very much at odds with insurance industry estimates; even those estimates lag behind Forrester Research's prediction that by 2004, $13.5 billion of insurance will be sold online. This is about 1.5 percent of the U.S. annual total of $900 billion.

WHAT SOLUTIONS DO CREDIT INSURERS PROPOSE?

The financial markets were the first to face the challenges of immediate assessment of debt. Their response: the creation of rating agencies whose risk assessments became known as credit ratings. Today e-commerce faces the same challenges:

- Immediate and secure trade debt risk assessment
- A product, easily available (web access, low cost), with the same meaning everywhere

To date, only two credit insurers have proposed solutions. One is a large U.S. insurer. It proposes an online "credit check" of buyers with a guaranteed three-day turnaround. This service is limited to the United States and Canada. The other is Coface Group, which has been working for more than two years on how to help clients cope with the new world of e-commerce. The Coface solution consists of their @rating product.

@rating has transposed the logic of rating to trade debts—but with a significant difference. For the first time, the rating agency has 50 successful years of experience in insuring the risk it rates. Also for the first time, an agency will put its money behind its rating in addition to its name, expertise, and reputation. It will do this by guaranteeing transactions placed through those e-commerce communities with whom it has an agreement. One such agreement, already signed, is with TradeCard, the leading B2B transaction manager.

An @rating displays the ability of a company to meet its short-term trade debts (up to six months). The rating is easily understood and available, whatever the size or location of the company. The rating is made possible by the two networks initiated by Coface, the Credit Alliance (grouping 44 credit insurers), and InfoAlliance (information providers in 66 countries).

@rating is inexpensive and flexible. For $300 a year a company can use it to indicate its financial solvency to the World Wide Web for marketing purposes. It can be accessed, free, as an indicator of the financial security of business partners. For $15 per customer it can be used to assess and monitor the security of a diversified trade debt portfolio. @rating already is becoming the tool for B2B e-commerce initiatives, platforms, and communities because it is an efficient way to check, certify, and, if necessary, guarantee the payment of online transactions.

Disclosure, especially when it relates to financial information, has always been a concern to American companies. E-commerce, even more so than other business models, requires complete transparency if a company is to succeed. Nevertheless, the key information that is vital to e-commerce business cannot be made freely available to everybody. There is a need for a third party in whom participants can have total confidence. @rating succeeds in this because it respects the confidentiality of the rated company. All data given is protected by a confidentiality agreement. This commitment has received extraordinary interest in countries with a strong tradition of confidentiality, such as Switzerland, where companies are reluctant to see their key information published. @rating has been successful because companies there have provided information only because they were sure that it would not be published.

In addition to being an important part of several B2B trade processes, such as the partnership with the TradeCard product, @rating already has teamed up with several other B2B trade facilitators. Most recent of these partners is Gemplus.

Together, Coface and Gemplus have launched an integrated solution for securing trade over the Internet. This will allow banks, businesses, and virtual markets to:

- Verify the identities of the parties in an electronic transaction
- Establish their delegated and contractual authorities

- Protect against the repudiation of the transaction by either party
- Ensure the successful completion of the contractual obligations

This solution solves the major concerns of e-commerce and makes Colface a leader in the current e-business market.

CONCLUSION

Internet use is rapidly growing and market dominance by North America will be eroded as user-access in other regions increases. A challenge for all businesses— not just credit insurers—hoping to grow their Internet activity is to successfully adapt to e-commerce. Some credit insurers have what it takes to migrate to becoming clicks-and-mortar operations, as Coface has clearly indicated. Coface succeeded because it had a clear view of where it wanted to go and had seasoned information technology professionals who have been in the organization for 10 to 15 years and who understand the business and how the information technology system must serve it. The challenge for the typical credit insurer is to define and build an e-business solution, accelerate its time to market, leverage existing systems, and maintain agility in a rapidly changing market. Those that do so will thrive. Those others who sit back and do nothing or try to protect their already entrenched positions will disappear.

17

Credit Insurance Case Studies

Eva Taylor

NCM Americas, Inc.

This chapter deals with the basic and enhanced uses for commercial credit insurance in general and its impact on international trade in particular. Credit insurance, in its most basic form, has been available in the United States for over 100 years. However, it has not been a widely used or highly recognized credit management tool—at least not until recently. Industry experts estimate the U.S. market penetration to range between 2.5 to 3 percent while Europe boasts a market saturation of close to 28 percent.

Although U.S. companies are less likely to use credit insurance than their European counterparts, it should be noted that U.S. market penetration has doubled in less than a decade. Analysts believe this to be due in part to recent technological advances and trade liberalization—the marketplace is evolving into a true world economy with U.S. exports on the rise. Increased foreign competition in the United States, profitable overseas ventures, and improved private sector trade services have all contributed to the 52 percent growth in U.S. exports over the last six years.

The rise in U.S. exports increases the need for commercial credit insurance and political risk coverage. Overseas trade opportunities can present new and unique problems. In addition to cultural differences and language barriers, exporters often encounter a tangle of different legal and accounting systems when national boundaries are crossed.

New, high-tech tools facilitate handling the complex issues of international trade. These tools allow for greater access to important customer and trade information through access to the Internet and employment of new hardware and software that assists with credit scoring, analysis, logistics, and communication.

Even with the assistance of new technology, businesses still confront the challenges associated with developing the most cost-effective credit management strategy necessary for corporate success. Besides assessing risk to commercial accounts receivable, finance executives usually are required to develop collection tactics and determine strategies that maintain sales initiatives while minimizing loss. When a company trades internationally, these same executives are often responsible for establishing guidelines for governing risk taken in complex overseas markets.

In order to gain a market advantage, multinational companies have added a number of alternative credit management tools to their credit management arsenal. Credit insurance is one of these tools. Knowledgeable credit executives have used these flexible programs to help mitigate risk, increase sales, and facilitate financing. By enhancing credit management programs with alternatives like credit insurance, resources can be redirected from a focus on multiple, detailed activities to high-level account portfolio management.

CREDIT INSURANCE DEFINED

In general, credit insurance policies protect an entity's commercial accounts receivable from unexpected and catastrophic losses due to the insolvency or nonpayment from that entity's buyers. In order to mitigate risk, the insurance underwriter constantly evaluates buyers, trade sectors, and countries worldwide.

This, however, is but one dimension of the picture. Increased competition is turning the world into a buyer's market. Because they have so many options, buyers are able to dictate the terms of sale by requiring open-account terms in lieu of more traditional methods of trade, such as international letters of credit. Not only does this elevate the risk factor, but it requires an increased investment in resources. Credit insurance can eliminate the risk and increased costs associated with managing an international receivable portfolio.

The accounts receivable portfolio is typically the largest asset on an organization's books. Assets, such as finished goods and equipment are insured, as are deposits in bank accounts that are insured by the Federal Deposit Insurance Company (FDIC). However, the largest corporate asset is often overlooked and left vulnerable to loss due to nonpayment and buyer insolvency. Typical causes for buyer insolvencies include undercapitalization, deteriorating markets, family disputes, and technology glitches. Strategic miscalculations and overexpansion also can cause insolvency. And information identifying the potential for these circumstances is not always readily available in the international marketplace. Credit insurance serves as a hedge to cover these risks. Additionally, premiums are tax deductible, and the reduced credit management costs with an unbiased, third-party opinion add to the value of credit insurance policies.

CATASTROPHIC LOSS SCENARIO

The added value can be seen when we evaluate a company that uses credit insurance to mitigate risk from a possible catastrophic loss. The company in question, the largest independent U.S. energy wholesaler with $150 million in annual sales, was experiencing good growth prospects and had a strong

Large exposure/potential loss	$800,000
By net margin	1%
Additional sales required	
to offset potential loss	$80 Million

Note: Required additional sales of approximately 53% to offset the loss and still meet corporate bottom-line profit objectives.

Exhibit 17.1   Catastrophic Loss Situation

balance sheet with average account receivables at $8.3 million. With less than 1 percent net margins and high exposures, the company needed to hold down peak seasonal demand because of potential catastrophic credit loss.

The energy wholesaler employed sophisticated credit management methods and personnel to manage the expected credit risk within its customer portfolio. However, it still needed a program that would eliminate the potential catastrophic risk associated with an unexpected situation. The solution was to implement a credit insurance program that covered all accounts for projected peak exposure, while maintaining a significant first-loss position for a truly catastrophic risk mitigation program. The deductible level was established by the wholesaler's ability to withstand any loss above the deductible covered by the insurance policy.

The results of this program allowed the customer to reduce limitations on peak seasonal sales while confidently entering into sizable contracts. These new contracts produced incremental profits that far exceeded the cost of the policy. For a true zero net cost, the insurance program provided catastrophic loss protection, reduced bad-debt allowance, and enhanced ability to negotiate with the lender. (See Exhibit 17.1.)

EVALUATING CREDIT INSURANCE POLICIES

Since credit insurance policies are flexible and may be adapted to meet very specific business needs, the first step in obtaining credit insurance is to evaluate the customer base to identify areas of risk and the company's level of tolerance of that risk. Next, set objectives that match corporate goals. Once these objectives have been established, the proper mix of credit insurance features can be determined.

The basic elements of credit insurance include credit limits, discretionary coverage, pricing, coinsurance, and deductibles. Underwriters determine credit limits based on financial information, trading experience with the buyers, mercantile agency information, and bank references.

Policy pricing is determined by industry, country and buyer risk, past loss history, the terms of payment, and retention. Coinsurance is typically 10 to 15 percent and is based on sales and loss experience, buyer and country spread, bad-debt history, and the company's risk appetite. Deductible options include per-loss deductibles or aggregate first loss (AFL).

Under most credit insurance policies, the insurance carrier immediately processes insolvent claims for payment. If one objective is to protect the cash flow from slow-paying but solvent customers, a protracted default endorsement should be added to the policy. This basic feature is very useful since even seemingly reliable buyers occasionally have difficulty paying in a timely fashion due to an unforeseen event leading to internal cash-flow difficulties. With a protracted default endorsement in place, a claim may be submitted after 180 days.

Typically, credit insurance is used to cover key customers. If, however, an organization sells to a number of smaller businesses, blanket coverage to a large group of these accounts is available through discretionary coverage endorsements (discretionary limit, or D/L). Based on the terms of the endorsement, the D/L provides blanket coverage to all companies within that discretionary authority. This allows for covered terms to smaller and often harder-to-insure accounts in addition to key accounts.

Another common credit insurance feature covers the cost of customized goods during the manufacturing process. The work-in-process (WIP) or predelivery risk endorsement provides coverage for costs incurred during the manufacturing process, less profit, in the event of an insolvency to the scheduled buyer prohibits the sale or delivery of goods.

EMPLOYING CREDIT INSURANCE TO MEET CORPORATE GROWTH INITIATIVES

The primary function of credit insurance is to mitigate risk to accounts receivable from bad-debt losses. However, some companies are discovering many more benefits from their policies. A major advantage of credit insurance is the role it can play in supporting sales and market expansion efforts.

In the current highly competitive marketplace, there is a great deal of pressure to quickly approve credit sales in order to capture new business, expand current business, and develop new markets. Credit management is a delicate balancing act between approving sales and minimizing losses. By helping to meet organizational growth objectives while maintaining a reasonable level of risk, credit insurance provides a means to gain a competitive edge.

Sales can be lost due to the time taken to analyze new customers. Slow response time can cause those new prospects to turn to competitors, that provide quicker turnaround in their credit decision-making process. Credit insurance programs can help capture new sales opportunities with fast buyer underwriting. Because credit insurance companies maintain large databases of credit and financial information on businesses throughout the world, they can respond soon after sales contact. This quick response contributes to a decrease in the number of lost sales opportunities.

Credit insurance programs can help increase sales to the existing customer base without increasing risk. This can be accomplished with buyer limit underwriting or discretionary coverage. The buyer limit analysis provides coverage up to the approved credit limit or discretionary limit. With credit insurance in place, the credit executive is able to request additional credit line coverage allowing for increases in sales volume. Preapproved credit lines can provide the security needed to take advantage of sales growth opportunities within a current customer base.

SALES EXPANSION SCENARIO

The benefits of using credit insurance programs to support growth initiatives is apparent when we look at a well-capitalized, established pet supply distributor with annual revenue at $120 million. The company in question was experiencing good growth opportunities within an industry that has witnessed a rise in demand along with several consecutive raw material price increases. This caused average account exposures to double in some cases, increasing the financial risk of a potential catastrophic credit loss.

Therefore, even though the insured had a few large accounts that offered additional sales opportunities, it was unable to extend credit since doing so would exceed an exposure level the firm felt it could handle comfortably. It was interested in a credit risk protection program that would allow it the ability to safely increase sales with reduced risks.

The solution was to cover the client's total portfolio, offering a better spread of risk to underwriting and allowing increased coverage on tougher risks. As a result, the coverage approved on just one account generated additional gross profit that not only covered the total cost of the protection program but it provided a return of more that 200 percent of the program's total annual cost. (See Exhibit 17.2.)

ADDITIONAL BENEFITS TO EXPANSION EFFORTS

Credit insurance also helps provide safe entry into new markets. Since all major credit insurance companies underwrite in international markets, they have comprehensive lists of terms for every country in the world. And because the insurance companies cover businesses throughout the world, they constantly analyze the areas they cover. This ongoing research provides insurance companies access to timely information on the political and economic status of any given region. Credit insurance companies typically possess in-depth

"Comfort" exposure level	$750,000
Approved insured coverage	$1 Million
Sales opportunity	$250,000
By account turns	8
Incremental annual revenue	$2 Million
By gross margin	10%
Incremental gross profit	$200,000

Note: With an annual program cost of $75,000, the company increased profits by $125,000.

Exhibit 17.2   Profit/Payout of a Sales Expansion Situation

knowledge of the countries where most businesses plan to expand marketing efforts. By sharing expertise and information, insurers can help add important measures of security and clarity to their clients' expansion strategies.

Another benefit of a basic credit insurance policy is its ability to free bad-debt reserves with deposit premiums. Freeing bad-debt reserves creates a new source for additional working capital to expand into new markets. A deposit premium is the scheduled premium payment for anticipated sales over the next 12 months. This schedule helps stabilize cash flow because premium payments can be built into the budget.

FINANCING FACILITIES ENHANCEMENTS

Recently, corporations have recognized a role for credit insurance in facilitating financing. Banks can be reluctant to lend amounts needed at attractive rates when a firm has more advanced needs such as major growth initiatives. So, to assist with the special needs of mutual customers, credit insurance companies and banks have helped customers create finance enhancements.

Adding a bank as a loss payee or a joint insured on the policy can increase working lines of credit. The loss-payee endorsement names the bank as payee on all eligible claims made to that policy. For example, if the bank is currently lending at 75 percent of eligible receivables, the loss-payee endorsement gives the bank the security to increase that percentage significantly on domestic and/or foreign receivables, as potential for loss is substantially mitigated. This increase in working capital and its subsequent impact on cash flow alone may offset the cost of the credit insurance policy through increased opportunity potential.

BORROWING ENHANCEMENT SCENARIO

Recently, a midsize U.S.-based steel service company with $20 million in annual sales (52 percent of which were export transactions) employed credit insurance as a borrowing enhancement tool. This steel company was experiencing good growth opportunities, especially in the international markets.

However, growth was being funded internally, which began to limit opportunities. The firm had average accounts receivable at $3 million and a financing relationship that was limited to lending on domestic receivables only. The steel company's main objective was to leverage assets within a borrowing arrangement, thus freeing capital to enable it to maximize on all selling opportunities.

To achieve this, the company implemented a domestic and export insurance program that eliminated all credit and political risk for both the insured and the insured's lender. As a result, the credit insurance transformed pledged accounts receivable into risk-free assets for the lender, which allowed it to increase advance rates, and include receivables that were previously excluded from the formula, and enabled them to borrow against open-credit invoices. Additionally, because the policy was written on "triple-A" rated paper, the lender was able to pass on a borrowing savings greater than the price of the policy. (See Exhibit 17.3.)

Average receivables	$3 million
Allowed receivables	$1.2 million
Prior advance rate (domestic only)	80%
Prior available capital	$960,000
New allowed receivables	$2.5 million
New domestic advance rate	90%
New export advance rate	70%
New available capital	$2 million
Additional Capital Provided	**$1,040,000**
Funds employed back in business at	20% gross margin
Additional opportunity	$208,000
By account turns per year	7
Potential incremental return	$1,456,000
Note: Total premium of insurance program was only $50,000	

Exhibit 17.3   Additional Capital/Profit from Borrowing Enhancement Situation

ADDITIONAL BORROWING ENHANCEMENTS FUNCTIONS

Credit insurance policies that name the bank as loss payee can help organizations move out of factoring agreements. Factoring can be very expensive; comparatively, insuring receivables and selling them to a bank or using them as loan collateral is far more cost effective.

Credit insurance also can facilitate off–balance sheet financing by enabling banks to purchase receivables outright, thus reducing corporate leverage. By enhancing their security value, credit insurance may enable banks to purchase receivables on a limited recourse basis. This true sale of accounts receivable may allow their removal, along with corresponding short-term liabilities, from the balance sheet. This off–balance sheet financing can be used to offer supplier credit to buyers for increased customer loyalty and to gain an advantage in the marketplace.

GLOBAL RISK MANAGEMENT

Multinational corporations and export traders face a variety of special challenges. Those challenges can range from mitigating risk in politically sensitive areas to developing international credit management strategies for subsidiaries or affiliates. When developing those strategies, credit executives include factors such as differences in culture, language, currency, and business and legal practices. Credit insurance and political risk programs can be applied to help organizations meet global business objectives.

Developing an international credit management strategy requires intensive research. Detailed investigations of the various methods of payment accepted by each country are required. Then foreign government officials must be queried to determine if they require letters of credit or documentation collection, or if they accept open-account terms supplemented by credit insurance. The associated cost for each method, including both actual expenses and the effects of gained or lost sales opportunities, must be factored into the formula. The analysis also should cover the benefits and risks of each method, available resources, and the projected return on investment. It is crucial that flexibility be built into the strategy in anticipation of unexpected political and economic changes.

Through policy requirements, companies must report all accounts that exceed 60 days from terms. If a company has aging reports that contain considerable past-due accounts, those reports would then be passed on to the insurer. Policies usually require collection on past-due accounts; therefore, sophisticated collection procedures for overseas accounts must be established. Once an account is over 60 days past due, the insurance company must be notified. The account is then referred to a collection agency whose fees may be covered by the policy. Overseas collection efforts can be complicated, and foreign legal systems can be quite frustrating. Credit insurance companies can assist by referring accounts to high-quality international agencies with expert legal staffs. In the event that collection is not obtained, the account may be claimable as a protracted default. This results in a much stronger aging report and provides for tighter security over the receivable process.

Credit insurance programs also can help ensure that subsidiary sales are limited to creditworthy customers through a joint insured endorsement. This feature allows organizations to proactively add domestic as well as international subsidiaries and affiliates on certain policies in order to cover their trade. If they are added and therefore under the same policy, subsidiaries and affiliates must adhere to the same terms and conditions. This feature can assist in procedural standardization.

This program is helpful when foreign subsidiaries find it difficult to convert currency for reporting purposes and to translate the definitions of the policy into their respective foreign language. Special credit insurance policies are also available to cover sales by a foreign subsidiary in local currency with currency endorsements.

Additionally, credit insurance increases global advantages by offering open-credit terms instead of secured credit terms (letters of credit, trade drafts, etc). Obtaining credit insurance may be necessary to remain competitive in the global market since it is widely used worldwide. While credit insurance is relatively unknown in the United States, almost one-third of European businesses rely on it to expedite sales with open-account credit terms. The insurance carrier's buyer underwriters will analyze the creditworthiness of business customers around the world. This allows for trade with competitive open-credit terms in the foreign marketplace.

Credit insurance companies can help relieve the expenses associated the assessment of overseas risk with through their vast buyer databases. These databases provide ready access to the credit and financial information necessary for approving open-account credit limits to international customers. Underwriters analyze this information and respond to the requested credit limits in an expeditious manner. And some insurance companies may provide online links for more immediate credit limit approval.

International trade also increases risk due to foreign crises, such as important restrictions, currency devaluation, foreign exchange restrictions, and acts of war. Companies trading in politically sensitive areas may want to consider an international credit insurance policy with political risk coverage. This provides protection to accounts receivable in the event of government moratorium, contract frustration, discharge of debt, war, and public buyer default. International policies provide comprehensive coverage that protects against the commercial risk of trading with foreign customers and the political risk of trading within the domain of foreign governments and economies.

If an organization has an established distributor network in a region that has become unstable, it needs to continue selling in politically troubled areas, or it will lose a valuable source of revenue. Special structures and pricing for international and global policies may allow for continued trade in these areas. Through these special policies, companies pay an additional market-rate premium to cover the increased risk.

If the company needs to sell expensive specialty items overseas and its buyer requires extended open terms in order to purchase those goods, international trade risk is compounded. Without credit insurance, the window of risk increases substantially. Special credit insurance features provide extended open terms, typically up to two years, or up to three years if the policy is written in conjunction with a predelivery risk endorsement.

POLITICAL RISK SCENARIO

The benefits of international credit insurance with political risk coverage is apparent when we analyze its usage by a manufacturer that produces high-tech, customized hydrogen gas chambers. The policy was purchased three years ago when the manufacturer had $8 million in exposures with a huge firm in Malaysia. At the time the policy was purchased, there were political and economic concerns regarding Asian markets. Recently, the company added a new buyer in India to cover $2.5 million in trade.

After the manufacturer began production of this highly customized product, the Indian government began testing nuclear weapons. In protest of India's actions, the U.S. government put sanctions against any manufactures selling high-tech and industrial equipment to entities in India. Due to U.S. political intervention, the $2.5 million contract was frustrated. The insurance company honored the claim as a political risk loss because the insured's export license to India was revoked by U.S. officials.

CONCLUSION

Credit insurance is more than just a policy to protect commercial accounts receivable portfolio. Credit insurance offers many enhanced features that add value to the receivable management process. Policies can be tailored to help credit departments run more efficiently, saving time, money, and effort.

Once the decision has been made to obtain a credit insurance program and all requirements have been identified, an insurance carrier that is capable of meeting specific corporate needs must be found. Most credit insurance companies offer the basic policy, but some enhanced features may differ from company to company. For unique requirements, work with an insurance company or specialist credit insurance broker that offers the flexibility to develop a program specifically designed to meet specific business needs.

In addition to basic and enhanced policy features, an insurer should be chosen based on how well it provides all requirements including deductible/coinsurance amounts, a premium payment plan, satisfactory policy language, and a comfort level with a broker or agent. Also investigate the quality and philosophy of the insurer's underwriting (i.e., Does it underwrite the insured or the insured's buyers?), and investigate its claims payment history. The key to securing the best credit insurance program is to be satisfied that it meets corporate needs and requirements before settling on the price of the premium.

PART SIX

FORFAIT

The forfait market, which has been long developed in Europe, is spreading to the United States. Chapter 18 explains some of the basics of forfaiting, how to set up a transaction, some of the questions to ask when transacting a trade, and some of the benefits.

A rather thorough case study follows in Chapter 19. It walks international credit professional's through a transaction and shows how the forfait market made it possible for a particular transaction to occur.

18

Forfaiting

Mary S. Schaeffer

IOMA

U.S. exporters are slowly turning to a technique long used by Europeans to finance their international trade: forfaiting. It is popular with credit and collection professionals because exporters receive their money up front, effectively removing all collection hassles (and of course improving cash flow). And it eliminates not only many of the risks associated with international transactions but the foreign exchange uncertainties as well.

HOW FORFAITING WORKS

Any forfaiting transactions requires both a forfaiter and an importer's guarantor. The forfaiter relies on the guarantee, typically given by a financial institution. This guarantee, called an *aval,* is unconditional, irrevocable, and transferable. The transferability feature makes it possible for an active secondary market to exist. Forfait debt obligations are actively traded, just as corporate bonds are in the United States.

The unconditional feature of the guarantee means the guarantor will pay the importer's obligations even if nonpayment is due to a contractual dispute. Other advantages of this type of arrangement include the speed with which it can be executed and its simplicity due to standardization of the documents used.

Typically, the forfaiter gives a commitment letter directly to the exporter. Once the product has been delivered, the exporter is given a series of promissory notes or bills of exchange. The exporter endorses them and returns the notes or bills of exchange to the forfaiter. The forfaiter deducts interest from the face value of the notes and forwards the net to the exporter. As the series of notes become due, the forfaiter presents them to the importer for payment.

WHAT IT COSTS

It is important to note that the exporter receives the discounted amount on the note, thus effectively paying the interest. The up-front payment reflects the forfait house's cost of funds *plus* a premium of 0.5 to 5 percent, depending on the transaction. When using forfaiting, the expense of the cost of funds plus a premium must be built into the pricing. Buyer and seller must agree to its use and incorporate it into the sales contract. International credit managers must make sure that the sales force understands the financial impact of the arrangements.

Forfaiting is generally used for longer terms, usually three to eight years, although it can be used for transactions as short as 90 days. It has also traditionally been used for larger transactions, ranging from $100,000 up to several millions of dollars or more.

Since the documentation is fairly standard, transactions are straightforward and can be completed in a relatively short period of time. This keeps down the costs and associated legal expenses. It is possible to get a definite commitment and a price quickly—sometimes in as little as 48 hours. Once the cost is known, it is easy to incorporate it into the price at a level that will ensure a profit for the company. This information can put the exporter in a very good competitive bidding situation. International credit managers who can arrange this will be heroes with the sales department.

HOW TO PICK A FORFAIT HOUSE

Most forfait houses are subsidiaries of Swiss, Austrian, East European, and, more recently, U.S. banks. Each house has its own slight differences, and perceptive exporters will interview several before deciding on the one that best suits their needs. International credit professionals first need to determine in which countries the forfaiter will do business. If it does not do business in the importer's country, then further investigation will be required to find a forfaiter who does business in the given country.

It is also important to inquire about the minimum and maximum transactions size. If the transaction in question does not meet the parameters, it will be necessary to locate another forfaiter.

Once ability to handle the transaction has been determined, references should be sought. It is also a good idea to locate several forfaiters who can handle the transaction in question. Then a competitive bidding situation can be set up. It will also help to set the price level and give the exporter some comfort and experience with several forfaiters. Doing so can be helpful in future dealings.

When obtaining quotes, credit managers must give all information, including time periods, country, amount, and the currency of the transaction, to the forfaiter. They must also find out what commitment fees are charged and how long the commitment will be good for.

QUESTIONS TO ASK A FORFAITER

All forfaiters are not created equal. It is important to select a forfaiter who is experienced in the countries in which the firm is selling. It is also critical that both the international credit person and the forfaiter are on the same page. To ensure that the best forfaiter is selected for a particular transaction, ask the following questions.

- Does the importer's country require a bank guarantee?
- If a bank guarantee is required, which banks are acceptable?
- Does the forfaiter charge a commitment fee?
- How long is the commitment good for?
- What currencies will the forfaiter accept for transactions?
- In what countries must the forfaiter transaction take place?
- Is the discount rate quoted a discount to yield or a straight discount?
- How many grace days does the forfaiter add to the discount calculations?
- Can the number of grace days be negotiated?
- Can the commitment be made on a fixed-margin basis?
- Will the forfaiter help calculate uplifts and incorporate variations into a final price?
- Is there a minimum amount or a maximum amount that the forfaiter will handle?

INFORMATION A FORFAITER NEEDS TO KNOW

Similarly, it is important that forfaiters be given all relevant information about the transaction under consideration. Here is a list of the information that should be given to potential forfaiters.

- Customer name, address, and type of goods involved
- Expected maturity
- Amount
- Currency
- Expected presentation date
- Type of instrument to be purchased
- Place of payment
- Information about the buyer's bank that is providing the security

CREDIT ISSUES

The use of forfaiting eliminates the need for credit analysis. No longer do exporters have to worry about the importer's credit or the political stability of the importer's country. Since these transactions are nonrecourse, exporters should make sure the documentation for the transaction indicates "without recourse." Credit professionals, most of whom are accustomed to granting credit for only one year, no longer have to be concerned about transactions lasting several years.

Forfaiting allows exporters simply to produce and ship the product. Once the correct documentation is completed, exporters have no additional role in the transaction. All remaining concerns are between the forfaiter and the guarantor. Compare this with the headaches often associated with letters of credit.

PRICING INTRICACIES

The international sales staff is continually being asked for extended terms. However, most international credit executives are reluctant to offer such terms, since longer terms bring the increased likelihood of nonpayment. Thus, forfaiting, long popular in Europe, is finding more devotees in the United States. To be used most advantageously, however, price is all important. Unfortunately, getting the best rate is not always straightforward.

GETTING STARTED

Whenever international credit executives start a new relationship with a forfaiter, they should learn as much as possible about the financier and his or her practices. The list of questions in the section entitled "Questions to Ask a Forfaiter" will help in the gathering of this information.

At the same time, the more information about the transaction given to the forfaiter, the more accurate the price will be. The information includes a start date, as most forfaiters will commit for some period into the future but charge a fee for doing so. The longer the commitment period, the higher the fee. Once forfaiters deem a customer an acceptable risk, it will be necessary to provide only minimal information (maturity, amount, currency, and start date) to obtain a forfait quote. More detailed information will be needed once the transaction is completed. The section entitled "Information a Forfaiter Needs to Know" specifies what forfaiters will need.

DISCOUNT PRICING

Most (but not all) forfait pricing is on a discount basis. Here is a very simple example of how discounting works, given the following parameters:

- Time period: one year
- Discount rate: 7 percent
- Amount: $1 million
- Commitment fee: $0

The seller in this example would receive $930,000 when the documents were presented to the forfaiter ($1,000,000–$70,000). One year later, the buyer would pay the forfaiter $1 million. In addition to receiving funds quickly, the seller has no collection worries or costs.

Many readers are probably saying that the 7 percent is not the "real" interest rate because the seller did not receive the full $1 million on which the rate was calculated. And they are correct. The 7 percent rate quoted is the "straight discount." When getting a quote from the forfaiter, ask whether the rate being quoted is the straight discount or the "discount to yield."

The discount to yield, while more difficult to calculate, provides a more accurate picture of the true interest rate being paid. It is generally expressed on a per-annum basis and is the yield a present value amount will achieve as it reaches its face value at maturity. If the time period involved is longer than 180 days, semiannual compounding may be involved.

ADDITIONAL PRICING CONSIDERATIONS

The rate quote given by forfaiters can be either a fixed rate or a fixed margin. Sellers like the fixed rate because it protects them against a rise in interest rates. However, forfaiters may not want to make such a commitment, offering instead a fixed-margin quote. Pricing quoted as a margin is typically the margin over London Interbank Offer Rate (LIBOR).

When a fixed-margin rate is used, international credit professionals must know which LIBOR is under discussion. Typically, it will be the one for the average life of the transaction. As in any other LIBOR transaction, the rate is set two days before the transaction starts. This can be an issue at year end if the sales force is trying to get a sale on the books before the close of the calendar year. Occasionally, the LIBOR market experiences wild gyrations during the last few days, or occasionally weeks, of the year. Anyone forced to set a LIBOR rate at this time could end up regretting it if the market misbehaves.

UPLIFTS

One of the first questions credit professionals ask about forfaiting is who pays the interest rate. Technically, sellers pay this, given the discount nature of forfaiting. However, not all sellers are willing to do this. To get around this, some forfaiters "gross up" the face amount so that sellers receive the entire amount to which they are entitled and buyers effectively pay the interest. If sellers do not wish to share this information with buyers, sellers must tell forfaiters so the calculations can be performed before a price quote is given.

Some forfaiters take this service one step further, permitting sellers to look like heroes by offering what appears to be an artificially low interest rate. Forfaiting is not inexpensive. However, if sellers wish to show a low rate, either to buyers or to management, certain forfaiters are willing to cooperate. Before traveling down this route, international credit executives should have a thorough understanding of all the calculations behind the forfaiters' pricing.

Forfaiting provides a wonderful opportunity for both buyers wanting quick cash flow and sellers needing extended terms. International credit executives who understand the pricing details of forfaiting will be able to negotiate the best rate for their companies while simultaneously helping the sales force compete in tight markets.

The following companies offer forfait services.

Forfaiting Companies

McKinney American Inc.
6420 Hillcroft, Suite 315
Houston, TX 77081-3103
Phone: 713-981-8168
Fax: 713-981-6172
E-mail: charles@mckinney.com

British American Forfaiting Company
1110 World Trade Center
121 South Meramec
P.O. Box 16782
St. Louis, MO 63105
Phone: 314-647-8700
E-mail: Forfaiter@aol.com

North American Forfaiting
135 East 57th Street
New York, NY 10022
Phone: 212-759-1919
Fax: 212-759-0118
E-mail: namerica@forfaiting.com

Bon Pour Aval Ltd.
Mark De Fraine
Phone: 44-171-329-2600
Fax: 44-171-329-2601
E-mail: bonpouraval@zdnetmail.com
Web site: *www.bpaval.co.uk*

Mezra Finance Ltd
Phone: 44-181-290-4110
Fax: 44-181-290-6621
E-mail: info@mezra.com
Free forfaiting spreadsheet

Meridian Finance Group
Los Angeles, CA
Phone: 310-442-3600
E-mail: info@meridianfinance.com
Web site: *www.meridianfinance.com*

Companies offering forfaiting in Switzerland: *www.forfaitswiss.ch*

19

Forfaiting Case Study

Riccardo Straino

The Internet Trade Finance Exchange

Forfaiting is traditionally viewed as a "supplier credit" form of trade finance where trade receivables, usually in the form of negotiable instruments, are discounted to a third party on a without-recourse basis. Benefits to the seller include better balance sheet management, a reduction in the number of days outstanding on receivables, and, since the sale of the asset is concluded on a without-recourse basis, full mitigation of credit, political, and transfer risks.

While supplier credit and discounting of receivables are hardly new or revolutionary, few companies manage to effectively integrate these "presale" and "postsale" activities into a single strategy to maximize sales and profits within the context of prudent balance sheet management. This integration is further complicated because in many companies, selling policies and practices are not tied directly to the cash management and balance sheet management functions. After all, how can salespeople maximize revenue without understanding the ultimate liquidation value of the receivables they are generating, and how effective can a company's treasury department be in liquidating receivables if the sales force is not building in enough margin to allow for liquidation without sustaining a loss?

When used properly, forfaiting is a sales tool, a cash and balance sheet management tool, and a risk management tool. This single technique can help a company integrate the *pre-* and *post*-sale functions to optimize a company's export sale performance.

To better illustrate an appropriate application of the forfaiting technique, this chapter details a transaction that initially occurred in 1996 in Sri Lanka. For the sake of confidentiality, the names of the company involved and the products they manufacture have been altered.

OPPORTUNITY IN SRI LANKA

In June 1996, the finance director of Secure Communications Corporation (SCC) received a call from the international sales manager. An exciting opportunity had emerged in Sri Lanka, where a new sales agent was making inroads with the Ministry of Finance. Sri Lanka needed to modernize its communications infrastructure and was about to release the terms of a new procurement contract for communications equipment.

While the technical specifications of the equipment were wide enough to allow over 20 manufacturers to submit bids, it was a condition of the contract that the selected supplier would be required to provide vendor financing for a period of not less than three years. As an additional incentive, the equipment provided by the selected bidder would become the technical standard for all future phases of the communications infrastructure modernization program. The potential for the Sri Lanka procurement program over the next four years could be worth in excess of U.S. $50 million to the selected bidder.

HISTORICAL BACKGROUND ON SECURE COMMUNICATIONS CORPORATION

SCC was a public company and, as a result, had some fairly rigid reporting requirements. The company manufactured numerous types of communication systems but found great success in one specific item that lent itself naturally to military applications. The company had flourished in the 1980s when U.S. defense spending was high and, as a by-product of having the U.S. government as its largest customer, developed a very conservative approach to risk and balance sheet management. With production running at over 90 percent of capacity, SCC was in a enviable position, requiring foreign buyers to pay cash in advance or under a sight letter of credit with confirmation by a U.S. bank acceptable to SCC.

With the end of the cold war and a significant reduction in defense spending, SCC found itself with excess manufacturing capacity and dwindling sales. Its products were still in demand, but suddenly prospective buyers were all in the emerging markets. And because of the military application of its key product, U.S. Export-Import Bank financing would not be available.

To further complicate things, the inflexible credit policies adopted by SCC in the 1980s were suddenly creating a significant problem for the company's sales professionals and its new network of agents, who were losing out to competitors with more aggressive credit policies. SCC attempted to compete by providing significant discounts to spur sales, but the company soon realized that the bids it won with the "loss-leader" strategy were marginally profitable at best and that such a sales strategy was not sustainable. Sri Lanka was the latest in a string of difficult new opportunities presented to SCC, but possibly one of the most profitable.

The international sales manager and the finance director considered the required financing terms for the transaction and tried to find a suitable solution. As mentioned, government export credit programs were not available due to the nature of the goods being sold, comprehensive insurance cover from the private market was unavailable at the time, and SCC did not have the resources or the stomach to carry a U.S. $11.0 million receivable from Sri Lanka on its own balance sheet. SCC approached its bankers, who for the same reasons were unwilling to provide financing for the transaction.

FORFAITING SOLUTION

SCC had been actively marketed by a forfaiter for some time, and while the discussions had been cordial, they had not been fruitful. The forfaiter made a scheduled follow-up call to the finance director as he was discussing the transaction with the sales manager and the agent in Sri Lanka. With little to lose, the finance director provided the forfaiter with all the salient details of the transaction and agreed to give the forfaiter a day to consider the viability of the transaction. The terms provided were as follows:

Contract Cash Value:	U.S. $11.6 million (approximately)
Delivery Date:	October 1996 (estimated)
Repayment Terms:	Six semiannual repayments over a three-year period, with the first repayment 6 months after bill of lading date and the last 36 months after bill of lading date.
Interest Rate:	The Government of Sri Lanka would pay no more than 2% above the one-year U.S. $LIBOR (London Inter-Bank Offered Rate) fixed for the life of the financing.
Security:	Usance letter of credit calling for drafts to be opened by Bank of Ceylon in favor of SCC. The letter of credit would call for SCC to draw six drafts or bills of exchange on the Bank of Ceylon, and these instruments would be accepted by the opening bank and returned to SCC if all documents supplied were in strict accordance with the terms of the letter of credit.

SCC was concerned about several issues when contemplating a forfaiting solution to its problem. Its concerns focused on three principal elements. The first involved determining if the forfaiter was credible counterparty. After all, if SCC concludes the contract with Sri Lanka and the forfaiter fails to deliver on his commitment, SCC is stuck with carrying a large three-year Sri Lanka receivable on its balance sheet. The second element was to ensure that the pricing the forfaiter was quoting was fair. And finally, SCC had to ensure that the proposal being crafted with the forfaiter would meet with the approval of Sri Lanka, the buyer.

Simultaneously, the forfaiter was busy completing his own analysis on the transaction:

1. Determine if there is a market for three-year Bank of Ceylon risk and what the market price to sell such a risk would be. Based on that, the forfaiter determines if his company is willing to commit to underwrite the transaction based on the belief that it could subsequently be sold in the market at a profit.

   To determine market pricing, forfaiters look at any existing bond prices, other types of outstanding debt issues, and polls other market participants. In some cases, forfaiters look to presell a specific asset to ensure that it will not stay on the forfaiters' balance sheets. In this particular case, the forfaiter found a one-year syndicated loan issued by the Bank of Ceylon, polled a few possible end investors to determine if the transaction could be sold, and if so, at what price. The price at which forfaiters expect to resell the transaction in the market is critical, because it is the base number above which all other pricing elements must be stacked.

2. Evaluate documentary structure of the transaction to ensure that it has maximum liquidity.

   In the forfaiting market, liquidity and price are driven by the length of the financing period, the country risk, the credit risk, and documentary structure. The first three points are covered by step 1. Forfaiters work diligently to make sure that any transaction contemplated has the simplest and most clear documentary structure possible. For this transaction, the forfaiter helped SCC evaluate the proposed letter of credit wording to ensure that it contained no clauses that would make the transaction more difficult and therefore expensive to sell.

3. Construct pricing models for SCC so that the contract price ultimately submitted takes into account the cash requirements of SCC, the interest rate requirements stipulated in the Sri Lankan bid specifications, the true market pricing for three-year Bank of Ceylon risk, and finally the forfaiter's own return requirement.

   Using sophisticated financial modeling software, the forfaiter developed several pricing models that would meet SCC's objectives, while making sure that the financing structure would still be acceptable to the buyer and leave the forfaiter enough room to resell the financing in the market at a reasonable profit.

Forfaiters use financial modeling based on present value calculations. These models are extremely sensitive to the date parameters used to construct them. It is important to note that while forfaiters create the financial models, most of the parameters must come directly from the exporters. Forfaiters make suggestions and give some conservative guidance to render the model more accurate and useful, but exporters ultimately are responsible for most of the parameters of the financial model.

The first thing the modeling does is calculate the anticipated costs of the transaction. The costs include the discount rate, commitment fees, and any other cost elements that exporters will be charged when selling the receivable to forfaiters. Once the model has detailed all of the forecasted expenses or cost items associated with selling the receivable, it calculates the amount by which the commercial contract needs to be increased so that after all of the financing costs are covered, exporters receive 100 percent of the required cash value. It is important to note that, up to this point, SCC has not given any pricing to the buyer in Sri Lanka. As a result, SCC still can create a contract price that will incorporate the forecast financing expenses. This may seem to be an obvious oversimplification, but all too many companies regularly enter into contracts without really quantifying all of the costs associated with the transaction, or at least they grossly underestimate them.

To complete the financial modeling, forfaiters use the following components:

- Key Dates
  - *Commitment date.* The date at which the forfaiter and the exporter enter into a formal commitment.
  - *Shipping date.* The date on which the goods are shipped. This date usually triggers the issuance of the debt obligations and the subsequent maturity dates.
  - *Discounting date.* The date at which the exporter exchanges the debt instruments for cash from the forfaiter. (Also known as the settlement date or the value date.)
  - *Maturity date(s).* The date for each expected repayment during the life of the financing.
- Key Values
  - *Net cash required.* How much net cash the exporter needs to receive after all expenses associated with the discounting of the receivable.
  - *Maturity values.* How much is received at each maturity date during the life of the financing.
- Key Interest Elements
  - *LIBOR.* The typical benchmark for determining the cost of funds of a transaction is based on the London Inter-Bank Offered Rate for the appropriate duration and currency. As such, a U.S. dollar transaction with a one-year duration would normally be priced as one-year U.S. $LIBOR plus any applicable margin.
  - *Margin.* The risk premium above the appropriate LIBOR charged by the forfaiter for a specific transaction. Note: forfaiters can price transactions in many different ways, depending on client needs.
  - *Commitment fee.* This fee is charged from commitment date up to discount date. Like a commitment fee on a mortgage, the

commitment fee compensates forfaiters for the opportunity cost of allocating a credit limit to a transaction that does not exist yet, as opposed to investing the cash into some other asset.

— *Flat fees.* Any flat fees applicable. Like points, flat fees sometimes can be used to lower the margin on a transaction.

— *Grace days.* Forfaiters often build extra days of interest in the discounting calculation to account for any forecast delays in receiving repayment based on experience. As an example, if a transaction has a life of 360 days, and it is discounted with five grace days, the discount calculation will be based on 365 days of interest. If the repayment happens at maturity or within five days of maturity, the forfaiter may have a small windfall. If payment is more than five days after maturity, the forfaiter takes a loss associated with each day of delay beyond the first five. The exporter, however, has no additional liability.

— *Importer interest rate.* Rate of interest paid by the importer.

Once completed, SCC received a financial model from the forfaiter that detailed:

• The total cost of selling the receivable to the forfaiter, on a without-recourse basis
• How much total interest Sri Lanka was willing to pay on the financing
• How much to increase the contract value based on the shortfall between the total cost of selling the receivable to the forfaiter, on a without-recourse basis, and the interest paid by Sri Lanka

Analyzing the transaction and creating the financial models took less than two days. In some cases, a proposal with financial models can be completed in just a few hours.

BID

In late June, SCC was prepared to submit its bid for the transaction. Prior to submitting the bid, it took a commitment option from the forfaiter to lock in the financing in the event SCC was awarded the contract. The commitment option was a detailed contract that bound SCC to sell the receivable to the forfaiter, bound the forfaiter to purchase the asset from SCC, and spelled out all the financial terms of the arrangement. Under the commitment option, if the contract was awarded to another bidder, SCC had the option to cancel the commitment with no further liability. With the option in hand to protect itself, SCC submitted its bid for the transaction. Two weeks later, SCC was notified that it had been awarded the contract.

At this point SCC and the forfaiter were committed to the transaction, and the commitment fee clock was running. Any substantial delays in the delivery of the goods would delay the discount date and increase the length of the commitment period. Such delays would result in additional unforeseen costs, which could reduce the profitability of the transaction. As a hedge against minor delays, the forfaiter advised SCC to factor in a 30-day delay in the delivery of the goods. If delivery went according to schedule, the financial model would have overstated commitment fees by 30 days, resulting in extra profit for SCC.

If shipping was delayed, SCC could manage up to a 30-day delay before the costs would start to eat into the company's profit margin. More important, the forfaiter's commitment is never open ended, so exporters need to be certain that they can conclude their transaction within the time frame they committed to the forfaiter; if not, the forfaiter's commitment may expire. At his or her sole option, a forfaiter may grant an extension but is not obligated to do so. Furthermore, the forfaiter may require additional fees or margin, rendering the transaction unprofitable for the exporter.

Within 10 days of contract award, Bank of Ceylon issued an inoperative letter-of-credit text for SCC to review. With the help of the forfaiter, SCC negotiated the terms of the letter of credit, paying particular attention to any portion that pertained to the drafts or bills of exchange drawn under the letter.

By October, SCC completed manufacturing and shipped all the products in accordance with the terms of the letter of credit. Once found to be compliant, the six bills of exchange were accepted by the Bank of Ceylon and returned by express courier to SCC. SCC endorsed the bills of exchange to the forfaiter without recourse and forwarded the bills along with supporting documentation to the forfaiter. The forfaiter received the documents, verified the validity and authenticity of the obligations of Bank of Ceylon, and released payment of U.S. $11.6 million to SCC. The net cash payment resulted in SCC receiving 100 percent of the cash that it would have required on a cash basis.

At this point, SCC was removed from any financial involvement with the transaction. It still had to honor all of its contractual obligations with respect to product support and warrantees, but the financial risks associated with the Bank of Ceylon bills of exchange maturing over the next three years had been sold to the forfaiter without recourse. The sale had been concluded, the asset had been sold, the balance sheet showed a debit to medium-term notes receivable and a credit to cash. SCC had successfully met the buyer's needs without compromising its own position.

Following the first transaction in Sri Lanka, the company redefined the role of the finance director to include direct involvement in the selling process. SCC management realized that financing, particularly in the emerging markets, is a more powerful selling tool than offering significant discounts on sales contracts, and much more profitable. In the process of concluding its first transaction, SCC learned to start the transaction process by defining the exit strategy for a potential receivable. Then, by carefully analyzing the estimated costs associated with the eventual sale of the asset, it determined how to construct the pricing of the sales proposal. If a prospective transaction is too difficult, risky, or complex to devise a viable exit strategy, the company would revert to its traditionally conservative credit policy and require confirmed letters of credit or cash in advance.

As a footnote, SCC subsequently used the identical documentary structure and financial modeling process to conclude six additional contracts in Sri Lanka in the following three years as well as numerous other contracts in countries such as Bangladesh, Indonesia, and Colombia.

PART SEVEN

GOVERNMENT PROGRAMS

Few companies think of federal export and finance programs when they run into a problem sale. Yet they should. The federal government has a number of excellent programs designed to help smaller and midsize companies export U.S. goods. These financing programs can mean the difference between a sale happening and one not taking place.

The government often offers coverage in countries where traditional credit insurers will not go. Chapter 20, on government programs, was written by a representative from the Department of Commerce and contains a very thorough overview of what is available.

The Data Protection Act, which went into effect in 2000, forces companies to change the way they obtain credit information. In the good old days, it was possible to pull a credit report on anyone without his or her authorization. In fact, some credit reporting systems were set up so that when a report was pulled on a company, links to the personal credit reports of company officials were included. With just a few clicks of a mouse, anyone's credit report was available. No more. Chapter 21 explains the implications of the new law.

20

Tapping Federal Export Finance Programs

John Shuman

U.S. Department of Commerce, International Trade Administration

One of the most overlooked and underrated resources credit professionals can use to limit risk are the programs offered by the Federal government. While many have limits and restrictions, these programs are of great use to those looking to sell into risky countries and those just beginning to export. The bulk of the $958.5 billion in U.S. exports of goods and services in fiscal year (FY) 1999 was financed without official support. Exports are financed through a myriad of means. They can be sold on open account directly to the foreign buyer, on letter-of-credit terms, or financed by commercial banks. Export factoring, forfaiting, and even barter and countertrade mechanisms help finance exports without support from federal agencies.

U.S. GOVERNMENT SUPPORT FOR U.S. EXPORTS

U.S. government finance agencies play an important role in financing exports. Their primary role is to bridge the gap when private sector financing is not available.

One such case is coverage for country risk, which occurs because certain markets are too risky for the private sector or the cost of private sector financing is prohibitive. This is the reason why little official finance is provided to

This chapter solely reflects the personal views of the author and not those of the International Trade Administration or the U.S. Department of Commerce. He gratefully acknowledges the assistance he received from the Office of Finance at the U.S. Department of Commerce and the Foreign Agricultural Service of the U.S. Department of Agriculture in the preparation of this chapter.

countries such as Canada, Western Europe, or Japan. The flip side of the coin is that the bulk of official financing is provided to certain countries in Asia, Latin America, Eastern Europe, and countries of the former Soviet Union.

Another type of market failure is for certain groups of exporters that do not have access to financing or where the cost is prohibitively expensive. Small businesses or businesses owned by underrepresented socioeconomic groups, such as those owned by women or minorities, fall in this group.

The major U.S. government agencies that support U.S. exports and investments overseas comprise the Export-Import Bank of the United States (Ex-Im Bank), the Foreign Agricultural Service (FAS), the Overseas Private Investment Corporation (OPIC), the Small Business Administration (SBA), and the Department of Defense (DOD). Also, the U.S. Department of Commerce helps facilitate export financing through an Internet matchmaker program and a seminar series. In addition, a number of states provide financing support to exporters located in their jurisdiction.

These five U.S. government agencies (excluding the Defense Export Loan Guarantee [DELG] program, for which statistics are unavailable due to national security concerns) supported some $22.8 billion in exports for fiscal year 1999, the most recent fiscal year for which data is available. This is roughly equivalent to 2.4 percent of U.S. exports.

This chapter contains a brief overview of the programs of the major U.S. government export financing agencies. For more details, please consult the web sites shown for each agency.

EXPORT-IMPORT BANK OF THE UNITED STATES

The Export-Import Bank of the United States (*www.exim.gov*) was established in 1934. It is an independent U.S. government agency that helps to finance the overseas sales of U.S. goods and services. Ex-Im Bank's mission is to provide a level playing field for U.S. exporters by countering the export credit subsidies of other governments and by bridging export financing shortfalls caused by market failures. The bank strives to create U.S. jobs while supplementing, but not competing with, private capital.

Ex-Im Bank currently has a staff of approximately 427 employees. In fiscal year 1999, it authorized $13.0 billion of financing to support $16.7 billion of U.S. export sales. Its overall outstanding exposure worldwide at the end of that fiscal year totaled $58.4 billion.

EXPORT-IMPORT BANK PROGRAMS

Ex-Im Bank will consider financing the export of any type of U.S. goods or services, including commodities. To qualify for Ex-Im Bank support, the product or service must have at least 50 percent U.S. content and must not affect the

U.S. economy adversely. Ex-Im Bank is prohibited from financing defense or military items, with certain limited exceptions for dual-use items and items related to counter narcotics operations. Ex-Im Bank offers the following programs in support of U.S. exports.

- Working capital guarantees cover 90 percent of the principal and interest on commercial loans to creditworthy small and medium-size companies that need funds to buy or produce U.S. goods or services for export. Guarantees may be for a single transaction or a revolving line of credit. Guaranteed loans generally have maturities of 12 months and are renewable. The commercial lender sets interest rates. Certain lenders, experienced in the program, have been given delegated authority that enables them to commit Ex-Im Bank's guarantee without seeking bank approval of individual transactions.
- Export credit insurance policies protect against both the political and commercial risks of a foreign buyer defaulting on payment. Policies may be obtained for single or repetitive export sales and for leases. Short-term policies generally cover 100 percent of the principal for political risks and 90 to 95 percent for commercial risks, as well as a specified amount of interest. They are used to support the sale of consumer goods, raw materials, and spare parts on terms of up to 180 days, and bulk agricultural commodities, consumer durables, and capital goods on terms of up to 360 days. Capital goods may be insured for up to five years, depending on the contract value, under the medium-term policy, which covers 100 percent of principal and interest on the financed portion. Ex-Im Bank's credit insurance allows exporters to finance receivables more easily by assigning the proceeds of the policy to their lender.

Ex-Im Bank's export credit insurance program provides valuable support to U.S. exporters. Foreign buyers often expect U.S. suppliers to offer open-account or unsecured extended payment terms rather than to pay by letters of credit, which can be very expensive, or by cash in advance. Since short-term interest rates are quite high in many foreign markets, the ability to offer customers U.S. dollar credit can mean a dramatic increase in sales to these customers. With Ex-Im Bank insurance, U.S. exporters can develop and expand their overseas sales by offering competitive repayment terms while protecting themselves against losses caused by default of a foreign buyer for political or commercial reasons. Exporters also can obtain export financing more easily from their commercial lenders by discounting their insured receivables or by using them as collateral.

Ex-Im Bank has been working to further improve its short-term insurance programs. Recently, it announced several improvements, including lower minimum premiums, faster review times, lower information requirements for small transactions, and more consistency in policy reviews. Ex-Im Bank will accept a greater degree of risk by expanding exporter discretionary authority and by assuming more exporter performance risk. Also, it will evaluate applicants according to its stated credit standards for both exporters and foreign buyers. This new transparency is designed to improve underwriting consistency and overall customer service.

- Guarantees of commercial loans to foreign buyers of U.S. goods or services cover 100 percent of principal and interest against both political and commercial risks of nonpayment. The guaranteed lender sets interest rates. Medium-term guarantees cover the sale of capital items such as trucks and construction equipment, scientific apparatus, food processing machinery, medical equipment, or project-related services, including architectural, industrial design, and engineering services. Long-term guarantees are available for major projects, large capital goods, and/or project-related services. Ex-Im Bank's Credit Guarantee Facilities also can be used to extend medium-term credit to buyers of U.S. capital goods and services through banks in certain foreign markets.
- Direct loans provide foreign buyers with competitive, fixed-rate financing for their purchases from the United States. Ex-Im Bank's loans, guarantees, and medium-term insurance cover 85 percent of the U.S. contract price (100 percent of the financed portion) in accordance with export credit guidelines from the Organization for Economic Cooperation and Development (OECD). The foreign buyer is required to make a 15 percent cash payment. Maturities are determined by the OECD country classification, contract size, and type of project and generally do not exceed eight and one-half to ten years. However, in accordance with OECD guidelines, certain power projects and aircraft transactions may qualify for longer terms. The fees charged by Ex-Im Bank for its programs are calculated in accordance with an OECD agreement governing the fees that may be charged by OECD export credit agencies.

EXPORT-IMPORT BANK AND SMALL BUSINESS

The U.S. Congress has mandated that Ex-Im Bank take three measures to address the financing needs of small businesses:

1. Ex-Im Bank is required by statute to develop a program that gives fair consideration to making loans and providing guarantees for the export of goods and services by small businesses.
2. Ex-Im Bank is required to designate a director to represent the interests of small businesses.
3. Ex-Im Bank is required to make available at least 10 percent of its aggregate loan, guarantee, and insurance authority to support small-business exports.

Support for small-business exports is strong. In terms of the total number of approved transactions, small business transactions accounted for 86 percent of the total in fiscal year 1999. In that year, Ex-Im Bank authorized $2.1 billion in financing to support exports by small businesses. This represents 16 percent of total authorizations, well beyond the 10 percent set aside for small business mandated by Congress. The figure includes nearly $1.2 billion of export credit insurance in support of 1,531 small-business export transactions, $383 million in working capital guarantees supporting 312 small-business transactions, $514 million in loan guarantees supporting 71 small-business transactions, and $37 million in direct loans supporting four small-business transactions.

In addition, Ex-Im Bank offers specialized programs geared at assisting foreign small businesses that wish to purchase U.S. goods and services. These programs serve to increase access to financing for small-business buyers, which often cannot obtain from their local banks the financing necessary to purchase U.S. goods and services.

U.S. DEPARTMENT OF AGRICULTURE FOREIGN AGRICULTURAL SERVICE

One of the missions of the Foreign Agricultural Service (*www.fas.usda.gov*) of the U.S. Department of Agriculture (USDA) is to promote the sale of U.S. agricultural exports into foreign markets. One of the agency's major tools for this is to provide financial insurance to exporters, guaranteeing them payment on the export sales transactions they have just made. Administered by the Commodity Credit Corporation (CCC) of the USDA, FAS' export credit guarantee programs encourage exports to buyers in countries where credit is necessary to maintain or increase U.S. sales, but where financing may not otherwise be available.

FAS' financing mechanisms include the GSM-102 and GSM-103 Export Credit Guarantee Programs, the Supplier Credit Guarantee Program, and the Facility Guarantee Program. For all programs:

- Sales must be registered with the USDA prior to export.
- U.S. exporters, U.S. banks, and all importers' banks must qualify in advance with USDA. No USDA qualification is required for importers.
- U.S. exporters pay a fee calculated on the guaranteed portion of the value of the export sale.

GSM-102 AND GSM-103 PROGRAMS

These two programs underwrite credit extended by the U.S. private banking sector or, less commonly, by the U.S. exporter to approved foreign banks using dollar-denominated, irrevocable letters of credit to pay for food and agricultural products sold to foreign buyers. The Export Credit Guarantee Program (GSM-102), the largest program in FAS in terms of program allocations, currently has $4.27 billion available for fiscal year 2000. In FY 1999, the figure was $5.12 billion. Of that, $2.96 billion represented actual export sale registrations in FY 1999. GSM-102, the oldest FAS credit programs, begun in 1980, covers credit terms up to three years. The Intermediate Export Credit Guarantee Program (GSM-103), begun in 1986, covers longer credit terms, up to 10 years. The current total program allocation for GSM-103 for FY 2000 is $143 million. It was $337 million for FY 1999, and supported $44.2 million of registered export sales.

The GSM-102/103 programs rely on an irrevocable, dollar-denominated letter of credit. After the exporter and importer enter into a credit sales transaction, the exporter applies to the CCC for a payment guarantee and then assigns the guarantee to its U.S. bank. Meanwhile, the importer's foreign bank opens a letter of credit in favor of the exporter. Because payment is guaranteed, the U.S. bank can offer competitive credit terms to the foreign bank, with interest rates linked typically to the London Inter-Bank Offered Rate on a rate-floating basis. The follow-on credit arrangements between the foreign bank and the importer are negotiated separately and are not covered by the CCC guarantee. The exporter ships the product, the U.S. bank pays the exporter, the foreign bank pays the U.S. bank principal and interest, and the importer pays its bank under the terms of their separate credit arrangement.

Many emerging market economies are susceptible to political, economic, and financial uncertainty. Such risks are often enough to preclude the financing of a sale. Thus, by ensuring against all risk of repayment by the foreign bank, whether due to economic, commercial, or political reasons, a CCC credit guarantee allows sales that otherwise would not have taken place, thus promoting and increasing U.S. agricultural trading opportunities into new, emerging markets. In the event of foreign bank default, for whatever reason, and upon a ten-day notice and six-month claim filed with the CCC by the U.S. bank, the CCC will pay the U.S. bank any outstanding payment arrearage, provided that the necessary documentation is in order. The CCC will then attempt recovery against the defaulting foreign bank and share any monies recovered with the U.S. bank on a pro-rata basis of the CCC's level of guarantee coverage.

U.S. exporters make a sale, perhaps one they could not have made before. U.S. banks get business they can feel confident about. Foreign banks receive better terms and may be able to provide more favorable terms to the importer, who then can order more U.S. goods.

GSM GUARANTEE

The CCC guarantee typically covers 98 percent of the port value of the export item, determined at the U.S. point of export, plus a portion of interest on the financing. Both programs provide a variable interest rate coverage, based on a percentage of the average investment rate of the 52-week Treasury bill (T bill). For GSM-102, interest coverage approximates 55 percent of the T-bill rate; for

GSM-103, approximately 80 percent. (For non–interest-bearing letters of credit with maximum 12-month terms, GSM-102 guarantees 95 percent of the export's value.) Guarantee coverage is usually limited to credit extended for the value of the commodity only, even though the sale may have been made on a cost and freight basis or a cost, insurance, and freight basis. However, under special circumstances, the CCC may offer coverage on credit extended for freight costs.

PROGRAM FEES

To participate in these programs, the U.S. exporter must pay in advance to the CCC a guarantee fee calculated on the dollar amount guaranteed, based on a schedule of rates applicable to different credit length periods. For GSM-102, guarantee fee rates are less than 1 percent of the value of the sale, varying from 15.3 to 66.3 cents per $100 of coverage. Fees are higher for the longer credit periods of GSM-103, varying from $1.17 to $3.00 per $100 of coverage. The exact fees are based on CCC fee rate schedule announcements.

PROGRAM PARTICIPATION

The CCC must qualify exporters for participation before accepting guarantee applications. An exporter must have a business office in the United States and must not be debarred or suspended from participating in any U.S. government programs. The importer does not need CCC-approved qualification; however, importers in some countries may be constrained by their own government's rules and regulations concerning the importation of certain products or the ability to set up the letter of credit as required by the CCC.

ELIGIBLE COMMODITIES

USDA announces the availability of guarantees covering specified agricultural commodities for specific countries or regions depending on market potential. Typical commodities are food, feed, fiber, and associated products. Forestry, such as lumber and pulp, and fishery products can also be covered. The commodity or product must be one entirely produced in the United States or a product that is determined to be of high value, of which 90 percent or more by weight, excluding water and packaging, is produced in the United States. Examples of the former can include such diverse products as wheat, oil seeds, feed grains, cotton, vegetable oil, hides and skins, breeding chicks, and telephone poles.

Examples of the latter can include such products as canned fruit, peanut butter, and processed meat. The GSM-103 program, with its longer tenure, is focused on a more limited number of products, emphasizing wheat, breeder livestock, and feed grains. Manufactured agricultural inputs, such as pesticides, fertilizers, and equipment, are not eligible.

ELIGIBLE COUNTRIES

Interested parties, including U.S. exporters, foreign importers, and banks, may request that the CCC establish a GSM-102 or -103 program for a particular country or region. The CCC will make a determination based on the potential market development, expansion or maintenance of U.S. exports that credit guarantee extension provides, the country's ability to service CCC-guaranteed debt, the country's political stability as it effects such debt service, and the country's current debt status.

ELIGIBLE BANKS

Financial institutions must meet established criteria and be approved by the CCC before they can participate in the programs. They will be evaluated on their financial status in servicing CCC-guaranteed debt. The CCC sets limits and advises each approved foreign bank on the maximum outstanding amount the CCC can guarantee for that bank. New banks may be added or levels of approval for others increased or decreased as information becomes available. Banks operating in the United States that are owned or controlled by the government of the eligible country or by the foreign bank issuing the letter of credit cannot receive an assignment of the payment guarantee.

DOCUMENTATION

A CCC-approved foreign bank chosen by the importer must issue a dollar-denominated, irrevocable letter of credit in favor of the U.S. exporter covering payment for the commodity. The letter of credit, the related sales contract, and the deferred payment/credit arrangements between the issuing bank and the U.S. bank will specify documentary requirements agreed to by each of the parties. As the exporter assigns the guarantee to its U.S. bank, that institution may specify further documentary requirements as well. Additional documentation includes evidence of export shipment submitted by the exporter to the CCC and entry documents provided by the importer to the U.S. exporter.

Additional details on the GSM-102 and GSM-103 programs are available on the FAS home page (*www.fas.usda.gov/excredits/exp-cred-guar.html*).

SUPPLIER CREDIT GUARANTEE PROGRAM

On August 30, 1996, the Supplier Credit Guarantee Program (SCGP) of the CCC became effective. CCC's credit guarantee programs are designed to increase the buying power or liquidity of U.S. customers of agricultural commodities and products.

The purpose of the SCGP, like the GSM-102 Export Credit Guarantee Program, is to encourage U.S. exporters to expand, maintain, and develop markets for U.S. agricultural commodities and products in areas where commercial financing may not be available without a CCC payment guarantee. The SCGP emphasizes high-value and value-added products but may include commodities or products that also have been programmed under CCC's GSM-102 program.

The SCGP can help U.S. exporters of U.S. agricultural commodities and products who wish to provide short-term credits (180 days or less) directly to their foreign buyers. In contrast, under the GSM-102 program, CCC guarantees repayment of credits extended (usually by U.S. banks) to foreign banks, which, in turn, provide financing to local importers of U.S. agricultural commodities and products. Under the SCGP, CCC guarantees a portion of the payment of such credits when secured by an importer's signed promissory note.

Advantages

The SCGP may be helpful in countries where GSM-102 financing is limited because the CCC has reached its exposure limits for private foreign banks. In these cases, buyers need different credit options to finance purchase. The SCGP may work well for commodities and products that normally trade on short-term open-account financing. It also may be helpful in increasing exports of high-value and value-added products where supplier credits are normally extended for 180 days or less.

Foreign importers will benefit by avoiding the cost and formalities of opening a foreign bank letter of credit required by other CCC credit guarantee programs. The SCGP also addresses the delay typically experienced by importers in opening letter of credits. Because the importer rather than a foreign bank is the borrower, the importer enjoys full benefit of the credit terms guaranteed by CCC.

Risks

While the SCGP offers certain advantages, it also poses corresponding financial risks to CCC. By taking importer rather than foreign bank risk, the CCC recognizes that a higher default in payments to exporters or their assignees could occur. Accordingly, the CCC requires the U.S. exporter to assume a higher share of risk than under other CCC credit guarantee programs. The credit guarantee provided under GSM-102 traditionally has been set at 98 percent of principal and a portion of the interest. Under the initial phase of the supplier credit guarantee program, the CCC guarantees 65 percent of the export value with no interest coverage.

Because the CCC does not normally conduct credit analysis of importers, this level of coverage provides an incentive to U.S. exporters and their assignees to evaluate carefully the credit risk of the importer yet allow expansion of export sales. Also, the CCC's registration fees under this program are higher than those under the GSM-102 program.

Marketing Tool

The SCGP is a tool that exporters may want to consider when developing a flexible financing strategy. For example, how can an exporter expand sales and maintain profits without increasing risk? Under the SCGP 65/35 risk-sharing scenario, exporters could more than double a line of credit to a particular importer without increasing net exposure.

In the first three years of use of the SCGP, many U.S. banks accepted assignments of the SCGP payment guarantees. Banks have generally recognized the guarantee portion of the exporter's foreign accounts receivable and have advanced working capital to the exporter for the portion of the sale covered by the guarantee. Other banks, if they are able to assess the creditworthiness of the importer, may be essentially purchasing the exporter's foreign accounts receivable at a discount rate negotiated with the exporter.

Further Information

Additional details on the SCGP can be found on the FAS home page at *www.fas.usda.gov/excredits/scgp.html.*

FACILITY GUARANTEE PROGRAM

This program guarantees credit extended by U.S. banks to approved foreign banks to pay for U.S. goods and services used for agricultural infrastructure in importing countries, such as storage, processing, and handling facilities. Sales must be linked to projects that primarily benefit U.S. agricultural exports.

The guarantee covers 95 percent of principal and some interest (after importer's 15 percent initial payment) for terms up to 10 years. The Facility Guarantee Program (FGP) terms are very specific: credit may be covered by the CCC only when payment is financed under a dollar-denominated irrevocable letter of credit issued in favor of an exporter by a foreign bank that has CCC approval to participate in the program.

Additional details on the FGP can be found on the FAS home page at *www.fas.usda.gov/excredits/facility/html.*

OVERSEAS PRIVATE INVESTMENT CORPORATION

The OPIC *(www.opic.gov)* was established by Congress as an independent agency in 1971 but is directly descended from the Marshall Plan. OPIC's mission is to mobilize and facilitate the participation of U.S. private capital and skills in the economic and social development of less-developed countries and areas and countries in transition from nonmarket to market economies, thereby complementing the development assistance objectives of the United States. OPIC's programs fill a commercial void, create a level playing field for U.S. businesses, and have a direct impact in states across America.

OPIC's unique programs provide U.S. companies with political risk insurance and financing support when private sector coverage is not fully available. OPIC's investment funds provide the equity needed for local companies to generate business and economic development.

OPIC finances and insures new ventures and expansions or privatizations of existing enterprises involving U.S. private investors. The projects OPIC supports are financially sound, promise significant benefits to the social and economic development of the host country, and foster private initiative and competition. As part of its overall mission, OPIC also advocates the interests of the U.S. business community overseas.

OPIC currently has a staff of approximately 200 employees. In fiscal year 1999, OPIC authorized $4.0 billion of financing to support U.S. investment overseas. OPIC had an active worldwide portfolio of some $19 billion at the end of that fiscal year.

OPIC FINANCING PROGRAMS

OPIC offers a number of programs in support of U.S. investment overseas. The two largest comprise political risk insurance, which provides coverage against currency inconvertibility, expropriation, political violence, and finance, which comprises either direct loans or loan guarantees, although the former are available only to small businesses. Also, OPIC leverages private equity through its private investment funds program.

- *Political risk insurance.* OPIC can insure up to $200 million per project, with coverage available for equity investments, parent company and third-party loans and loan guarantees, technical assistance agreements, cross-border leases, capital market transactions, contractors' and exporters' exposures, and other forms of investment. OPIC offers special insurance programs for small businesses, infrastructure development, financial institutions, natural resources, and oil and gas projects.
- *Finance.* Offering loan terms up to 15 years, and a range of flexible financing structures and security packages, OPIC can help U.S. companies secure timely and appropriate financing for international projects. OPIC can lend up to $200 million per project on either a project finance or corporate finance basis in countries where commercial financial institutions are reluctant or unable to lend on such a basis. Project finance looks for repayment from revenues generated by the project itself, rather than relying on project or sponsor guarantees. Corporate finance looks to the credit of an existing corporate entity other than the project company to support debt repayment. OPIC financing support is available to ventures involving significant equity or management participation by U.S. businesses.

- *Private investment funds.* To address a lack of sufficient capital for equity investment in targeted regions or sectors in emerging markets, OPIC has made long-term loans to privately managed private equity investment funds. By providing access to long-term growth capital, management expertise, and new technologies, these direct investment funds act as a catalyst for private sector activity fundamental to the development of market economies. Investments by these funds also assist U.S. businesses of all sizes by developing new markets and opportunities overseas. OPIC funds have attracted major private sources of equity, including pension funds and other institutional investors. OPIC currently supports some 26 funds operating in every region of the world. Operating worldwide, sector-specific funds concentrate on environmental projects, on water, and on investments involving U.S. small businesses. OPIC-supported funds have helped bring economic development to people in more than 40 developing countries.

SMALL BUSINESS ADMINISTRATION

The Small Business Act established the SBA in 1958. It is an independent U.S. government agency that assists, counsels, supports, and protects the interest of small-business concerns and assists these in their start-up and growth. SBA is congressionally mandated under the Small Business Act to provide four primary areas of assistance to American small businesses: (1) advocacy, (2) procurement, (3) management, and (4) financial assistance. SBA currently has a staff of approximately 2,979 employees. In fiscal year 1999, SBA held a portfolio of guaranteed loans totaling more than $45 billion and extended management and technical assistance to more than 1 million small businesses.

SBA FINANCING PROGRAMS

SBA operates two main vehicles that specifically support exports of U.S. SMEs. These vehicles are the Export Working Capital Program (EWCP) and the International Trade Loan Program. However, SBA also finances exports through its domestic finance programs, most notably the Regular Business Loan Program and Certified Development Company Loan Program. Note that Congress has only appropriated funds for the agency to extend *guarantees,* not loans, under these programs. In FY99, SBA approved guarantees for 1,098 export-related loans totaling $392 million.

The EWCP accounted for 332 loan guarantees totaling $120 million in FY99. This program helps small businesses obtain working capital to complete export sales. SBA can guarantee up to 90 percent or $750,000, whichever is less, of a private sector loan. Loan maturities are for 12 months or less.

The International Trade Loan Program accounted for $40 million in guarantees for 97 loans in FY99. This program provides long- and short-term financing to small businesses involved in exporting as well as to businesses adversely affected by import competition. SBA can guarantee up to $1.25 million for a combination of fixed-asset financing and working capital. The working capital portion cannot exceed $750,000. Proceeds may be used to purchase or upgrade facilities or equipment or make improvements that will be used within the United States to enable the borrower to produce goods and services for export.

Under the Regular Business Loan Program, one of SBA's primary lending programs to small businesses unable to secure financing on reasonable terms through normal lending channels, SBA approved 43,639 loan guarantees totaling slightly over $10 billion in FY99. The proceeds from these loans can be used for most business purposes, including exporting. For the latter, SBA approved about 545 guarantees totaling $178 million in FY99.

Under the Certified Development Company Loan Program, where SBA works with regionally based certified development companies to provide financing to enable small businesses to create and retain jobs, SBA approved 5,280 loan guarantees totaling some $2 billion in FY99. For international trade, SBA approved 123 such guarantees totaling $54 million in FY99.

SBA TECHNICAL ASSISTANCE PROGRAMS

SBA also offers a wide array of technical assistance programs through its broad network of multipliers. These programs include:

- *Risk management.* SBA has developed an Internet-based tool to allow lenders to assess the foreign credit risk associated with export loans. This tool, called AExR Online@, enables financial institutions to make decisions easily about three primary risks in most export transactions: (1) country risk, (2) buyer risk, and (3) bank risk. Using SBA's AExR Online@, financial institutions will be able to quickly determine if SBA would consider the underlying foreign transaction eligible under Export Working Capital or International Trade Loan programs.
- *TradeNet's Export Advisor.* This is a one-stop online information resource for exporting (*www.tradenet.gov*).
- *Export Technical Assistance Partnership.* This partnership targets export-ready small businesses with customized training and counseling.
- *Export Legal Assistance Network.* This network sponsors a free initial consultation with an attorney to discuss international trade questions.
- The *Office of International Trade's web site.* This site (*www.sba.gov/oit*) contains a wealth of information for exporters.

DEFENSE EXPORT LOAN GUARANTEE PROGRAM

The DELG (*www.delg.org*) program allows the secretary of defense to guarantee payment of private sector loans extended to eligible foreign sovereign governments for the purchase or long-term lease of U.S. defense articles, services, and design and construction services. The purpose of the program is to enhance U.S. national security objectives and enable U.S. defense contractors to better compete in the international marketplace. The DELG guarantee commits the full faith and credit of the U.S. government.

The FY96 National Defense Authorization Act grants the U.S. Department of Defense (DoD) the authority to issue guarantees up to $15 billion in outstanding contingent liability.

DELG's documentation, procedures, country risk assessment, and foreign content regulations are similar to the Ex-Im Bank program. However, there are the following important differences:

- Limited export eligibility
- Limited country eligibility
- Comprehensive, sovereign guarantees only
- Longer repayment schedules
- No subsidies
- Nonfinanced exposure fee
- Credit agreement required
- One-dimensional legal relationship—DoD's relation is only to U.S. banks
- Governing law is New York

A DELG guarantee covers up to 85 percent of the contract value or 100 percent of U.S. content, whichever is less. Financing terms include:

- Disbursement periods for as long as five years, during which only interest is charged
- Repayment periods for as long as 12 years

The DELG program charges the eligible foreign country an exposure fee to cover the cost to the U.S. government of a potential default.

DELG guarantees are available for loans to eligible countries that are extended by approved lenders to cover the cost of defense items that meet certain criteria, including domestic content requirements. DELG eligibility requirements are as follows.

- Eligible countries fall within one of four categories as specified in the authorizing legislation:
  1. Members of the North Atlantic Treaty Organization (NATO)
  2. Major non-NATO allies
  3. Emerging democracies of Central Europe (as designated by the secretary of defense)

4. Noncommunist members of the Asia-Pacific Economic Cooperation Conference (APEC)

DoD will not guarantee a loan to a country that is ineligible for guarantees from the Ex-Im Bank of the United States. A country can be added to the list of approved if the authorizing legislation is changed. If a country loses its eligibility for Ex-Im Bank loan guarantees, it will be deleted from the list of approved countries.

- Maximum amount eligible for the DELG guarantee:
  — DELG guarantees are applied to eligible export items that contain a minimum 50 percent U.S. content. (U.S. content is defined as the contract amount less the foreign content.)
  — The maximum amount of DoD's guarantee is the lesser of 85 percent of the sales contract value (less ineligible foreign content) or 100 percent of U.S. content.
- Eligible export items are defined in the Arms Export Control Act (22 U.S.C. 2751, et seq.) and described in the U.S. Munitions List (22 CFR, Chapter I, Part 121). Appropriate export licenses from the U.S. Department of State are required before DoD will issue a final loan guarantee.

DELG guarantees may be applied to both direct commercial sales and sales made through the U.S. Foreign Military Sales (FMS) program. To participate in the DELG program, a lender must qualify for loan guarantees under the procedures of the Ex-Im Bank and execute the DELG Master Guarantee Agreement (MGA). This agreement provides the terms and conditions under which DoD will guarantee loans extended by the lender.

Approved lenders negotiate a credit agreement with the eligible foreign country for each specific loan transaction. DoD must review the credit agreement to determine if its terms are consistent with DELG policies and procedures.

DELG procedures closely follow those of similar programs administered by the U.S. Ex-Im Bank, which is generally prohibited from supporting defense exports. There are important exceptions, however, which include the following:

- Eligible exports are limited to those defined as defense articles and services in the Arms Export Control Act (AECA).
- The borrowing country must pay fees sufficient to cover all program costs.
- The exposure fee, which is calculated to cover the risk of a potential default, may not be included in the guaranteed loan amount.

DELG policies and procedures provide details on these important differences and others. Information on qualifying for Ex-Im Bank loan guarantee programs can be obtained by contacting the bank at 212-466-2952. Eligible lenders may execute an MGA by submitting a written request and $2,500 application fee to the DELG program office. The DELG program is a government-owned, contractor-operated program. The program is administered by

GRC International, an AT&T Company. All inquiries should be directed to Barbara Castanon or Lee Ann Wettherhan, program manager/deputy, respectively, at 703-506-5857/5450, bcastanon@grci.com/lwetterhan@grci. com, or by mail to GRC International, Inc. DELG Program, 1900 Gallows Road, Vienna, VA 22182. Interested persons may check the DELG web site (*www.delg.org*) or call the public information line at 703-697-2685.

U.S. Department of Commerce International Trade Administration Export Finance Matchmaker

On March 9, 2000, the U.S. Department of Commerce's International Trade Administration announced the availability of a dynamic new free interactive web site that exporters can use to quickly find financial firms that finance sales to overseas buyers. This service, the Export Finance Matchmaker (EFM) (*www.ita.doc.gov/td/efm*) contains the most comprehensive database of banks and other export finance service providers that offer a direct link to export financing needs. The program also facilitates the tedious task of locating new customers. By opening the door to a variety of export financing options offered by a diverse group of export finance firms from coast to coast, EFM provides U.S. businesses with a marketing tool to succeed in competitive international markets.

EFM was developed by the Office of Finance, a part of the International Trade Administration's Trade Development Unit. The program supports both the Department of Commerce's goal to be truly an e-commerce department as well as the International Trade Administration's mission to help U.S. companies sell products and services abroad in support of U.S. jobs at home. EFM supports a variety of export financing products, including preexport working capital, direct loans to foreign buyers, forfaiting, export factoring, documentary credit products, export credit insurance, and various other miscellaneous financial services.

Export financing firms define their target customer. Such firms know what they are looking for in terms of attracting exporters that are right for their risk appetite and fit their overall business strategy. On the other hand, the exporting business community knows its business and the direction in which it wants to go. EFM brings the parties to the table, moving them closer to successfully completing an export transaction, and at a faster pace than otherwise attainable.

EFM is quick and user friendly. Exporters simply fill out the online form providing information about a proposed export and sit back and watch EFM match their business to an export financing firm. The more thorough the exporters are in completing the form, the more precise is the match. Once EFM has matched an exporter to one or more export financing firms, the exporter can contact the export financing firm via e-mail through EFM. In the event no match is made, EFM suggests that the exporter modify its search and try again.

In addition to the matching function, the EFM web site contains extensive information on export financing, including practical references to other relevant government web sites.

For more information log on to the web site or contact the Office of Finance, U.S. Department of Commerce, International Trade Administration at 202-482-3277.

CREATIVE EXPORT FINANCING WORKSHOPS

The International Trade Administration's Trade Development's Office of Finance organizes workshops around the United States for exporters to learn the value of export finance as a sales tool and for staff at U.S. Export Assistance Centers to enhance their financing knowledge to better counsel clients.

These workshops highlight the competitive strengths and weaknesses of trade finance providers of preexport working capital, foreign receivables financing, and medium-term finance, helping exporters decide which type is best for their transactions. To help craft an international credit policy, experts focus on how to factor foreign company and foreign credit risk into a sales policy. Private sector financing firms are always highlighted. A current schedule may be accessed on *www.ita.doc.gov/td/sif/of.*

21

Data Protection Legislation in the United Kingdom

Mike Barry

Independent Credit Management Consultant

Protecting the rights and privacy of the individual is always a concern when it comes to credit checking and reporting. Unauthorized use of personal credit information is addressed through data protection legislation.

INTRODUCTION

In 1984, the United Kingdom government introduced legislation—the Data Protection Act—designed to protect any living, identifiable individual from the misuse or unauthorized disclosure of personal data about him or her. The act applied to data held on a computer system.

It was introduced at a time when there was a growing demand for credit in both the consumer and the commercial sectors, and that demand had created a need for lenders to have information about potential borrowers. As a result there was a rapid expansion in the credit status reporting market, resulting in credit agencies building huge databanks of information about individuals, their credit worth, and their payment performance. That information came from a variety of sources, including Public records, such as the Electoral Roll and the Register of County Court Judgments, and from information provided by the customers themselves.

In addition, lenders could feed information into credit agencies. Many large agencies developed sophisticated computer systems that enabled them to store and collate that information so that, in effect, they could provide a complete credit history of a person.

They then sold this information to lenders to assist the credit-granting decision. The lenders held that information in their own files, and developed their own databases of information relating to their customers and potential customers.

A lender obviously needs some information from potential borrowers to enable the credit-granting decision to be made. Borrowers gave the requested information to assist in the decision making. However, once that information was on record, it became available to others who might be interested in seeing it and using it for some other purpose—a purpose that customers had no knowledge of when providing it to the original lender.

A need was identified to control the way such data was obtained, held, and processed, and the use to which it was put. For example, an individual provided personal information to a lender, for the purpose of obtaining some form of credit. The 1984 act specified that the lender was required to advise the individual that the information was required for credit-checking purposes and that a search would be made with a credit reference agency, which would be recorded by that agency. The individual was required to give his or her consent to that.

The personal information provided was given for a specific purpose and the 1984 act directed that the information could only be used for that purpose. In the preceding example, the individual provided information for a specific purpose—credit checking. So that is all the information could be used for. It was not to be used for direct marketing or for any other purpose.

The act established a supervisory body, the Office of Data Protection, under the control of the registrar of data protection. The function of the registrar was to ensure compliance with the act, and to license those holding personal data. That included not only credit reference agencies but also credit granters who would themselves hold personal data about their customers.

The act required those holding personal data to obtain a license from the registrar of data protection and to specify, when registering, the uses that would be made of that data. So a business might register that the data it obtained would be used for the purposes of "credit assessment, debt recovery, and the prevention of fraud."

The 1984 act then set out eight data protection principles, designed to ensure that information was lawfully obtained and processed, used only for the purpose for which it was obtained, was accurate, kept up to date, and kept secure. However, the act dealt only with data held on a computer system. Manual records were not covered. So a person or business holding information on a computer or computer system required a license and was bound by the legislation. A person or business holding similar information in some manual form—in a filing system or a card index—was not subject to any of the provisions of the act.

DATA PROTECTION ACT OF 1998

The fact that the 1984 legislation dealt only with data held on a computer created the anomaly just explained. A large, and no doubt growing, volume of information concerning individuals was still held in some manual form.

The Data Protection Act of 1998 went into effect in March 2000. Under that act, data held on computer and in manual systems is controlled. In addition, the data protection principles were amended to extend the protection afforded to individuals.

As a result, data protection legislation will apply to the vast majority of businesses in the United Kingdom—all of which must be in possession of some personal data concerning their customers, held in manual form or on computer. As a result, the licensing process has been replaced by registration with the Office of Data Protection. The title registrar of data protection has been changed to commissioner.

Similar legislation is in place in all other European Union countries.

DATA PROTECTION PRINCIPLES

The Data Protection Act of 1998 redefines and amends the eight data protection principles introduced in 1984. Broadly, they define that:

1. Data must be obtained fairly and lawfully.
2. Data shall be obtained for only one or more specified and lawful purposes and shall not be further processed in any manner incompatible with those purposes.
3. Personal data shall be adequate, relevant, and not excessive in relation to the purposes for which it is processed.
4. Personal data shall be accurate and, where necessary, kept up to date.
5. Personal data shall not be kept longer than the purposes require.
6. Personal data shall be accessible to the individual concerned who, where appropriate, has the right to have information about him or her corrected or erased.
7. Appropriate technical and organizational measures shall be taken to prevent unauthorized unlawful processing, accidental loss, destruction, or damage to personal data.
8. Personal data shall not be transferred to a country or territory outside the European Economic Area unless that country or territory ensures as adequate level of protection for the rights and freedoms of data subjects in relation to the processing of personal data.

PERSONAL DATA AND PROCESSING

Personal data is information concerning a living individual (including expressions of opinion about him or her) that:

- Is being processed by means of equipment operating automatically in response to instructions given for that purpose

- Is recorded as part of a relevant filing system or with the intention that it should be processed by means of such equipment
- Is recorded as part of a relevant filing system or with the intention that it should form part of a relevant filing system
- Does not fall into the latter but forms part of an accessible record

In short, any personal data held concerning a living individual is covered by the act. "Processing" is defined as "obtaining, holding, amending, using and destroying."

MISUSE OF PERSONAL DATA

The legislation seeks to prevent information provided for one purpose being used for any other purpose without the consent of the individual concerned. Further, it prohibits the processing of data concerning individuals, unless the individual concerned has given his or her consent. That consent is given for a specific purpose, and the data obtained can be used only for that purpose. It cannot be used for any other purpose. To use it or to disclose it for any other purpose constitutes a misuse of the data.

One issue illustrating this misuse—and one that the commissioner is already addressing—is the Electoral Roll. An individual is required by law to provide information to enable an Electoral Roll to be created, which entitles that individual to vote. The law requires the individual to give that information "for voting purposes."

The commissioner questions whether, in those circumstances, the Electoral Roll should be made available to credit reference agencies, which use it for totally different purposes. The information is given for one purpose and is then used for another.

Initially, the commissioner suggested that an individual should have the right to opt out. To opt out by law, he or she must complete the Electoral Roll form but to say that the information on that form is to be used only for electoral purposes and no other.

At the time of this writing (summer 2000), the issue is still to be resolved, but is an example, perhaps an extreme one, of information provided for one purpose being used for another. The legislation seeks to address this problem by introducing the concept of advise and consent.

CONCEPT OF ADVISE AND CONSENT

Information must be obtained fairly and lawfully. This means that individuals asked to provide information must be advised as to who wants it, what it is required for, and the purposes to which it will be put. The individual must then give his or her consent to processing.

In the consumer credit market, it has long been the practice to include the required advice in the form of an agreement or application completed by the applicant and to obtain consent by means of the applicant's signature to that form.

It must be noted that this has not been the practice in the commercial credit market, where those applying for trade credit have not generally been advised of or given their consent to any credit searches that are made. Further, sole traders and partnerships are individuals; as are company directors.

So, if a trade supplier wishes to comply with the act, the "Advise and Consent" requirements must be complied with. If a supplier makes inquiries to check the financial status of a company or to hold information concerning a company, then as the company is not "an individual," the act does not apply. However, if the supplier wishes to process information regarding a director of a company, the director is an individual and is protected by the act, and the "Advise and Consent" requirement applies.

"Advise and Consent" will also impact on all businesses that, as a matter of best practice, carry out credit reference checks through a credit reference agency, take up trade references, subscribe to credit groups or credit circles, or use factors or credit insurers.

OBLIGATIONS OF THOSE HOLDING DATA

Those holding data must register with the commissioner of data protection. They must comply with the eight data protection principles and the "Advise and Consent" requirements.

Registration is affected by providing the commissioner of data protection with:

- The name and address of the data holder
- Whether there is a nominated representative of the data holder for the purposes of the act and, if so, the name and address of that representative
- A description of the personal data involved and the category or categories of data subjects to which it relates
- Details of the purposes for which the data will be processed
- Names of any countries outside the European Economic Area to which the data will be directly or indirectly transferred

Failure to register when required to do so is a criminal offense. Data users can commit other offenses, including:

- Holding personal data of any description other than that specified in their register entry
- Holding data for a purpose not specified in their register entry
- Obtaining personal data from a source not described in their register entry
- Making disclosures of personal data not described in their register entry
- Transferring data to a country not described in their register entry

The evidential requirement in respect of this offense requires that the data user must have acted "knowingly and recklessly."

A breach of the data protection principles does not constitute a criminal offense.

However, if the commissioner of data protection is satisfied that there has been a contravention, he or she has power to serve an enforcement notice obliging the data user to change its practices and remedy the breach. Failure to comply with an enforcement notice is a criminal offense.

TRANSFER OUTSIDE THE EUROPEAN ECONOMIC AREA

As noted, the legislation prohibits the transfer of data to any country or territory outside the European Economic Area (EEA), unless that country or territory has an adequate level of data protection for data subjects in place. The EEA comprises all existing countries of the European Union, together with Norway, Iceland, and Liechtenstein.

Clearly, if the intention of the legislation was to protect living individuals from the misuse or unauthorized disclosure of their personal data, allowing data to be transferred to a country or territory that had no data protection legislation might result in data becoming public knowledge. For that reason, the prohibition was introduced.

However, the Commissioner can allow transfer to countries or territories outside the EEA if:

- The transfer is necessary for the completion of a contract
- The data subject (the individual) has given consent for such transfer
- The commissioner of data protection is satisfied that there is an adequate level of protection in the country or territory to which transfer is proposed

RIGHTS OF THE INDIVIDUAL: THE DATA SUBJECT

As might be expected from the basis of the legislation, the individual (the data subject) is given significant rights under the act.

An individual has the right to claim compensation, through the courts, if he or she has been damaged by any contravention of the act. "Damage" covers financial loss or physical injury but not "distress." In normal circumstances, damages will not be awarded for "distress" alone. If a court is satisfied that the individual has suffered actual damage and that there is a real risk of further contravention concerning the data, then it can order the rectification, blocking, erasure, or destruction of the data.

There are, however, a range of other rights given to the individual.

A Right to Access

An individual has the right to make a request in writing to a data holder for:

- A copy of all data held concerning him or her
- Details of whom that data has been passed to
- The source of such data
- Details of decisions made about him or her by solely automated means

The data holder may charge a fee of up to 10 pounds for complying with the request and must provide the information within 40 days of the request. The response must be in a permanent form, unless this is not possible, or if the applicant agrees to some other form. Any "unintelligible terms" must be explained. The data held must not be changed between the receipt of the request and the dispatch of the information.

Some data is exempt from production. For example, confidential references given for the purposes of employment but not "credit references" are exempt, as are corporate financial information, examination scripts, and data that is subject to legal or professional privilege.

If an automated decision is made using personal data, and if that is the only basis for any decision significantly affecting the individual, then he or she must be advised as to the logic involved in making the decision.

An individual has the right to apply to a credit reference agency for a copy of his or her credit file. The agency must provide such a copy within seven days, on payment of a statutory fee.

Right To Prevent Automated Decisions

An individual can give written notice requesting that no decision that significantly affects him or her be based only on the automated processing of personal data relating to him or her. The data holder must respond in writing within 28 days of the request advising the individual of the action that will be taken to comply with that request.

In any event, if such a decision is made by automated means and even if the individual has not given such notice, the individual must be notified that the decision has been made by that process. That individual can then, within 21 days of such notice, request that the decision be reconsidered by means that are not automated.

That request need not be complied with if the automated decision is made in respect of a request to enter into a contract with the individual and the decision is to do so. In practice, this provision means that only automated decisions that result in "declines" give rise to the exercise of this right.

Right To Prevent Processing

If the processing of personal data is causing, or likely to cause, substantial damage or distress to an individual, then that individual is entitled to give written notice to the data holder to stop or not to begin processing.

The data holder then has 28 days to respond, in writing, stating compliance or an intention to comply with the request or stating any reasons for considering the request unjustified and whether and to what extend it intends to comply. Compliance can be refused if the processing is necessary for compliance with some legal obligation or is required "in the vital interest of the data subject."

Right to Accurate Information

Clearly, it is in the interests of the individual, as well as those of credit granters, to ensure that information held is accurate and up to date. Thus, an individual is entitled to see what information is held concerning him or her and, where appropriate, to have inaccurate information rectified.

The commissioner of data protection has power to issue an enforcement notice in respect of any breach of this individual right. Further, an individual has the right to apply to a court to have inaccurate information amended, erased, or destroyed. A court also may order that any third party that has been provided with the inaccurate data be notified of any rectification or erasure.

IMPACT OF LEGISLATION

It is obvious that the legislation will have an impact on the credit-granting function. Consumer credit agreements and documents used in account opening in the commercial credit sector will need to comply with the "Advice and Consent" requirements. U.K. businesses holding data on individuals will need to register with the commissioner and will need to ensure compliance with the eight data protection principles.

There will also, however, be an impact on the collection process and on the work undertaken to trace absconders.

The first data protection principle requires that "Data must be obtained fairly and lawfully." A credit granter has a duty to keep customers' financial details confidential. Passing such information to a collection or tracing agency is justified, but disclosing it to the customer's family, friends, neighbors, or employers would constitute unlawful processing.

Although it is permissible to write to an employer if a debtor has absconded, asking for information as to the debtor's whereabouts, the approach should not reveal the debtor's financial position; nor should deception be used, such as telephoning the employer pretending to be a friend or relative, or some official body. That would be obtaining information "by deception," and the information would then not have been obtained "fairly and lawfully."

If letters are sent to the debtor in care of the employer, the envelope needs to be marked "Private and Confidential." If an employer or some other third party agrees to forward mail, then such mail should be sent to the employer or third party sealed and marked in the same way.

Principle 3 requires data to be "adequate, relevant, and not excessive," and principle 5 stipulates that personal data "shall not be kept for longer than the purposes require." In the course of investigations to trace a debtor, information will be obtained from various sources—and it must be obtained fairly and lawfully. Information as to previous addresses or previous employers may be obtained and may help the tracing objective. However, once a piece of information becomes irrelevant to the task, it should be deleted so that the data held is not "excessive."

Data protection principle 4 requires that "Personal data shall be accurate and, where necessary, kept up to date." Inaccurate data held by those charged with account collection can cause distress or damage to the individual concerned—for example, if an individual is wrongly accused of owing money—particularly if that false information is passed to some third party.

The sales ledger needs to be accurate; customer records need to be kept up to date. Addresses, postal codes, and telephone numbers must be accurate and amended as necessary.

Those employing collection and/or tracing agencies need to be aware that those who act by an agent act themselves; the business employing the agency may be liable for any breaches of the legislation committed by their agents. Thus, it is important that a business deciding to employ an agency:

- Takes up references
- Promptly investigates any complaints about its agent's conduct and takes appropriate action
- Establishes a contract with the agency requiring it to comply with the provisions of the data protection act

The commissioner has issued guidance notes to assist in compliance with the legislation and has said that "Creditors cannot turn a blind eye" regarding the conduct of collection and trace agencies. While creditors are not required to regularly investigate and audit their agents to ensure compliance, they are expected to take some basic precautions.

Further, regarding information provided by an agent that may have been gathered by underhand means, the commissioner would be less likely to take action against a client who could point to a contract with and the agent covering these issues and, more important, that takes steps to enforce the relevant terms of that contract when problems arise.

Creditors, or their agents, who obtain information by deception will be in breach of the legislation. Further, if the techniques used to obtain that information were not only deceptive but also caused distress to any person, the commissioner might well regard that offense as more serious and worthy of prosecution. In this area, the commissioner is a prosecuting authority in his or her own right and will generally prosecute a case if available evidence justifies such action.

CREDIT CIRCLES AND CREDIT GROUPS

Credit circles and credit groups operate in some industries as forums for the exchange of information concerning the conduct of customers' accounts. Information concerning bad debts and payment performance is exchanged for mutual protection. The legislation does not prohibit the existence or operation of such organizations. However, a credit granter who is a member of such a body needs to advise a customer who is an individual that information concerning his or her payment performance may be shared among members of the circle or group. The individual concerned must consent to that so again, the "Advise and Consent" requirements apply.

SUMMARY

The legislation is complex and, while the consumer credit market, as a result of the 1984 act, has adapted its procedures to ensure compliance, the commercial sector will need to adapt also.

The commissioner of data protection has issued, and will no doubt continue to issue, guidelines designed to help businesses to understand the legislation and to comply with it. Although the legislation gives the commissioner power to take enforcement action, she has stressed that the general approach taken by her office is to encourage compliance with the data protection principles through advice, education, and negotiation.

To assist data users, the commissioner has devised lists of standard purposes, descriptions of data, sources, disclosures, and overseas transfers. The Office of Data Protection will give help in identifying appropriate standard purposes. Data users who do not wish to use one of these, or for whom a suitable standard does not exist, can register in their own words.

Further information, registration forms, and guidance notes can be obtained from the Office of the Commissioner of Data Protection, Springfield House, Water Lane, Wilmslow, Cheshire, SK9 5AX, UK.

PART EIGHT

BARTERING AND COUNTERTRADE

Some think of bartering as transactions that firms with poor-quality goods and little cash enter into. While this may occasionally be the case, it is no longer the only reason companies enter into such arrangements. Chapter 22 provides an overview of the topic, some useful links, and information for those who are considering countertrade as a real option. Chapter 23 offers a real-life case study of one company that found success through the barter market.

22

Countertrade

Mary S. Schaeffer

IOMA

When looking to sell into a less-developed country (LDC), international credit managers often find their professional skills tested to the limit. Many of the companies have no way to meet regular credit standards. To make matters worse, there are often additional foreign exchange issues. But this does not mean that the sale cannot be made. Few realize it, but countertrade is an often-workable solution. In fact, it is also used in semiindustrialized countries and when selling into central and Eastern European countries. Yet little is known about this long-standing practice.

WHAT IS COUNTERTRADE?

Countertrade is a resourceful way to arrange for the sale of a product from an exporter to a company in a country that does not have the resources to pay for it in hard currency. The problem is usually with the importer but may also be with the country's limited reserves. International credit executives who arm salespeople with an innovative countertrade solution give the sales force a competitive advantage. In some cases, the company that cannot come up with a countertrade initiative will not be able to sell in certain markets.

BARTER

The best-known form of countertrade is barter, the simultaneous exchange of goods. Countertrade experts say it is also the form least used.

COUNTERPURCHASE

Conversely, counterpurchase is the most common. This involves two parties, one of whom has goods that someone in the less-developed country wants and the other of whom wishes to purchase something, usually a commodity, from somebody in the LDC. In the simplest form of counterpurchase, payment never enters the LDC. Currency passes between the two other parties. More likely, a bank will be involved, slightly complicating the transaction.

Here is a simple example of a counterpurchase transaction. An LDC with a good supply of a commodity, such as soybeans, needs some personal computers. If a computer manufacturer needed some soybeans, the two could exchange the goods. However, not many computer manufacturers use soybeans. A company involved in the production of food products might—but the food company is not looking for computers. So the computer manufacturer ships the computers to the LDC, which in turn ships the soybeans to the food company. The food company then pays the computer manufacturer.

Occasionally, there are circumstances when the goods are not as disparate as personal computers and soybeans, and a barter can be made. However, arranging a perfect match can be difficult.

BUY-BACK

Those selling capital equipment or technology sometimes accept partial payment in the form of the goods manufactured with their equipment. This is known as compensation or buy-back. In these arrangements, the supplier of the equipment gets some currency in addition to the goods.

In a buy-back transaction, a producer of steel might send its goods to a foreign company, which would use the steel to manufacture a product, such as shelving. The steel producer would then buy back the shelves at a reduced price, in effect partially paying the manufacturer with the raw steel.

OFFSET

When two industrialized countries are involved in high-value contracts, such as aircraft or other defense items, offset is sometimes used. These arrangements tend to be reciprocal. As part of a high-dollar purchase agreement, say a $100 million worth of airplanes, the seller agrees to purchase $100 million of computer equipment from the buyer's country.

BILATERAL TRADING AGREEMENTS

Bilateral trading agreements between two governments are also considered countertrade. Bilaterals are used most frequently when the countries involved have centrally planned or controlled economies along with foreign exchange shortages. This assures a market for the goods of the controlled economy, which tend to be raw materials or farm products. The bilateral agreement assures the producer of a market for its goods and can be either a formal arrangement or simply an agreement to "develop mutual trade." Finding a counterparty for these transactions is not simple. Large commodity traders, banks, and independent agents arrange countertrade transactions.

If your company has a product for countertrade, do not overlook the newest resource to help international credit professionals: the Internet. There is a wealth of information and leads out there. With a little bit of digging, international credit managers will be able to provide the sales department with the leads they need to get started.

COSTS AND RISKS

On top of the typical costs associated with any type of international trade, there are the fees charged by the party who arranged the countertrade. Given the complex nature of these transactions, consideration should be given to the additional risks associated with these contracts. Delivery and performance, always a consideration, take on new layers of concern when timing differences occur.

The interdependency of two or more trades greatly increases contract risk. Many experts recommend writing separate commercial contracts for each leg rather than having one master countertrade contract for the entire transaction. The separate contracts can then be linked by countertrade documentation.

DOCUMENTATION

Never assume that the other party will perform in a certain way when entering a countertrade arrangement. The documentation, typically prepared by the party arranging the transaction, should:

- Connect all parties together
- State the purpose of the trade
- State the responsibilities of the participants
- Summarize how the transaction will run

The documentation should include:

- Terms of the underlying contract(s)
- Requirements of each party
- Any local regulations that affect the trade
- Timing
- Any financing requirements
- How the arranger will receive its fee

WHY COMPANIES TURN TO COUNTERTRADE

Risk Reduction

Initially, countertrade was seen as a risk mitigation solution. However, those embarking on this route should be aware that some countertrade transactions are quite complicated. The complexities can increase risk as the number of parties and currencies involved rises. Thus, to make sure that risk is really reduced, those considering a countertrade transaction should

- Fully research all countertrade regulations in the country of the trading partner
- Also research import/export regulations in the countries of all trading partners
- Make sure to include all costs associated with the countertrade transaction when calculating the profit and/or loss with the transaction
- Consider using a consultant for the first few transactions

Develop New Markets

Some multinational companies use countertrade to develop markets and increase sales of their base products. In the following case study in Chapter 23, an international credit professional explains how countertrade was used to facilitate trade into China. In this case, it allowed the company to enter a market that it would not have been able to enter using traditional selling terms.

Reduce Inventory

The cost of carrying inventory can sap away the profits from any corporation. A number of companies have discovered that they can reduce these costs by entering barter or countertrade transactions. A number of organizations will help firms arrange such transactions. These include:

- International Reciprocal Trade Association (*www.irta.net*)
- Corporate Barter Council (*www.corporatebarter.com*)
- Attwood Richards Inc. (*www.arintl.com*)
- Barter Corp. (*www.bartercorp.com*)
- Tradewell Inc. (*www.tradewell.com*)

GOVERNMENT POLICY

The U.S. government does not prohibit countertrade. The official position of the Commerce Department is that "the U.S. Government views countertrade as generally contrary to an open, free trading system but will not oppose participation by U.S. businesses in countertrade transactions unless such activity could have a negative impact on national security. All normal import and export regulations must be observed, as there are no special exemptions for countertrade transactions." In spite of this position, the Department of Commerce offers advisory assistance.

ADDITIONAL INFORMATION

International credit professionals who want to learn more about countertrade have a number of options at their disposal. For starters they can visit the web sites listed at the end of this section. The U.S. Department of Commerce has a useful publication, *International Countertrade—A Guide for Managers and Executives,* produced in conjunction with I-Trade. Commerce Exchange International's *The World of Countertrade* and the American Countertrade Association's *Countertrade Term Definitions* will both prove useful. In those situations where even extended terms will not get you the sale, consider a countertrade alternative.

In its online publication, *International Countertrade—Individual Country Practices,* the Commerce Department describes some of the requirements, commodities, goods, and services used in countertrade for different countries.

Some useful countertrade web sites are:

- *www.commerce-exchange.com*
- *www.countertrade.org*
- *www.i-trade.com*
- *www.barternews.com*

POTENTIAL PROBLEMS

Evaluate the risks involved in the countertrade transaction. These include:

- Assuring the quality and consistency of the goods to be obtained
- Assuring the delivery times of goods to be received
- Determining the reliability of the supplier

If delivery of goods takes place months or years in the future, consider the effects of changes in the value of goods over time. For example, the value of oil next year could be very different from today's oil prices.

23

Countertrade Case Study

H. A. (Hal) Schaeffer Jr.

D&H Credit Services, Inc.

During my years as division credit manager for the Optical Systems Division of Bausch & Lomb in Rochester, New York, I had my first taste in dealing with what at that time was referred to as "bartering," now more commonly referred to as countertrade. Countertrade as defined by the American Countertrade Association refers to the reciprocal and compensatory trade agreements involving the purchase of goods or services by the seller from the buyer of the product, or arraignments whereby the seller assists the buyer in reducing the amount of net cost of the purchase through some form of compensatory financing. Bartering is the exchange of goods or services of equivalent value without the use of currency.

A more concise definition in the case that I am about to present reflects the selling of one set of products to the people of another country in exchange for delivery of a different type of product normally sold to a firm's U.S. customers.

BACKGROUND

In this case, Bausch & Lomb (B&L) wished to sell its contact lens products to the People's Republic of China (PRC). At that time, confirmed letters of credit by a U.S. bank were not available through the PRC. B&L was left with a dilemma, since all businesses were government owned. With hundreds of millions of potential customers in China but no guaranteed way to get its payment out of the country, B&L had to become very creative.

In 1986 B&L owned the Optical Systems Division, which manufactured industrial and professional microscopes. B&L wished to enter the student microscope market, but it had no quality microscopes in production that would easily fit high school and college students' needs. Plans had been designed but no manufacturing had been set up to accommodate this market.

When hearing about the Contact Lens Division's problem with getting its funds out of the PRC, a plan was developed to have a manufacturing facility in China produce the student microscopes needed for the new high school and college market. Engineers from the Optical Systems Division were flown to the PRC to inspect the manufacturing facility that was being considered to create these microscopes. Engineering specifications were created along with quality controls for inspections and replacements of defective products. A contract that covered both the sale into and the sale out of the PRC was drafted to put this barter operation into action.

INTERNATIONAL CREDIT'S PART

As the division credit manager, I was involved in reviewing the final draft of the legal contract covering both shipments into the PRC of contact lenses and shipments out of microscopes to the United States. My greatest concerns were that the product received would be in insufficient quantity to cover new orders, political and economic risk of dealing with the PRC, the quality of the merchandise, the delays that could result from the manufacture of goods from a factory not owned or controlled by B&L, and the shipping of fragile goods from that great of a distance.

Having met with our engineers, who had inspected the plant and had worked directly with plant staff, I was assured that sufficient safeguards were in place in the manufacturing process. They also assured me that before any goods would be inventoried by us, a random sampling of the finished product would be conducted. Deductions caused by defective product are a constant nightmare that every business (and credit manager) must live with but can be minimized with instituting constant due diligence at all times.

HANDLING DEDUCTION ISSUES

When the first batch arrived, I became a fixture in the inspection area. Our microscopes had an exceptional reputation; I was not going to allow anything to diminish that reputation. As I had suspected, the first batch of microscopes were not up to our standards. The entire shipment was returned to the manufacturer at their expense.

The second batch sent to us (this after a very hasty trip by our chief engineer to the PRC plant facility) faired far better. We now had quality product to fill the orders of our valued customers. So was it time for me to relax? Not on your life! While we now had product to ship, we still had to make sure that when it got there, it still was in perfect working order. If it arrived damaged for any reason, we had to have product in inventory to replace it at a moments notice or suffer problems with not only our reputation but also our receivables. While it is always easier to have the local factory replace defective goods, it would be much more difficult to guarantee replacement if the plant in the PRC had problems.

I had recommended that for every 10 microscopes that were shipped out to our customers, we maintain two to three replacement ones until we had sufficient built up stock or were satisfied with the flow of goods from the PRC. Since the credit manager is typically responsible for deductions taken against invoices, he or she can be the "fire alarm" that notifies top management of deduction problems that are occurring on a constantly increasing basis.

The credit and customer service departments play a vital role in preventing deduction problems from becoming receivable problems. Communication and cooperation between departments must be the order of the day if a company is not only to survive but also to prosper and grow in today's very competitive marketplace.

TODAY'S MARKET

Today countertrade has become a very exciting way to sell goods to customers of all types and sizes all over the globe. Many large firms act as intermediaries, such General Electric, General Motors, 3M, Westinghouse, and so on. Countertrades resulted in sales of $4.3 billion in 1996 by over 350,000 businesses, according to Tom McDowell, executive director of the National Association of Trade Exchanges. Considering the volume and dollars surrounding this way of doing business, it is in every firm's best interest to consider countertrades before either giving up on a sale as being too risky or simply "fire-selling" excess inventory.

Some variations to countertrade exist and should be defined.

One variation is offset. It is (as defined by the American Countertrade Association [ACA]) compensatory, reciprocal trade agreements for industrial goods and services as a condition of military-related export sales and services. It is also used in the purchase of civilian aircraft and has become the norm in the aerospace/defense sector. Offset is divided into two categories, (1) indirect offset and (2) direct offset. Indirect offset involves goods and services unrelated to the aerospace/defense material being sold. Direct offset involves compensation in related goods and usually involves some form of coproduction, license, or joint venture.

Counterpurchase is an agreement whereby the initial exporter buys or undertakes to find a buyer for a specified amount or value of unrelated goods from the initial importer during a specified time period.

Technology transfer is the transfer of technology mandated as part of a countertrade or offset agreement, other than coproduction or license production. It may be in the form of research and development, technical assistance and training, or patent agreements between manufacturers. Technology transfer is central to many Third World enterprises, public and private, and is the focus of a large number of countertrade and offset deals.

I will discuss how the credit manager can live up to his or her motto of "maximizing sales, minimizing risk" and win a few brownie points in the meantime. If a firm sells internationally, there are always "land mines" to avoid in just conducting business on a day-to-day basis. Political, economic, and monetary risks are added to the normal risk involved in extending credit to a customer when a firm sells internationally. While not all countries that customers reside in are a gamble, credit professionals still need to deal with the local country's laws, customs, and currency fluctuations.

ADDITIONAL INFORMATION

The Internet

So where do you go to get the expert advice needed to open doors to the world for your products? Your first stop should be to the Internet to look for firms that perform this type of brokering for many other companies. Some of the largest include firms such as 3M, General Electric, General Motors, Westinghouse, and many, many more. Review carefully what they have on their web sites and look for what services that they offer. As an example, 3M offers credit services, customs clearance, financing for buyers, financing for suppliers, sales and marketing services, sourcing, state-of-the-art communications network, and transportation and competitive freight rates. Other firms may offer unusual or customized services that a more general firm may not offer.

You also need to be concerned about where your products are going to end up. If you have marketing agreements with other firms in certain countries, you will not want to jeopardize your relationship with those customers by having the same products as they sell for you show up in their area at a reduced price. A nondiversion contract can help with this and can be extended to buyers of your goods so they likewise cannot sell your goods in a restricted area.

The next very important area that you need to research is what will it cost (fees). While countertrades are an excellent way to sell slow-moving or excess inventory and your firm will certainly realize a better return on its inventory than "fire-selling" it, there still are costs involved. Some intermediaries charge an annual fee, a per-transaction fee, and a percentage of the sales fee. They also keep track of these transactions for the Internal Revenue Services so that taxes can be paid on the sale of these goods or services.

American Countertrade Association

Another area of expertise are associations, particularly the ACA. It calls itself an association of key U.S. manufacturers, exporters, and international trade financiers involved in selling and investing in a variety of industries (often of infrastructural and/or "big-ticket" items), including—but not limited to—electronics, commodities, telecommunications, power generation, defense, and aeronautics.

The purpose of the ACA is to provide a forum to educate and network to create ways to facilitate trade flows and investments into countries that either have difficulty externalizing hard currency or impose certain counterpurchase or offset obligations on vendors selling their products, projects, and technologies. ACA members tend to focus on ways to create financing and investment solutions to mitigate sovereign/political and commercial risk.

Financing facilities often deploy countertrade techniques that may utilize barter, clearings, credit insurance and enhancements, structured financing using offtake arrangements, counterpurchase, and so on.

On a much smaller scale there are barter brokers that handle only lower-dollar, less-sophisticated transactions between U.S. firms. They deal in mostly consumer-type products and services and help smaller firms either sell off slow-moving inventory or sell services during their slack time. The firms then use their built-up "credit" with the broker to "buy" goods or services that they need. Doing so allows firms to keep their cash flow intact yet still be able to "buy" what they need to run their business. There are some downsides to these types of transactions. One is that you still must pay taxes on the transactions but you can always write off your costs. Membership fees and transactional fees are involved with every "sale." Do not look to use this method of selling your goods or services as a means of "storing up credits"; you could lose them if something happens to the broker, or you may not be able to find a way to adequately "spend" them for goods or services that you truly need. No broker has access to all goods and services that a firm may desire so shop around for the right organization. Since you will also be owed "credits" to use for purchases, you should also make sure that the broker firm is creditworthy; that is, would you extend the broker firm credit equal to what it owes you in "credits"?

CASE STUDY CONCLUSION

Now that I have walked you through the world of bartering and countertrade, I will finish the case of B&L and the PRC. Once a steady flow of quality student microscopes was established, B&L felt confident to sell equally large quantities of its contact lenses and solutions to the PRC. Optical Systems Division engineers visited the PRC quarterly, and goods received at the U.S. plant were inspected vigilantly.

In 1988, B&L sold its Optical Systems Division to American Optical. At that point B&L had to devise another creative way to continue selling its contact lenses and solutions in the PRC. Likewise, the PRC was not receptive to discontinuing the manufacture of student microscopes that B&L engineers had worked so hard to help them design and produce. A three-way deal was worked out where the new owners of the Optical Systems Division would obtain the student microscopes and could sell them to the former B&L customers. Contact lens products would still be sold in the PRC, but now the new Optical System Division owners would pay B&L for the microscopes that they received.

B&L would receive a shipment inventory list from the PRC and would then bill the goods directly to the new owners. This was a win-win situation for all parties involved as quality inventory was received in the United States, quality goods were received in the PRC, and everyone profited from the sale and co-operation.

Does this mean that there were no problems or disputes? Not really, but thanks to the diligence of the credit staff involved in both U.S. companies, disputes were kept to a minimum. This was done by monitoring the quality of goods received into both the United States and shipped to the PRC as well as by staying on top of the receivables, inventory, and cash flow throughout the entire three-party business circle.

As a final note to this case, we as credit professionals must always be innovators when it comes to finding the most creative way to make a sale happen. While it is always important to be alert to credit risk and losses, we cannot afford to pass on an opportunity to grow and financially strengthen our firms. Risk must always be weighed against rewards; how our decision affects the company as a whole both negatively and positively must always be in the forefront of our decision-making process. Mere credit decisions are no longer acceptable; they must be sound business credit decisions that look at all factors not only from a credit point of view but also in light of internal and external factors that can affect a company as a whole. Always be alert to opportunities and be ever watchful of potential land mines.

PART NINE

LETTERS OF CREDIT

Letters of credit are the payment/security mechanism of last resort for many credit professionals. Many have a love/hate relationship with them. Regardless of how they feel, many must work with them. The most successful are those who understand what is involved and learn how to avoid the obvious mistakes.

24

Letter-of-Credit Basics

Mary S. Schaeffer

IOMA

Letters of credit are extremely useful in international trade, if used correctly. This means making sure that the letter of credit is filled out correctly and conforms to business requirements. Additionally, there must be adequate time for the business side of the goods to be delivered, the necessary paperwork completed and delivered, and the documents to be presented to the bank. All this sounds simple enough, but as anyone who has had anything to do with letters of credit knows only too well, "simple" is not a word used in conjunction with letters of credit.

WORKING EFFECTIVELY WITH LETTERS OF CREDIT

While letters of credit often fall under that old umbrella of "you can't live with them but you can't live without them," managers must find ways to use them effectively. A number of credit managers have come up with new ways to use these exacting instruments. While some of the following techniques may appear deceptively simple, they are often overlooked.

Standardization

With a one-size-fits-all approach, errors become less likely. Also, since fewer variances were allowed, the staff becomes more familiar with the fine nuances of their method. This policy also helps reduce errors since deviations are not permitted.

Customer Instructions

Send customers instructions on how to open letters of credit along with an application for opening accounts. By letting customers know all the fine points needed regarding the letters of credit, problems can be prevented before they occur.

Many assume that customers know how to get letter of credits. While this very well may be true, so many details must be put in a letter of credit that customers easily may put in something that does not match your documents. This does not make one party right and the other wrong, it just guarantees that the paperwork for the letters of credit will not agree and thus will be rejected by the bank.

Providing detailed instructions also makes it easy for the sales force to give the letter-of-credit information to customers. Most are not proficient at passing along all the necessary letter-of-credit data anyway. Finally, since everything is written down, customers can object if anything is not as it should be. This opens the topic for discussion before the goods are shipped and alleviates misunderstanding.

Working Closely with Banks

Many credit professionals report that a better understanding of letters of credit leads to more business written against them—business that might have been lost if they had not discovered this alternative to selling on open account.

Refinements

By using letters of credit that match the terms a company would normally request, a firm may be able to do business with entities that do not meet normal credit criteria without adding risk to the receivables portfolio. Letters of credit are one way to expand sales without increasing risk.

One-Source Routing

By routing as many letters of credit as possible through your main bank and its foreign affiliates, you will be able to improve the consistency of your presentations and payments. This helps minimize discrepancy fees. It also improves bank communications, which helps speed up payments.

By focusing on as few banks as possible for letter-of-credit activity, it is possible to speed things up. Ideally, this activity will be limited to only one or two banks. The added volume will make you a valued customer, which should in turn lead to improved service when things go wrong. Focusing on just a few banks also makes things easier on the staff, who then have to learn only how one or several banks do things. By limiting the number of bank procedures that the staff must learn, you also limit the number of errors made.

REQUIRED INFORMATION

Letters of credit contain much information. In order that such letters not be considered discrepant, every t needs to be crossed and all i's must be dotted. Make sure that your letters of credit:

- Are irrevocable
- Are dated

- Specify the beneficiary and the account party
- Specify the amount
- Are numbered
- Are issued on bank stationary
- Are signed
- Allow drafts at specific tenors to be drawn on the bank
- List the documents required

BANK FUNCTIONS

While a rose by any other name may still smell sweet, a bank by another name will not still perform the same function when it comes to letters of credit. The number of different types of banks involved in letters of credit and their respective functions can be confusing, even for those with extensive international credit and collection experience.

To help clarify, Fuller International's Louise S. Leone prepared the following list and distributed it at the international group meeting at National Associates of Credit Managements (NACM) Credit Congress. The list also defines the banks' roles in letter-of-credit transactions:

- *Issuing bank* initiates the letter of credit extending its guarantee to pay on presentation of proper documentation.
- *Advising bank* is usually located in the beneficiary's country. It delivers the letter of credit to the beneficiary.
- *Confirming bank* is usually located in the beneficiary's country and adds its guarantee of payment. It can be the same as the advising bank, but it also can be another bank.
- *Negotiating bank* accepts documents for examination for payment.
- *Paying bank,* where drafts are drawn, is nominated to make payment. It is also sometimes referred to as the drawee.
- *Reimbursing bank* is where the issuing bank maintains balances to fund the paying/drawee bank's payment to the beneficiary.

UNIFORM CUSTOMS AND PRACTICES 500

International transaction should be subject to the Uniform Customs and Practices (UCP) for Documentary Credits. The latest version, published in May 1993, is referred to as UCP 500. As those dealing in China have discovered, for example, the Bank of China is reluctant to include such a requirement. This has caused some concern in the credit community. Credit managers should be wary of any company that refuses to include the "subject to UCP 500" provision in a letter of credit.

The International Chamber of Commerce (ICC) views one of its core tasks as making it easier for companies in different countries to trade with each other.

The means for achieving this include the ICC rules for the conduct of trade and payments. The UCP is one such set of rules.

It had been revised to address new developments and technological applications and to improve the functionality of the rules. One of the complaints about UCP 400 was the number of discrepancies that appeared in documents allowing them to be rejected. It is not crystal clear that this problem is eliminated in UCP 500. Still, UCP 500 provides a level playing field for international trade. Remember, China will not include UCP 500 language.

For more information, contact the International Chamber of Commerce at 212-685-3454.

INTERNATIONAL STANDBY PRACTICES 98

As of January 1, 1999, standby letters of credit are governed by international agreement. The new rules in *International Standby Practices 98* (*ISP 98*), issued by the Institute of International Banking Law and Practice, standardize the rules for using standby letters of credit worldwide and allow international credit managers to negotiate standbys accurately, without being experts.

Once associated primarily with the U.S. market, the standby is now a fast-growing international product, exceeding commercial letters of credit in value terms by five to one. In 1997, over $450 billion in standbys were held by non-U.S. banks in the U.S. market alone. The *ISP 98* rules reduce the cost and time of drafting, limit problems in handling, and avoid disputes and unnecessary litigation that result from the lack of internationally agreed-on rules for standbys.

NEW STANDBY LETTER-OF-CREDIT RULES

The new, internationally recognized *ISP 98* rules are to standbys what the UCP 500 has been to commercial credits. They contain definitions of key terms, such as "original" and "automatic amendment"; cover the standby process from "obligations" to "syndication"; and contain basic definitions should the standby involve electronic presentation of documents.

International credit executives can obtain a copy of the *International Standby Practices ISP98* from International Chamber of Commerce Publishing, 156 Fifth Avenue, New York, NY 10010; phone: 212-206-1150; fax: 212-633-6025; e-mail: iccpub@interport.net (Publication No. 590); cost: $14.95.

SPECIAL SERVICES

Letters of credit can create such a hassle and take up so much time that several companies have sprung up to handle them for international credit professionals. These firms know letters of credit inside out and for a modest fee will handle the work. Among these companies are:

- Letter of Credit Expediters run by Steve Slavik. Phone: 503-280-0454 or e-mail: lcepays@teleport.com
- Quality Letter of Credit run by David Clemens (*www.qualitylc.com*)

TYPES OF LETTERS OF CREDIT

Many international credit and collection professionals have learned the hard way that all letters of credit are not created equal. While most managers are familiar with the details of the basic letters of credit, there are six other types, each with its own land mines waiting for the unwary:

1. Standby letters of credit
2. Revolving letters of credit
3. Deferred payment letters of credit
4. Transferable letters of credit
5. Back-to-back letters of credit
6. Red clause letters of credit

We will discuss standbys last as they have many uses and can be used to alleviate risk in rather different ways.

All types of letters of credit are used primarily, but not exclusively, in international trade, where they facilitate the process of paying for goods sold in another country. But they also can be used to guarantee a transaction. In those instances, there is no intent to draw against the letter of credit unless the prearranged payment is not made.

There are two other points to be made when considering any letter of credit.

1. All letters of credit should be confirmed, ideally by a financially sound bank. Some credit professionals insist on a U.S. bank, but a reputable European or Asian bank is just as good.
2. All letters of credit should be irrevocable. If they are not, they are not worth the paper they are written on. After all, when is a bank likely to revoke the letters of credit? Only at the point where the buyer's financial situation becomes so precarious that payment is in danger— and that is the very point at which the protective features of the letters of credit are needed.

Professionals who understand all the ins and outs of the different types of letters of credit are in the best position not only to use them wisely but to select the type most appropriate to their situation.

Revolving Letters of Credit

These letters of credit are typically used in those instances where there is repeat business. Obtaining one letter of credit to handle multiple shipments reduces the administrative work with the bank. Limits can be placed on the amount and the timing of each draw. In these instances, the letters of credit are intended to be drawn against. In order to do so, the seller presents the specified documents to the bank. Monitoring of such letters of credit is of vital importance; a missed date can mean not getting paid on a timely basis.

Deferred Payment Letters of Credit

These letters of credit are similar in many respects to revolving ones except that payment does not take place immediately. Deferred payment letters of credit are used in those cases where sellers agree to offer extended terms to buyers. With this type of letter of credit, sellers present documents to the bank as soon as they are received but do not receive payment until some agreed-on date in the future. Besides the security feature, there is the advantage of having such a letter of credit over selling on open account. Sellers can use the bank's promise of future payment to obtain credit from their own bank, effectively trading on the credit of the bank that issued the letter of credit.

The period of deferment usually exceeds six months, making this an attractive instrument in only a few cases—usually those involving heavy machinery or other goods where extended terms are more common.

Transferable Letters of Credit

When the seller of goods is actually only acting as a middleman, it may be necessary to have a transferable letter of credit in order to complete the transaction. Typically, letters of credit are not transferable. However, it is possible to have them marked as transferable. In these instances, the rights are passed on to the transferee (of which there can be more than one). All transferees must comply with the terms and conditions spelled out in the original letter of credit.

Usually, before any transfer is made, the beneficiary must request in writing that the bank effect such a transfer. This is one more step in a process filled with paper and details. It also presents another opportunity for discrepancies to creep into the documents and another opening for banks to bounce those that are not properly completed. Any problems will inevitably add time to the process. Those considering using this type of letter of credit should factor this potential problem into their time equation and make sure the letter of credit is issued for a long enough period to cover delays.

Many banks will not make transfers until they have been paid for their services—another cause for delay. Most experts recommend that when such letters of credit are used, the dates should be prior to and the amounts less than the date and the amount of the original letter of credit.

Some experts refer to transferable letters of credit as assignable letters of credit. The two are the same.

While the use of this type of letter of credit often adds complications to an already complex process, it is sometimes unavoidable. By knowing the possible weak points, the international credit manager will be able to gain the most from these letters of credit.

Back-to-Back Letters of Credit

These letters are usually preferable to transferable letters of credit, although banks are not generally thrilled with this type of an arrangement either. Again, they are often used by a middleman, typically one who might have trouble obtaining credit based on his own financials. With back-to-backs, the middleman asks a bank to issue a second letter of credit in favor of the ultimate supplier, using the letter of credit issued by the buyer as collateral for the second one.

In this arrangement, the terms and conditions of both letters of credit are identical except the amounts and dates in the second one must be smaller and earlier. The risk with this type of letter of credit is that the performance of the original letter of credit is contingent on the timely and perfect execution of the second. People using such instruments are advised to ensure plenty of time is allowed for delays.

Red Clause Letters of Credit

These type of letters of credit are useful to those sellers who do not have adequate capital to produce (or purchase) goods that larger customers have ordered or would like to order. These letters permit beneficiaries to acquire an advance of all or part of the amount of the credit depending on the details spelled out in the letter of credit. Upon instructions from the buyer, the issuing bank authorizes the confirming bank to make a cash advance to the beneficiary.

The beneficiary (i.e., the seller) must provide a written guarantee against documents evidencing that shipment will be presented in compliance with the terms spelled out in the letter of credit. A close partnering arrangement between the buyer and the seller is usually necessary for this type of arrangement to work. It requires a financially strong buyer and a seller with a desirable product but limited financial resources. When production is complete, the seller presents final documents to the bank for payment. At that time, the bank will make payment less any funds advanced.

If the goods are not shipped, the paying bank looks to the issuing bank for reimbursement, not only of the funds advanced but interest charges as well. This amount is then charged to the buyer's account—regardless of whether the goods are ever received. Obviously, this instrument is rarely used. However, it can be helpful in limited circumstances.

Standby Letters of Credit

These types of letters of credit are used most frequently to guarantee performance or for services. They can be found backing bonds, loans, or future interest payments. They are put in place as a type of insurance with the intent that they never be drawn. However, if the underlying obligation is not met, the beneficiary can, and often does, draw on the letter of credit. The bank honoring the obligation will then either debit the bank account of the issuer or convert the obligation into a loan.

As with other types of letters of credit, in order to draw upon it, the beneficiary must present documents to the bank. The exact documents needed, as with other letters of credit, are spelled out in the letter of credit itself. If this type of letter of credit is accepted by an exporter, it must be monitored just like all others to ensure that it does not expire before it is no longer needed. If this is the case, make sure to extend it—or draw on it if the other party refuses to cooperate.

Uses of Standby Letters of Credit. Under a standby letter of credit, a bank promises to pay the exporter/seller if its customer/buyer does not meet payment obligations as defined in the sales contract. The bank charges the buyer a fee for this. The Federal Reserve's board of governors (Regulation "H") defines standby letters of credit as "any letter of credit or similar arrangement, however named or described, which represents an obligation to the beneficiary on the part of the issuer:

- to repay money borrowed by, advanced to or for the account of the account party;
- to make payment on account of any indebtedness undertaken by the account party; or
- to make payment on any default by the account party in the performance of an obligation."

With use of a standby letter of credit, both commercial documents and funds generally flow outside the letter of credit (between buyer and seller). The letter of credit is "standing by" for an event of default or nonperformance before it can be drawn on.

Special Purpose of Standby Letters of Credit. Many people view the standby letter of credit as a special-purpose letter of credit. In such cases, the intent is that it will never be drawn but serves only as a "guarantee" of performance or payment.

Innovative Uses of Standby Letters of Credit. Letters of credit can be used in a wide range of situations. To help international credit professionals see some of the possibilities, the following list contains some of the more common uses for standby letters of credit. Many international credit professionals do not automatically think of standby letters of credit when analyzing a tricky credit situation. The list provides possibilities that might be applicable to their own operations. Then they can determine whether using a standby letter of credit will help them. Even if it is not something that will work now, it might be a good idea at some future point.

In addition to the uses specified in the section "Uses of Standby Letter of Credit," such letters may be used to:

- Guarantee payment or performance after a contract or bid has been awarded

- Advance funds to the seller to purchase materials for a project
- Back up the obligations of the seller should it not perform in accordance with a contract
- Provide assurance during a warranty period that a project will run smoothly after completion
- Back up underwriting obligations
- Allow a company to self-insure for workers' compensation
- Collateralize a loan
- Securitize a company's accrued vacation liability in order to accelerate the expense
- Help with local bid requirements for guarantees issued on the strength of the issuing bank's letter of credit in foreign countries
- Help companies backstop their environmental cleanup liabilities
- Improve the credit ratings of securities, bonds, notes, or commercial paper supported by a letter of credit
- Mitigate portfolio risk when securitizing assets
- Encourage investment in an area by enabling companies to access less-costly tax-exempt financing
- Subsidize investment in equipment that will protect the environment with tax-exempt financing
- Backstop a state's obligation when it issues notes that will later be repaid through taxation (this also provides a liquidity facility)
- Back up a commercial paper program that will provide low-cost, short-term financing and a liquidity facility

As you can see, standbys can be used in many different circumstances.

25

Letter-of-Credit Problems and Solutions

Mary S. Schaeffer

IOMA

Discrepancies and letters of credit go hand in hand. It is not possible to talk about letters of credit without talking about the problems that plague them. These problems are one of the reasons many international credit professionals would prefer not to use letters of credit. However, since letters of credit are such an ideal instrument for avoiding risk and getting paid, many international credit executives bite the bullet and work on minimizing the errors in them.

One such executive is John W. Dunlop, president of AVG Trade Group. He has developed a service that allows international credit professionals to initiate and transmit letters of credit over the Internet. The site, *www.avgtsg.com,* also has a letter-of-credit tutorial. International credit executives can direct their staff to visit the site to learn about letters of credit—for free.

Dunlop says that errors in letters of credit result in what he calls "unworkable letters of credit." He believes sellers contribute to the problem because they would rather take the risk of a bad letter of credit than lose the sale. The problem ends up on the desk of the international credit manager, who must figure out how to get paid *without* the letter of credit.

UNWORKABLE TERMS

"An unworkable letter of credit," says Dunlop, "is one that contains conditions that the beneficiary cannot comply with. The result is a discrepant submittal of negotiable documents and the loss of the protection."

Dunlop is quick to point out that unworkable letters of credit are different from unfavorable letters of credit. While there may be conditions in the latter that are not to the beneficiary's liking, these conditions can be met. With an unworkable letter of credit, it is physically impossible to meet the conditions either because two conditions contradict each other or because of timing or other impracticalities. The most common unworkable terms in letters of credit focus on:

- *Performance conditions.* Since the buyer does not wish to tie up credit for any longer than the minimum amount of time, the latest shipping date, the expiration date, and/or the presentation date are apt to be inadequate.
- *Document requirements.* This might include a requirement for documents that the beneficiary cannot produce or procure before shipment—for example, a signed inspection certificate from the applicant and a certificate detailing the origin of each component in an assembled product. Even if this information were known, American chambers of commerce will only certify American products, so any product with a foreign component would not be given a certificate, and this requirement would not be met.
- *Additional conditions.* These are requirements with which the beneficiary cannot comply. For example, consider the case where an applicant asks a beneficiary of a carriage insurance freight (CIF) shipment to supply a copy of the carrier's insurance policy instead of a certificate of insurance. Such policies are typically umbrella policies to cover the ongoing operations of the carrier and are not available to freight forwarders or their customers.
- *Ambiguities.* When two contradictory requirements are included in a letter of credit, the beneficiary has no way of complying. Use of the INCOTERM FOB (free on board) in one place and then a requirement that freight be prepaid to the destination is an example. Other vague terms such as "an original copy" or a "certified fax" make it impossible for the beneficiary to comply.
- *Country issues.* Certain countries have policies that make it difficult to use letters of credit. Most people are familiar with the Chinese abhorrence of confirming their letters of credit. Certain Middle East countries require certification that the carrier's ship will not make stops at ports they consider "politically incorrect." Japan prefers split bills of lading.

MINIMIZING UNWORKABLE CONDITIONS

While it is probably impossible to completely eliminate these unworkable items, international credit professionals can do many things to make sure these issues are either eliminated or dealt with in a timely fashion. Here's what you can do:

- *Identify the unworkable issues.* Start with the list of common items and add to it ones that recur.
- *Work with the buyer.* Often, buyers are not aware that these conditions exist in the letter of credit. Once buyers understand the seller's issues

with the letter of credit, they can negotiate with the bank to have them stricken from the letter of credit.

- *Communicate with the buyer about these conditions in writing.* In this manner, the new wording can be included, and buyers can give it directly to the bank. The change will come in the form of an amendment that should reflect the seller's recommended wording. The letter sent to the buyer should, if at all possible, include references to the letter of credit not conforming to Uniform Customs and Practices (UCP) 500. This information will be useful to buyers if their bank insists on its own language.
- *Provide the buyer with letter-of-credit instructions* that spell out the terms and conditions that should be included. If at all possible, make this a standard document that the sales force gives to all customers who are required to provide letters of credit.
- *Review the amendment as soon as it is received from the bank.* If it does not conform to what was requested of buyers, assess whether it is worthwhile to accept the amendment as is or request another amendment. Remember, in all likelihood, time will be running out.

For more information on letters of credit or handling letters of credit over the Internet, visit AVG Trade Group's web site (*www.avgtsg.com*).

COMMON PROBLEMS

Letters of credit cause more headaches for international credit and collection professionals than do any other collection mechanism. The reason for this, as anyone who has worked with letters of credit will tell you, is discrepancies. Yet despite all the complaints associated with letters of credit, they continue to be used by a large percentage of exporters. International credit and collection managers who want to be successful at their jobs need to learn how to minimize these discrepancies. Some theorize that banks like to bounce letters of credit because they then earn additional fees. Whether this is true or not, eliminating discrepancies is in the international credit manager's best interest.

By identifying the most common reasons for these errors, those using this wonderful tool for international trade will be able to avoid them in the future. These discrepancies tend to fall into three areas: (1) the goods themselves, (2) the procedures related to the presentation of the letter of credit for payment, and (3) the associated documents. Problems in any of these areas can result in the letter of credit being bounced back, additional charges being levied, or, in the worst-case scenario, the letter of credit expiring before payment has been received.

AVOIDING MERCHANDISE PROBLEMS

Sometimes the problems with letters of credit start before the documents are ever presented for payment. When a partial shipment is made, the shipping documents will not match the letter of credit. If customers increase their order, the documents will not match either. In both of these cases, the letters of credit need to be amended before they are presented to the bank for payment. If they are not, there will be a discrepancy, which will give the bank the opportunity to return the documents.

The goods described on the bill of lading must exactly match the description on the letter of credit. Similarly, the value of the shipment and its volume also must match. If there is a discrepancy in any of these matters, you will have a problem. So, get it fixed before the letter of credit is presented.

Occasionally, an exporter doing a lot of business with one customer will mix up shipments and end up presenting documents with the wrong letter of credit. Make sure all documents and letters of credit are reviewed carefully before they are taken to the bank. Careful review of the material has saved more than one credit pro from making this simple mistake, which, while not devastating, will delay payment for several days.

AVOIDING DOCUMENTATION PROBLEMS

The documentation itself presents numerous headaches. The volume alone can be stupefying. One of the biggest problems for exporters is missing documentation. Exporters can rectify the problem if they can locate the missing documents and if the letters of credit have expired. Do not let the time tick away on this one. Better to get the letter of credit extended then to chance its expiration. Often, this is easier said than done—especially if missing documentation is not the fault of the importer who may then be uncooperative in arranging for the extension.

Bills of lading present numerous openings for problems to creep in. Examine them closely as soon as you get them. Any changes made to a bill of lading must be signed or initialed by the steamship company or its agent. Even a missing date on the bill of lading can cause the letter of credit to be rejected.

Equally problematic are insurance documents, which also must match. The policy must cover the risks that are outlined in the documents. All the facts must match exactly. Descriptions of goods, pricing, and value are just some of the areas that can lead to problems. Dating is also an issue. Again, the endorsement by the insurance company, its agents, or the underwriters must be correct.

Not only must each of the documents be correct, but they must all conform to each other. Any discrepancies that are found must be corrected before the expiration of the letter of credit. Generally, if no time frame is specified, the beneficiary has 21 days from the shipping date to make these corrections. While that might seem adequate, 21 days can tick away quite quickly if no one is paying close attention.

AVOIDING PROCEDURAL PROBLEMS

One of the most common problems with letters of credit is that they get presented after they have expired. That's right, no one pays adequate attention to the expiration date, and, then, before anyone notices, the time period has elapsed. This can happen because a shipment was delayed and no one thought to go back and have the letter of credit extended. Sometimes the original time period for which the letter of credit is drawn is not realistic. In other cases, the time frame reflects everyone's best-case scenario, and we all know how often that target is hit.

When requesting a letter of credit, it is best to build in some leeway. Once again, this is often easier said than done, as the sales rep may not want to reveal to the customer that shipment may not occur under the ideal time frame. In international matters, it becomes imperative that the sales force or foreign reps, if they are used, stay in close contact with the credit and collection department responsible for the letter of credit.

If the time frame in the letter of credit is not realistic, do not wait until the last minute to ask for an extension. Ask for an extension as soon as the need for one becomes apparent. The salespeople may not be happy with you about this, but consider how happy upper management will be if the letter of credit expires after a shipment has been made and an extension cannot be obtained.

If you are going to present stale documents (i.e., missing documents after the 21-day grace period), call ahead to make sure the bank will accept them.

While some of the techniques discussed here may seem basic, they are very important to any exporter accepting letters of credit. It is easy to get caught up in the hundreds of things that busy professionals must do each day and let the mundane tasks, such as reviewing bills of lading, insurance documents, and letters of credit, fall by the wayside. This sort of carelessness has cost many firms and cost them dearly. Do not let it happen at your company.

COMMON MISTAKES

The following list was prepared by Bill Ezzo, vice president of Connecticut Bank of Commerce, and identifies the most common mistakes made in the handling of letters of credit and the specific section in UCP 500 that governs each issue. Based on this information, if a letter of credit is rejected, the international credit and collection manager can go to UCP 500 and read the section to determine if the bank action was warranted. The most common errors are:

- If the invoice value exceeds the credit amount, UCP allows the bank to reject the documents. Refer to page 44, article 37b of UCP 500.
- Unless specifically provided by the credit, the applicant must be the party commercial invoices are issued to, and invoices must be issued by the beneficiary. Refer to page 44, article 37a.

- Description of the goods in the commercial invoice must exactly match the description in the letter of credit. Many who have used letters of credit tell hair-raising stories about minute discrepancies in this area that have caused banks to reject their letters of credit. Refer to page 44, article 37c.
- The quantity of goods may not vary by more than 5 percent from that specified in the credit. There is no tolerance, however, in the credit amount unless specifically outlined. Refer to page 45, article 39b.
- In installment credits, any installment not rendered on a timely basis cancels the letter of credit for the remaining installments. See page 46, article 41.
- Documents must be presented within 21 days of shipment under a documentary credit unless the credit specifically amends this requirement. This is the type of detail that can fall through the cracks when the letter of credit is first set up and can come back to haunt the international collection manager trying to collect under the letter of credit. It illustrates the importance of getting feedback from everyone involved before setting up the letter of credit. It also demonstrates the importance of tracking dates.
- Allow sufficient time for document presentation and for all invoices to run past due prior to the expiration date of a standby letter of credit. What seems like a sufficient amount of time up front can turn out to be woefully inadequate in the face of day-to-day reality. Related to this is the matter of watching the clock once it has begun ticking. It is imperative that a tickler be set up so that the credit manager can have the letter of credit extended if the original time frame turns out to be deficient.
- Freight and insurance charges in the commercial invoice should agree with those in transport and insurance documents. This is one of those tiny discrepancies that banks love to use to bounce a letter of credit—and earn extra fees.

By identifying these common handling mistakes, international credit professionals will be able to catch their letter of credit fumbles before they happen—or at least before they get to the bank. This will save time, money, and perhaps a few gray hairs.

Pay attention to the details and watch the number of discrepant letters of credit plummet.

PART TEN

TECHNOLOGY

The credit world is changing dramatically and technology is a big part of the reason for those changes. The Internet might not have been part of the vocabulary of most people reading this book just five years ago. Similarly, on a shorter time horizon, encryption is not something most companies are doing routinely as part of the e-mail systems but will be at some point in the not too distant future. As fancy technology concepts become more commonplace, the credit world is adapting. Credit scoring, once used primarily in the consumer arena, is pushing its way into the business-to-business market and the international community as well. What is next remains to be seen.

26

Technology

Mary S. Schaeffer

IOMA

Technology is changing many facets of international trade. Exchanging information, the handling of letters of credit, and new payment and financing alternatives are just a few of the areas affected. This chapter takes a look at three representative new methodologies.

TRADE PAYMENT WIZARDS

Business-to-business transactions over the Internet are the wave of the future. The trick for international credit executives is to find a way to facilitate the receipt of payment of these transactions. John W. Dunlop, president of AVG Trade Group, has come up with an innovative way to accomplish this. Called AVG Trade Payment Wizards, it was developed with the support of California Bank and Trust's International Banking Group.

Concept

The Trade Payment Wizards (TPW) provides business-to-business Internet web sites with an international payment method that is trade-finance based. It can be used for any size transaction, and transactions between two countries can also be managed. The only software required is Adobe Acrobat 4.0. The TPW consists of the

- Transaction information form
- Bank collection request and demand draft or letter of credit instructions

All the blank forms are located on the AVG web site *(www.avgtsg.com)* and can be downloaded for free. The seller completes the transaction information form with the buyer information, wire transfer instructions, and the sales terms.

The information form populates the corresponding fields of the CBT International Documentary Collection and Bill of Exchange to accomplish the payment function. The choices of waiver, protest, tenor, and notification are preset to eliminate delay and confusion.

All bills of exchange are two-party drafts between the buyer and the seller.

How It Works

Business web sites can link to the TPW (*www.avgtsg.com/wizards.htm*) page. Sellers can then select one of the required payment methods.

- *Cash-in-Advance TPW.* It uses the process of an international documentary collection against draft or clean collection. The bill of exchange with sight tenor is sent without documents for wire transfer payment to the seller.
- *Payment Against Documents TPW.* It uses the process of an international documentary collection against documents. The bill of exchange with sight tenor is sent with attached documents. These papers represent title that are exchanged for payment. Payment is wire transferred to the seller.
- *Payment against Acceptance TPW.* It uses the process of an international documentary collection against trade acceptance. The bill of exchange is sent with a time tenor of up to 180 days with attached documents.
- *Commercial Letter-of-Credit TPW.* It uses the export letter-of-credit instruction sheet to advise the buyer of the amount and the terms and conditions of the credit for payment.

Complete the TPW field information for the buyer, seller, and include the seller's wire instructions. Print the form, sign it, and attach the draft and shipping documents to the collection request. Send them to California Bank & Trust in Los Angeles. The bank will send the collection to its corresponding bank for presentation to the buyer and wire transfer to the seller's account.

If a letter of credit is used, print it out, sign it, and send the letter-of-credit instructions to the buyer. The bank will advise the exporter when the letter of credit has been issued. Of course, the exporter may contact AVG to manage the credit and prepare documents.

AVG offers a letter of credit over the Internet (*www.avgtsg.com*).

If users desire, they can become customers of the bank and have access to the bank's proprietary Internet-based trade-finance system to track all their transactions. Although there is no charge for use of the wizards, normal banking fees will apply.

Benefits

Dunlop points out a few of the many benefits to the TPW. They include:

- Simplicity of the system over the Internet
- Low cost with all fees being deducted from proceeds
- Acceptance in 200 countries that accept UCP/UCC standards
- Digital signature and Internet transmission enabled

International credit executives who are intrigued by this exciting new mechanism can visit *www.avgtsg.com* or e-mail at johnwdunlop@avgtsg.com.

OFFER EXTENDED TERMS TO CANADIAN AND BRITISH CUSTOMERS USING TRADE ACCEPTANCE AGREEMENTS

Help has arrived for those credit executives selling in Canada and the United Kingdom who need to offer extended terms. The Trade Acceptance Agreement (TAD), patented by Actrade International, provides that, once the buyer signs it, the seller will receive full payment within 48 hours.

Setting Up a TAD

An international credit professional interested in using a TAD would call Actrade and give it a list of potential customers and the following information, so the company can complete its credit investigation:

- Three trade references
- Banking information
- The latest financial statements (preferably audited)

Buyers like this program because it is off the balance sheet. Sellers like the program because it is nonrecourse—once the TAD has been signed, the credit and collection issues belong to Actrade.

The structure typically requires monthly payments by the buyer for whatever the time frame may be. For example, a 90-day TAD would necessitate three equal monthly payments. However, the seller receives its money up front.

The minimum transaction size is $2,500 and the maximum depends on the creditworthiness of the potential customer. TADs can be used for large transactions.

Costs and Fees

Actrade charges a 2.5 percent processing fee plus 1 percent per each monthly installment. Thus, a three-month transaction would have a 5.5 percent discount. On a hypothetical $60,000 transaction fee, the seller would receive $56,700 and the buyer would pay $60,000 in three $20,000 monthly installments.

Actrade has one special deal: a 30-day note at 2.5 percent. While at first glance this may seem costly, it is attractive to sellers who typically sell 2/10 net 30 and have customers who take the discount regardless of the payment timing. Not only does it guarantee the seller the money on time, it takes away the collection costs and hassles normally associated with chasing down delinquent payers.

Advantages

The main benefit experienced by users of TADs is improved cash flow. Any device that allows a company to collect in a few days instead of 30 or more will help. Use of a TAD lowers Days Sales Outstanding (DSO) figures, an attractive feature to international credit professionals whose performance is monitored on this criterion. The company can improve its relations with customers because it will not always be chasing them for payment.

The international credit professional who brings this program to the sales force should find that relations with it improve. Finally, companies that offer TADs to sell slow-moving products will not have damaged their reputations by marking down their merchandise to bargain-basement prices. They can simply offer extended terms and take a discounted payment from Actrade.

Nonrecourse

Although it may seem that the nonrecourse feature will put an end to the handling of unauthorized deductions and the like, this is not the case. The TAD operates like a lease. Customers will still bring dispute issues to sellers. However, the payment will not be affected.

BOLERO

As international credit professionals well know, ocean shipments can include one entire container filled with paperwork: bills of lading, bankers' acceptances, and letters of credit. Now an international initiative called Bill of Lading Electronic Registry Organization (Bolero) is aiming to change that by bringing bills of lading, the documents that represent ownership of goods shipped at sea, into the electronic age. A Bolero bill of lading provides all the benefits of an electronic waybill in addition to providing greater security and control over the export goods.

What Is Bolero?

Bolero International Ltd. evolved under the cross-industry stewardship of SWIFT, the Belgium-based global banking telecommunications cooperative with over 3,000 banks worldwide, and Through Transport Club (TTC), the London-headquartered mutual cargo insurance organization owned by over 5,000 transport operators. In unison with the Bolero Association, a 200-member special interest group formed in 1995, and a project team conducted two years of extensive market, legal, and technical research involving hundreds of companies and industry organizations around the world. The initiative is backed by a user group consisting of exporters, importers, bankers, freight forwarders, insurers, and carriers, most of whom have been part of the planning and will participate in the trial.

Why Switch from Paper?

The estimated global cost of administering paper bills of lading and other nonnegotiable trade documents is a staggering $400 billion annually. That is not all: The process is also inefficient, time-consuming, and wide open to fraud, forgery, and error. Bolero's secure, single window of communication to the entire global trade community can potentially reduce problems of fraudulent presentation of counterfeit documents at dockside and lower the incidence of goods being held by ports and terminal operators due to discrepancy of documents.

In addition, today's paper-based system is unable to meet the growing pressure from exporters and importers to eliminate delivery delays and to further just-in-time processes.

How Bolero Works

Bolero uses a central electronic registry and encrypted digital "signatures" to replace bills of lading and their actual ink signatures. Participating users will be organized into trading "strings" made up of specific exporters, importers, forwarders, ocean carriers, insurers, and banks. Instead of receivers of goods appearing at ports with bills of lading, the trading strings will carry out electronic exchange of ownership through a computerized registry.

Title transfer, along with exchanges of payment, delivery, and shipping instructions, will be secured through the encrypted signatures. These will consist of unique combinations of the computer codes of senders and receivers in addition to elements of the message sent. Users will be able to communicate with Bolero over either public or private networks.

Bolero's centralized application will allow export managers to send messages from point A to point B either by manually preparing them on a forms-based interface or on a Netscape Navigator web browser. Communication with Bolero can take place through a proprietary information technology network or the Internet with free, downloadable plug-ins. Another alternative is an automated gateway through which an application will feed messages automatically into Bolero's system. Interfaces, card readers, and business applications can be developed by third parties.

Bolero "Rule Book"

What will govern trading in this paperless universe, given the vast body of often conflicting national laws and international conventions that currently exists? All users will be required to agree in advance to the terms and procedures of the Bolero "Rule Book," a binding multilateral floating agreement between participating parties.

The rule book applies only to communication over the Bolero system and is designed to allow ownership transfers in cyberspace without generating lawsuits. The Bolero system will not own the data it holds; documents will retain their integrity since the system will not manipulate any data. The rule book is based on exhaustive work by a team of lawyers.

Paper Will Not Disappear

Export professionals should note that for the foreseeable future, paper bills of lading will still exist, due to several factors:

- Most developing countries are not wired for electronic commerce and require paper bills of lading for many goods.
- Some exporters may insist on paper bills of lading at the demand of banks issuing letters of credit.
- The Bolero system is not intended for payment messaging or financing transactions.
- Although the intention is to expand Bolero to air freight eventually, for the present the system is focusing only on ocean transactions.

International credit professionals wishing to learn more about this project should visit the web site *(www.boleroproject.com)*.

Getting Started

The Bolero organizers state that there are no size restrictions for companies wishing to participate. Joining Bolero is not difficult. Since it affects both shipping and credit, credit professionals might want to discuss the matter internally with the logistics manager or export manager. Once a company has joined, it has the opportunity to offer input to future working groups.

Users will have to sign the Bolero rule book and the Bolero service contract. In addition, to use the process, users will need certain hardware and software—none of which is excessively expensive and most of which you may already own.

What Is Needed

At the simplest level, users need to connect to the Internet with a Pentium PC that has

- 233 megahertz
- 64 megabytes of RAM
- Windows 95 or NT or higher

Additionally, users will need:

- Downloadable Bolero freeware
- An Internet browser
- A smart card and reader

The last requirement will enable users to generate the necessary digital signatures to secure the messaging. Large-volume users might want to hire a vendor to develop automated gateways and fully integrated applications to interface with their back-office processing systems, but these are not required to use the system.

A Word about the "Rule Book"

Key to making a process like this work is establishing a set of rules that everyone will abide by. Establishing such guidelines for companies in every country around the world was not easy. The Bolero rule book allows any dispute to be resolved in the same way as it would be with paper documentation. Signing the globally patented rule book will be a precondition to using Bolero.

Bolero offers a common set of rules that allow participants to replicate the commercial and legal outcome of transactions that were previously paper-based. One of the main precepts of Bolero is that its use does not affect the underlying transaction.

The rules were established through an exhaustive process that began with analysis of the traditional functions, documents, and methodologies. Based on this analysis, a set of rules was drafted. The rules were then tested against the law in major commercial jurisdictions and redrafted to take into account results of the testing phase. They were also circulated to potential users, industry trade associations, practicing lawyers, and academics. The Bolero rule book is a contract that melds technology to the legal framework and is crucial to the success of Bolero.

Those interested in finding out more about the Bolero project or joining it can do so by accessing its web site (*www.boleroproject.com*).

The issues discussed in this chapter are just a few of the innovative ways executives are starting to use technology to change the face of international credit. We believe it is only the beginning.

27

Encryption

Mary S. Schaeffer
IOMA

The Internet has brought massive innovation to many facets of corporate life but has also caused a myriad of new concerns, many revolving around the issue of security. One of the ways that companies are beginning to deal with this problem is to encrypt data. What follows is based on several talks given by Chevron executives at conferences. It shows how one company looked at the issues and then devised a way to work with the technology and limit risk.

CHEVRON'S CORPORATE POLICY

Chevron's corporate policy states that:

Information and the systems supporting it are key company assets, requiring prudent and proactive protection by information owners and users alike. It is the policy of the company to secure these assets from external and internal threats through a combination of technology, practices, processes and monitoring, based on risk and the value of the assets. The goal is to minimize the potential for damage either purposeful or accidental, to the company's computer and communications systems, company data and information.

This policy allows Chevron to focus its resources to protect its most important asset—information. Like other companies, Chevron needs to protect itself from hackers, pranksters, dishonest insiders, competitors, and information terrorists. It is concerned about viruses, interception, prying eyes, alteration or loss of data, communication blocks, and system disruptions. However, the biggest concern is unauthorized access.

ORIGINS OF THE PROBLEM AND SOLUTIONS

Security breaches can arise in any of the following ways:

- An intruder masquerading as an employee
- Eavesdropping
- Data being changed en route
- e-mail addresses being changed en route
- Cracked passwords and IDs

Defenses that stop unauthorized access to computer information transferred over the Internet are:

- Authentication (digital signature-private key/hash)
- Encryption
- Digital certificates (ID validation/nonrepudiation)
- Firewalls
- Strong passwords

The consequences of not having these defenses can be severe. Financial loss, damage to the company's reputation, loss of business, legal actions, and the loss of strategic information are only a few of the possible results. When an employee has a laptop stolen, the biggest loss is not the cost of the laptop but the strategic information stored on the hard drive. Thus, Chevron relies on what it calls "secured messaging."

SECURED MESSAGING

Secured messaging is the use of encryption and digital signatures. Before defining what a digital signature is, let us focus on what it is not. It is *not* a digitized signature—the manual signature by an individual on an electronic device such as those used by certain department stores for charge card purchases.

- *Digital signature.* Unique to the person and using a private key, digital signatures can be verified as belonging specifically and used solely by that person. It is linked to data, so any change to the data will invalidate the signature. It is also nonreputable, which means that people can prove they sent a communication and, conversely, cannot deny that they sent it. It is the equivalent in the paper world to getting a document notarized.
- *Encryption.* This is the ability to transform electronic information into an unreadable format that can be converted back to its original readable state only by specific individuals previously authorized to do so.
- *Encryption engines.* Also known as encryption algorithms, are encryption engines powerful enough to generate truly random keys, taking this responsibility out of the hands of people. It also allows for session keys that can be used once or multiple times and then discarded.

J	U	L	I	U	S		C	A	E	S	A	R
10	21	12	9	21	19		3	1	5	19	1	18

The sum for Julius = 92   The sum for Caesar = 47

$9 + 2 = 11$ $4 + 7 = 11$

$11 + 11 = 22$

$2 + 2 = 4$

Therefore, the hash total for Julius Caesar is 4.

Exhibit 27.1   Encryption Hash Example

BACK TO MATH CLASS

The word "algorithm" may remind some readers of their high school math classes. An algorithm is a detailed sequence of calculations performed in a specific number of steps to achieve a desired outcome.

A hash algorithm is a function that reduces a message to a mathematical expression and is called a one-way hash because the expression cannot be reversed. For example, if every letter of the alphabet were assigned a number (a = 1, b = 2, etc.), any name could be reduced to a single digit. One of the earliest users of encryption was Julius Caesar. Exhibit 27.1 shows how to encrypt the name Julius Caesar.

Altering any original message or file, including a change in the spelling of a word, eliminating apostrophes, or changing a comma to a period, will result in a different hash.

PUBLIC KEY INFRASTRUCTURE

Two sets of electronic keys are used to encrypt and decrypt documents: public keys and private keys.

Public keys can be shared while private keys are known only to their specific owner. An encrypted document is created using the sender's private key and the receiver's public key. The receiver decrypts the document using the sender's public key and the receiver's private key. The public key is the certificate authority. Separate pairs of keys can be used to encrypt or digitally sign to strengthen security.

Whatever is locked by a private key can be unlocked only by the corresponding public key and vice versa. Encrypting and sending with the sender's private key and the receiver's public key can therefore be decrypted only with the receiver's private key and the sender's public key. Use the private key to create the digital signature/hash.

Currently, a huge debate is going on over standards for the PKI. As a number of entities have a vested interest in becoming the standard setter, the debate probably will not be settled soon. Encryption concepts may be new to many readers, but it is imperative that anyone who works for a company that uses the Internet understands them. Remember, not too long ago, the whole idea of the Internet seemed alien.

CASE STUDY: USING ENCRYPTION AT CHEVRON

Project Scope

Chevron had three main objectives for the technology solution it devised:

1. Employ commercialized software to support encryption needs throughout the company.
2. Install software that would initially be used to encrypt e-mail and documents for storage and distribution.
3. Develop an application for the payment request process using encryption and digital signatures.

Chevron felt that it was important to use encryption to:

- Protect data from unauthorized access
- Transport confidential data across the Internet
- Have digital signatures for the authorization of transactions such as payment requests
- Ensure that the person who sent the encrypted note is the author and also to provide confirmation of receipt
- Prevent exposure of confidential data when laptops are lost or stolen
- Select an industry leader as a software provider to increase the chances of interoperability

Although many people within Chevron already use encryption with e-mail, it was the goal of this project to include those submitting payment requests and the international sales staff in that group.

Pilot Application

Participants in the pilot had very definite ideas about what they wanted. However, what they wanted and what was available were not quite the same. The pilot program had a number of objectives, many of which were technical and set the groundwork so the program could be expanded after the initial portion had been successfully implemented. The specific goals included:

- Creating an automated payment request form incorporating digital signatures

- Marketing the electronic form to company personnel
- Linking the payment request form to encryption (digital signatures and validation)
- Addressing the legal implications of digital signatures and human resources issues for inappropriate use

Developing an Electronic Form

The company now had the opportunity to reengineer its existing practices through the development of an automated payment request form. Specifically, it:

- Replaced all existing payment request forms
- Made blank forms available through the company intranet, eliminating the printing and storing of forms issue
- Included all pertinent fields for both domestic and international payments
- Included a pop-up window with help information for each field
- Employed encryption software for digital signature functionality
- Required multiple digital signatures for preparation and various approvals
- Prevented unauthorized changes due to the digital signature lockdown feature
- Allowed for the verification of each digital signature against the certificate authority file
- Included instructions for completion of the form and processing steps

Thoughts About Passwords

Use robust passwords, or those that include both upper-and lower-case letters and alphabetical and nonalphabetical characters. In addition, never share passwords.

Pilot Survey and Results

To make sure they were on track and to uncover any unforeseen problems, the team at Chevron conducted a pilot survey. Specifically they asked about the:

- Enrollment form and process
- Downloading and configuring of encryption software
- Downloading and configuring of electronic form software
- General instructions
- Ease of using encryption and electronic forms
- Technical support
- Results and recommendations

The company was pleased to find that user satisfaction was very high. However, it discovered that users wanted a hard copy of the documentation rather than being pointed to the Internet for instructions. The team was also able to identify who should be using encryption based on customer feedback.

It is likely that other companies will emulate the Chevron project as the technologies discussed in this chapter become more commonplace. Those who think that encryption is something likely to be used only at a few technologically innovative companies should remember that not too long ago, the word "Internet" was not even part of the vocabulary of most international credit executives.

28

Credit Scoring

Mary S. Schaeffer

IOMA

Credit scoring, long the domain of the consumer market and highbrow intellectuals, may finally be making inroads into the international arena. This chapter reports on a meeting of influential credit executives and influential organizations where the first steps were taken to formalize the credit scoring approach for international credit. An Associate of Financial Credit and International Business Executives, commonly known as the FCIB, joined forces with the Department of Commerce to begin discussions with 50 industry leaders on the use of credit scoring for international accounts on Tuesday, February 7, 2000. The talks successfully stimulated audience participation.

HISTORY OF CREDIT SCORING

Edward I. Altman, the Max L. Heine Professor of Finance at New York University, gave an overview of credit scoring. Credit-scoring models, he says, quantifies the probability that you will not be paid. These models are built by looking at a number of variables that affect this likelihood, then assigning weights to each factor. "Size," he warns, "is no longer a proxy for health." There is no such thing as too big to fail.

Most of what credit professionals know as credit scoring fall under the discriminate models category. This group can be further broken down as follows:

- Consumer models such as FairIsaac
- Z-score
- Zeta score
- Private firm models, which tweak some of the aforementioned
- EM (emerging market) score
- Others, such as bank specialized models

Z-SCORE

Specifically, Altman used the Z-score, the model readers may be most familiar with, to develop the EM scoring model, which is used for international accounts. See Exhibit 28.1 for an explanation of the Z-score. Now before your eyes glaze over, let me assure you that the example is just simple high school algebra and that you only need to know multiplication and addition.

Altman, who built his first model over three decades ago, does not see the original Z-scoring model as perfect. He says that the setting of the weightings can be a problem unless "you are brilliant." Unfortunately, few of us are brilliant all the time, and those who are tend to get promoted.

He also points out that when a company initially gets into trouble, some of the ratios actually improve before taking a nosedive. He gives the example of the current ratio, which with its increased accounts receivable and inventory would give the appearance of a successful company rather than one with bloated receivables and inventory, which may be overvalued and never sold.

Additionally, Altman does not like the fifth component (sales/total assets). He feels it does not differentiate between a healthy and an unhealthy company. He also says that variations from industry to industry and country to country are not reflected. A number of the participants throughout the meeting reiterated this last view.

Altman also insists that the credit-scoring model must be linked to a public bond rating. The score should be equated to a bond-rating equivalent that can be used to predict the number of years until default. Altman says that the initial rating of a company offers some indication of its eventual mortality.

$$Z = a1x1 + a2x2 + a3x3 + a4x4 + a5x5$$

where Z = the discriminant score

and x1 = working capital/total assets
     x2 = retained earnings/total assets
     x3 = EBIT/total assets
     x4 = market value of equity/value of total liabilities
     x5 = sales/total assets

     a1 = 1.2
     a2 = 1.4
     a3 = 3.3
     a4 = .6
     a5 = .999

Exhibit 28.1 Traditional Z-Score Model
Source: Edward Altman.

EMERGING MARKET MODEL

Altman took the traditional Z-score model and refined it to take out all the biases he saw in it. He also took it to ground zero, where a company that has a score higher than 0 was not likely to default and one that has a score below 0 was likely to default. He looked at companies one year before bankruptcy and determined that their score at that point was -3.25. Thus, by incorporating a constant into the equation, he was able to get to the 0 point. He says that a score of 0 is equivalent to a D rating from Standard & Poor's (S&P). (See Exhibit 28.2 for an explanation of the basic EM model.)

His model varies from the S&P and Moody's model in one significant way. He says these two institutions have a policy of "Thou shalt not have a rating higher than the sovereign rating." He does not ascribe to this policy and allows companies to have a rating higher than their country rating if the numbers so indicate. Here are Altman's steps to calculating a rating on an international company:

1. Convert the rating to a U.S. bond equivalent rating.
2. Adjust the bond rating for the vulnerability of the foreign currency to fluctuation. Altman does this by analyzing each bond for the issuing firm's vulnerability to problems servicing its debts that are in foreign currency if the local currency is devalued. After making this determination, he assesses and revalues the rating.
3. He then adjusts for industry risk, penalizing those in high-risk industries and improving the ratings of those in low-risk industries.
4. He then adjusts the rating for a company's competitive position in its industry.

Score = 3.25 + a1x1 + a2x2 + a3x3 + a4x4

where x1 = working capital/total assets
     x2 = retained earnings/total assets
     x3 = EBIT/total assets
     x4 = book value of equity/value of total liabilities

Constant = 3.25

    a1 = 6.56
    a2 = 3.26
    a3 = 6.72
    a4 = 1.05

Exhibit 28.2 Emerging Market (EM) Score Model
Source: Edward Altman.

5. He also adjusts for the market value versus the book value, if the company is publicly traded.

6. He makes bond-specific adjustments.

One of the biggest issues, not only for Altman, but also for any credit professional attempting to do credit scoring, is the quality of the data, particularly when evaluating international companies. Altman says that if you do not have confidence in the data, you should give your rating a haircut. This is an extremely complex topic, and this chapter only touches on the highlights of the EM scoring model. Credit professionals who would like to read more about Altman's method are advised to purchase his book, *Managing Credit Risk: The Next Great Financial Challenge.* The book is available on Amazon.com.

BENEFITS OF CREDIT SCORING

The benefits, says Jacky Jamieson, vice-chair FCIB-NACM and director of The Credit Department, are many. Credit scoring can improve performance by streamlining the process that allows credit professionals to focus on the exceptional accounts and become more oriented toward servicing internal and external customers. Use of credit scoring gives credit professionals the exposure perspective while providing flexibility in mitigating risk. Credit managers can then focus on the overall quality of the accounts receivable portfolio.

Finally, and perhaps the reason many like credit scoring, it can focus credit managers' attention so cash flow can be accelerated. Those credit professionals who see some portion of their compensation tied to Days Sales Outstanding like this feature.

SOVEREIGN RISK

The subject of sovereign risk ratings putting a ceiling on corporate ratings was raised. Crowe Chizek & Company's project manager Ivo Antonov pointed out that sovereign default is not necessarily an indication of loss of payment, although often it is. So how should sovereign risk be factored into international credit-scoring models? One member of the audience indicated that his model used a 5 percent weighting for the sovereign rating. Bank failures are often linked to "the heavy hand of government," says Eric Falkenstein of Moody's. They do this through exchange controls, deposit moratoria, and Eurobond rescheduling.

TYPES OF SCORECARDS AVAILABLE

Credit scoring can be used for a variety of purposes. Dun & Bradstreet's Jan Rowland broke the applications down into two categories: applications and portfolio. She says that application-type models might be used to:

- Automatically approve or reject new accounts
- Set credit limits
- Price for risk

The portfolio models could:

- Monitor benchmarking
- Dynamically update credit lines
- Trigger collections activity on delinquent accounts
- Issue an "early-warning signal" on troubled accounts

Using credit scoring to review new accounts, a model could automatically accept or reject 60 to 80 percent of the new accounts, with an analyst reviewing those in the gray area.

Another innovative use of credit scoring was suggested by IBM's Mark Marinello, who indicated that it could be used not only to determine who would go severely delinquent but who would pay when a collector called. This would allow credit managers to get the most productivity from their collectors.

DeutscheBank's managing director, Gene D. Guill, suggested that credit derivatives could be used when looking at the entire portfolio. Doing so effectively transfers the risk away from the customer to the derivative's counterparty. Several credit insurers in the room pointed out that the same could be done using credit insurance.

SPECIAL INTERNATIONAL CONCERNS

American Express's Jan Wojciechowski spoke about some of the issues AmEx faced when trying to set up credit scoring to be used in many different countries, "You have to deal with cultural differences," he says. He gives the example of bankruptcy in Japan, which would bring great personal shame, more than it would in, say, the United States. These variations must be factored into the model.

WHAT CREDIT EXECUTIVES THOUGHT

The credit managers who attended the presentation were generally interested in pursuing the concept of credit scoring. "Our company is very interested in helping develop a reliable scoring model to use to establish customer credit lines and to alert us to weakening credit risks so we can take protective measures before a serious default occurs," says Novus International's Dave Marsh.

29

E-commerce and International Credit Executives

Dorman L. Wood

Dorman Wood Associates

Personal computers, the Internet, and now e-commerce have all made a serious impact on the way the credit and collection functions are handled. Moving forward, this change will snowball, and credit and collection professionals who wish to succeed will need to continue to learn to adjust in order to stay even. A quick review of some events over the last century show just how far we have come.

A number of events took place that progressively made our planet seem smaller. These include

December 17, 1903	Wilbur and Orville Wright successfully flew their *Flyer I* at Kitty Hawk, North Carolina.
May 20–21, 1927	Charles Lindbergh piloted his *Spirit of St. Louis* across the Atlantic.
June 1931	Wylie Post flew his Lockheed Vega around the world in 8 days, 15 hours, 51 minutes.
May 5, 1961	Astronaut Allen Shepard made a fifteen minute suborbital flight into space.
December 1967	The Concorde, the world's first supersonic commercial aircraft, made its maiden flight. AirFrance and British Airways later began transcontinental service with flights between Paris and London to New York in less than four hours.
1972	E-mail and the Internet made their first public appearances at the Internet Computer Communication Conference.

BACKGROUND

As historical as these milestones were, the development and burgeoning usage of the Internet must be considered as the most important. International credit executives worldwide are struggling with the growing challenges of doing e-business or e-commerce—more frequently referred to as business to business (B2B). These challenges include, but are not limited to:

- Instant credit approval
- Legal aspects
- Digital signatures on digital documents
- Security of information
- Information exchange
- Learning new technology

Call it what you will, e-commerce is changing the way business has previously been conducted—both domestically and globally. It is also forcing companies to reevaluate their organizational structures and corporate cultures. How big an economic force e-commerce becomes is the subject of much speculation by analysts. While estimates vary, most experts agree the increase will be huge.

OLD BUSINESS MODEL

The pre–e-commerce way of doing business was often slow and time consuming. The sales process, depending on the type of product or service involved, could span days, weeks, or months. The process often involved a physical visit (or several) by a salesperson. Product was often delivered for evaluation. Once a buyer had made a decision and submitted a purchase order to the seller, the order was entered into the seller's business system; then the seller's credit staff would begin their time-consuming credit investigation, analysis, and approval process.

The order cycle could take several hours or days, depending on factors such as dollar amount of the order and availability of credit and/or financial information on the buyer, to name two. Once the credit department had approved the order, it was submitted to manufacturing or to a warehouse for fulfillment. Following order fulfillment and shipping, an invoice was generated and mailed to the buyer. On the net or discounted due date of the invoice, the buyer made payment. Once the seller received the payment, it was applied to the buyer's account to clear the invoice. Under ideal circumstances, the entire process could consume 30 to 45 days.

NEW EXPECTATIONS

E-commerce has not only changed the business process but has changed buyer expectations. Through an Internet web page, also known as a web storefront, buyers from anywhere in the world can browse online catalogs of companies worldwide; view products (often in three-dimensional images with audio); download and test software or utilize temporary subscriptions to databases; place an order, choose a payment method, and complete a credit application; receive shipping advice and order status; make payments; and manage transaction records all through their desktop computers.

The e-commerce order cycle can be completed in a matter of minutes. The entire process is easily completed without buyers leaving their office, or even from their homes. Orders can also be completed during nonbusiness hours.

E-commerce seems to be ideal for speeding commodity orders worldwide and providing important information for fair pricing without regard to time zones. However, the anything-goes attitude that seems to prevail in the United States does not exist in many of the countries that are our most important trading partners.

Two factors that many companies cite as reasons for jumping on the e-business bandwagon are the promise of increased productivity and the creation of immediate supply and demand. The advantages that these companies hope to gain are:

- Less paperwork
- Fewer errors in placing and filling orders
- No time-zone worries
- Less on-hand inventory
- Betters records of product inventory and demand
- On-demand tracking of shipment status

EFFECT ON CREDIT

The promise of increased productivity has become a source of frustration for many international credit executives. The speed with which transactions can be completed via the Internet has created buyer expectations that may not always be met. The challenge of instant or very rapid credit approval tests even the most experienced credit executive. Although technology is now providing tools for gathering information, credit scoring, financial statement evaluation, and decision making, supply has not yet caught up with demand.

Consumer credit grantors have utilized such software or modeling for decades. However, the number of vendors offering these tools for commercial credit granting is limited. The available tools have been based on those used for consumer credit and are being adapted for commercial use. eCredit.com and C/LEC are two such providers of credit scoring for commercial credit grantors. Other players include CreditView, NMC Technologies, and Beaver Corp. Ltd.

Commercial credit information on international companies is available through a number of sources, including Dun & Bradstreet, Graydon America, and Veritas. International credit executives are now able to access, view, and download credit information through their desktop systems. Unfortunately, the information may not always be available instantaneously. Depending on the location of a potential or existing international customer, a credit report may not be available for 10 or more business days. In such cases, the credit executive is challenged to approve a new customer's order as rapidly as possible, while attempting to ensure future payment.

Additionally, international credit executives are still facing the challenge of keeping up with local political and economic conditions of the country in which their company's do business. Many international credit executives still believe that the best sources for such information are those they have privately and personally cultivated in-country through on-site visits and frequent contacts via telephone.

While credit executives usually have some basic, if not extensive, knowledge of the laws governing business within their own countries and/or states, many faced uncertainty when selling to foreign customers. Unlike the United States whose states recognize the provisions of the Uniform Commercial Code (UCC), foreign countries have not attempted to adopt such standardization regulations of business transactions.

ELECTRONIC SIGNATURES

Early in 2000, the United States enacted the Electronic Signatures in Global and National Commerce Act. Section 101 of the Act, entitled "General Rule of Validity," reads in part:

> *(a) General,—Notwithstanding any statute, regulation, or other rule of law (other than this title and title II), with respect to any transaction in or affecting interstate or foreign commerce—(1) a signature, contract, or other record relating to such transaction may not be denied legal effect, validity, or enforceability solely because it is in electronic form; and (2) a contract relating to such transaction may not be denied legal effect, validity, or enforceability solely because an electronic signature of electronic record was used in its formation . . ..*

While electronic signatures are readily recognized and accepted within the Unites States, many foreign countries have not been taken to this new method of contractual agreement with such enthusiasm. Consumers have come to accept various terms and conditions posted on the web pages they regularly utilize for shopping, travel, or seeking general information. "Do you agree to the terms and conditions stated above? If so, please click on 'Agreed' below." This is commonly known as a "click agreement"; by "clicking" you send a digital signature, which indicates your approval. This is the same basic type of digital signature that can be placed on a credit application form, contract, terms of sales, and so on, between two commercial firms. This information can then be archived for future reference.

EXPORT CONTROL ISSUES

The privacy issues associated with e-business affect companies and individuals alike. Many companies and individuals have concerns about "Big Brother" government monitoring e-commerce transactions through encryption programs. The United States and 32 other countries participate in the Wassenaar Arrangement (1996), the first global multilateral arrangement on export controls for conventional weapons, sensitive dual-use goods, and technologies.

Included on the list of sensitive dual-use goods and technologies covered by the Wassenaar Arrangement are high-end encryption programs. The United States prohibits export of such programs.

CREDIT-RELATED ISSUES IN E-COMMERCE

Although the design of a company's web storefront is not usually among the functions or responsibilities of a credit executive, if a company is going to conduct business over the Internet and extend credit, the credit executive should be involved. He or she can ensure that any credit-related documents posted on the web page are correct and request the required information.

Entering the global world of e-commerce may be an appropriate time for a company to reexamine its credit and collection policies and procedures. Disciplinary boundaries between the technical, economic, business, and legal aspects of e-commerce are blurred and porous at best. Currently, global standards for doing e-business do not exist. Therefore, it is suggested that companies address all pertinent legal issues (i.e., electronically submitted credit applications, purchase orders, sales contracts, "click agreements" to terms and conditions of sale, pricing, and database security.) Taxation and export issues should also be included in such reviews. Additionally, companies should check out the banking structure and customary methods of payment in the countries they are targeting. For example, China's banks are not set up to support e-business and credit cards are not yet popular there.

CREDIT GROUPS AND CREDIT CIRCLES

The Internet has also spawned online industry credit groups. While the exchange of credit information via the Internet or e-mail may seem like an idea that is long overdue, the practical application is not without its pitfalls.

The confidentiality of credit information exchanged at a face-to-face industry credit group meeting between creditors can be controlled and protected. Credit executives the world over know the value of the confidential exchange of credit information. They build trusting relationships with their peers through periodic credit industry group meetings and the resultant networking activities; they know with whom information is being exchanged.

For additional information on how credit circles are affected in the United Kingdom, refer to Chapter 21.

As the business world and e-commerce force change, the field of credit management is on the brink of a whole new frontier. All credit professionals need to determine what skills will be needed to remain a player in the new millennium and then decide what they have to do to acquire those skills.

30

Professionalism in
International Credit

Mary S. Schaeffer

IOMA

International credit executives have many sources for information. However, that information is sometimes hard to find, can be out of date, and frequently is not based on an adequate sampling. Consider the following scenario. A domestic credit manager in search of industry information can turn to the Credit Research Foundation, an industry trade group, or his or her own experiences with other customers in the same industry. Complicate the issue by taking it to the international arena and the credit executive may have some problems.

For starters, the universe has just gotten exponentially larger. Now the credit executive needs not only to find information about the given industry but the given industry in a certain country as it pertains to U.S. exporters. It is not uncommon to find international credit executives in search of Days Sales Outstanding (DSO) numbers for a given industry in one particular country. This information is extremely difficult to find. For starters, even if it were possible to find domestic DSO numbers in the given country, importers may pay their foreign suppliers differently. More to the point is the fact that in order to obtain meaningful numbers, it is crucial to have a decent sample size and this just may not be the case, especially in smaller countries.

Thus, international credit professionals must be more resourceful than their domestic counterparts. Information is available. It just is not what they are accustomed to finding for domestic situations, and it is sometimes harder to find and interpret. Given these difficulties along with cultural differences and added complexities of doing business in another country, international credit executives must gather data to make profitable credit decisions wherever they can.

ORGANIZATIONS

A number of organizations are devoted to providing information to international credit executives. Some make it their entire focus while others include international topics as part of their educational efforts.

FCIB

The best known of the international credit groups is the Association of Executors in Finance, Credit and International Business (FCIB), a branch of the National Association of Credit Management (NACM). The entire focus of this group is international. The FCIB has four luncheon roundtable meetings each year in New York. These meetings may include an educational speaker. However, the focus of the gatherings is the country-by-country reviews by the attendees. Information is submitted prior to the meeting and summarized by the FCIB staff. Attendees offer their views and experiences in the given countries.

Questions, both those submitted in advance and from the floor, are answered by other members. It is not uncommon to find very knowledgeable bankers in the audience offering advice in response to a question. Some of the discussions are spirited. It should come as no surprise to those reading this that the bankers do not always agree. Recent attendees have benefited from advice from ABN-AMRO's Bob Long and Walter (Buddy) Baker and Fleet Bank's Ken Nadler.

The FCIB also runs two annual conferences in the United States. The first is usually held in November in New York and the second in April in Chicago. These educational events run for a day and a half and feature experts on topics of interest to the members. Roundtable discussions are typically part of the gatherings as well.

Three times a year, in various European cities, additional conferences are held. There has been some talk of expanding the locales to include other international locations.

The FCIB has also introduced a professional certification, the Certified International Credit Executive (CICE), discussed in the section entitled "Certification —CICE" later in this chapter. Information about this program and other FCIB information can be obtained from its web site (*www.fcibglobal.com*).

Riemer

The well-known and highly respected Riemer Group is best known for its many industry credit trade groups. One of the groups is an international group. Meetings are held several times a year to discuss trade experiences. An educational speaker is usually part of the meetings.

Each fall, as part of its annual conference, the Riemer Group brings in a number of educational speakers who focus on international matters. Typically, the conference occurs in early September, and the first two days are devoted to international topics. For more information about Riemer activities and services, go to *www.riemer.com*.

Unz Co.

Originally a publisher of export-related forms, Unz has expanded its focus to include educational activities as they relate to international trade. The company offers a number of seminars on topics such as INCOTERMS, letters of credit, and so on. For more information, go to *www.unzcompany.com*.

Other Associations

While not specifically focused on credit topics, a number of export-import associations have information useful to international credit executives. The Association for Importers and Exporters and Women in International Trade are two such groups.

Also, some international credit executives with a finance or treasury bent find the Association for Financial Professionals extremely useful. This group holds an annual conference, a number of regional conferences and has local chapters, many of which hold monthly luncheon meetings. For more information, go to *www.afponline.org*.

Banks

Banks with international operations are often overlooked when it comes to international credit information. These banks include the big money center banks, some European and Asian banks, and some regional banks with an international presence. Turn to them for advice, especially when it pertains to banking- and/or finance-related questions.

Institute of Credit Management

The Institute of Credit Management is the professional credit association for the United Kingdom. Each year it offers over a 100 day-long and 2-day seminars. Anyone visiting the United Kingdom is advised to check out its web site to see if they can fit a seminar into their schedule. For additional information, go to *www.icm.org.uk*.

THE INTERNET

There is a plethora of international credit information on the Internet. You just have to find it. Several credit portals offer international credit professionals information and links to other sites of interest. I am not going to attempt to list all the international credit sites but rather just a few that offer the most links. They are:

- *Creditworthy.com*. Probably the first web site built for credit professionals by a credit professional (Rich Hill), creditworthy.com has links to every possible credit-related site, both domestic and international. Additionally, it offers a free biweekly e-mail newsletter and discussion groups. However, the focus is mainly domestic with a healthy dose of international information. For more information, go to *www.creditworthy.com.*

- *Creditman.co.uk.* This UK site also offers a free e-mail newsletter, links to many other sites, and discussion groups. It, too, was developed and is run by a knowledgeable credit executive (John Arnold). Keep in mind that this is a UK site. Thus, when reading the dates, they will be in day/month/year format. Also, the topics are all related to the United Kingdom. This is a great site for those doing business in the United Kingdom. For more information go to *www.creditman.co.uk.*

- *creditriskmonitor.com.* Relatively speaking, this is the new kid on the block when it comes to credit information web sites. It has tons of useful links but currently is mainly focused on domestic issues. While the cornerstone of this site is its fee service, much free information is available to international credit executives. The site is the brainchild of the Fensterstocks (Sam and Albie). For more information and to see if, perhaps, once again, the Fensterstocks are offering a free trial of the fee portion of their service, go to *www.creditriskmonitor.com.*

- *Other web sites.* As indicated, many other web sites contain information of interest to international credit executives. Many of the contributors to this book have their own web sites. Check their biographies at the beginning of the book to find those sites and more about their services. Many of the NACM affiliates carry international links and articles. Check out the local sites. Links to these sites may be found on *www.nacm.org.*

CERTIFICATION—CICE

The CICE is a voluntary professional designation program sponsored by the FCIB. CICE holders are expected to have managerial expertise in the areas of international credit and risk assessment, treasury, collections, and trade-related services, as well as a thorough understanding of the commercial business practices and courtesies necessary to manage and lead in the global business environment of the future.

Who Can Apply?

Senior-level international business and trade finance executives with a minimum of six years of senior-level management experience can apply. The candidates must demonstrate a mastery of skills in one or more areas of international credit, finance and business management, corporate and country-risk assessment, international business management, or customer financial services, or must document contributions to the international credit or trade-related service profession. Experience may be drawn from all international credit and trade finance professions and activities including those of service-related institutions such as banks, forfeiters, factoring houses, credit insurance underwriters, brokers, legal representatives, and credit reporting agencies.

Application Process

1. Complete the CICE application form and submit it to FCIB. A $250 nonrefundable application fee must accompany the application.
2. Along with the application, CICE candidates will submit a proposal for a research paper or management study report. The topic must be original in nature and relate to international business credit management, collections, risk management, finance, treasury, or related trade service functions. Applicants will receive the status of their CICE designation eligibility within 30 days.
3. Within six months of receiving approval of the research paper topic, candidates will submit the final work. The Accreditation Committee will judge all papers. By submitting the research paper, the CICE applicant is granting publishing rights to FCIB and waiving all intellectual property rights unless otherwise requested in writing by the applicant.
4. Continued designation status will be contingent on ongoing participation in the international business credit or international trade-related services profession and payment of a U.S. $100 annual renewal fee. Recertification is required every three years and carries no recertification fee.

Research Paper: An International Credit/Financial Management Study Report

Applicants will write and submit a piece on an international business credit and related trade services topic. The committee will consider any topic of interest to international business credit professionals. The Accreditation Committee must approve the outline for the paper, which will include its topic and scope. All papers must be submitted within six months of receiving topic approval.

All papers will be judged on both content and writing style. It is understood that all papers are submitted and accepted with the implied permission for FCIB to publish them at some future date, with appropriate attribution, unless otherwise requested in writing by the applicant.

Those international credit executives interested in obtaining CICE accreditation should visit *www.fcibglobal.com* for more extensive information and to download the application form.

As technology and competition eat away at the number of credit jobs available, those interested in international credit might want to consider this certification. It is just one more way of letting management know that you are keeping up to date in all the latest developments in your field.

31

Closing Thoughts

Mary S. Schaeffer

IOMA

The international economy continues to expand—and get smaller at the same time. While it was once a serious consideration to contact someone in another country, we now think nothing of sending an e-mail to get a quick answer to a simple question. As the marketplace becomes more competitive, companies look to expand their markets and often do so by becoming global players. Those who are most successful realize that in order to do business in the international arena, they must adapt to the way their customers do business rather than trying to force their customers to do business the way they are accustomed to transacting sales.

Ideally, there would be one standard for transactions that everyone would use. But this is not to be—although in some areas, most notably terms of sale, accounting and legal issues—have shown some modest movement. We expect bigger changes down the road but some preliminary movement has already taken place.

TERMS OF SALE

Americans are frequently criticized for their insistence on using U.S. shipping terms, which are totally irrelevant to the rest of the world. Most international trade is transacted using INCOTERMs. INCOTERMs have many advantages, including the fact that they spell out exactly who is responsible for what as far as insurance and shipping fees. They also make it clear when title changes hands. The International Chamber of Commerce (ICC) recently updated the terms to reflect changes in the global economy.

International credit executives are advised to insist that all contracts use INCOTERMs. INCOTERMs 2000 should be used to define the responsibilities of buyer and seller in contracts effective from January 1, 2000, and contracts should reference INCOTERMs 2000. For more information, visit the ICC web site at *www.iccwbo.org.*

INTERNATIONAL ACCOUNTING
STANDARDS COMMITTEE

Accounting standards worldwide vary greatly, with none being more stringent than generally accepted accounting procedures (GAAP). The International Accounting Standards Committee (IASC) is an independent, private sector body. Its goal is to harmonize the accounting principles used by businesses and other organizations for financial reporting around the world.

It states that it wishes:

> to develop, in the public interest, a single set of high quality, understandable and enforceable global accounting standards that require high quality, transparent and comparable information in financial statements and other financial reporting to help participants in the world's capital markets and other users make economic decisions; to promote the use and rigorous application of those standards; and to bring about convergence of national accounting standards and International Accounting Standards to high quality solutions.

For more information, visit *www.iasc.org.uk.*

ARBITRATION

Mention undertaking legal action in another country to most business executives who have done so and you will hear horror stories. Thus, many entering the international arena prefer to have arbitration clauses in their agreements. While arbitration clauses are not perfect, there has been some success in this area, most notably with international organizations set up to handle international disputes.

The ICC has had some success in this area. In 1999, 529 requests for arbitration were filed with the ICC, concerning 1,354 parties from 107 different countries (state or parastatal entities represented 8 percent of the parties). The places of arbitration were fixed in 48 different countries on five continents; arbitrators of 57 different nationalities were appointed or confirmed under the ICC rules. The amount in dispute exceeded U.S. $1 million in 58 percent of new cases, and 269 awards were submitted to the ICC court.

Those who use the arbitration process like it because decisions are final and binding. Although arbitral awards may be subject to being challenged (usually in either the country where the arbitral award is rendered or where enforcement is sought), the grounds of challenge available against arbitral awards are limited.

Arbitral awards enjoy much greater international recognition than judgments of national courts. About 120 countries have signed the 1958 United Nations Convention on the Recognition and Enforcement of Foreign Arbitral Awards, known as the New York Convention. The convention facilitates enforcement of awards in all contracting states. Several other multilateral and bi-lateral arbitration conventions may also help enforcement.

Those who are not willing to have the process binding sometimes use con-ciliation. ICC conciliation offers a means of resolving a dispute amicably with the full and unqualified consent of the parties without recourse to arbitration.

For more information about theses processes, visit *www.iccwbo.org/index_court.asp.*

THE INTERNET

To say that the Internet is changing the way business is transacted is certainly an understatement. New technologies, ways of doing business, and ways of finding information are just the beginning. As we go to press, the Federal Trade Commission approved the formation of Covisint, the business-to-business web site that will streamline the parts purchases of large automakers. Some experts estimate that effective usage of this purchasing mechanism will reduce the costs of an automobile by as much as $1,000. If these cost savings are even halfway accurate and the project is a success, we expect other networks to fol-low.

This is just the latest way that the Internet has made the world a smaller place to do business. Using a reverse auction process, this network lets every-one compete on a level playing field. How credit will be analyzed and approved in this brave new world remains to be seen.

International credit and collections will become ever more important in this fast-paced electronic environment. Those who are successful will be those who keep up with all the latest advances and find ways to incorporate these advances into their daily work process. It is going to be fun.

Good luck.

Index